596

I0354135

93

18 x 109.

Delany, Sheila.
    Writing woman : women writers and women in
literature, medieval to modern / Sheila Delany. --
New York : Schocken Books, c1983.
    218 p. ; 21 cm.

    LC: 83042725   ISBN: 0805238697 : $26.50

    1. Women and literature.   I. Title.

696

Women Writers and Women in Literature, Medieval to Modern

Sheila Delany

Writing
Woman

Schocken Books · New York

To my students, especially the ones who argued back

First published by Schocken Books 1983
10 9 8 7 6 5 4 3 2 1   83 84 85 86
Library of Congress Cataloging in Publication Data
Delany, Sheila.
  Writing woman.
  1. Women and literature. I. Title.
PN481.D4   1983   809′.93352042   83–42725

Designed by Jacqueline Schuman
Manufactured in the United States of America

ISBN 0–8052–3869–7 (hardcover)
     0–8052–0756–2 (paperback)

Permissions acknowledgments
Grateful acknowledgment is made to several journals for permission to reprint material previously published by them:
  Queen's Quarterly. For "Confessions of an Ex-Handkerchief Head," which originally appeared in *Queen's Quarterly,* vol. 89, no. 4 (Winter, 1982).
  Science & Society. For *Flore et Jehane,* which originally appeared under the title "*Flore et Jehane:* A Case Study of the Bourgeois Woman in Medieval Life and Letters" in *Science & Society,* vol. 45, no. 3 (Fall, 1981). Copyright © 1981 by *Science & Society*
  The Chaucer Review. For "Womanliness in *The Man of Law's Tale,*" which appeared in *The Chaucer Review,* vol. 9, no. 1.
  The Minnesota Review. For "Sexual Economics," which originally appeared in *The Minnesota Review,* NS 5 (Fall, 1975).
  Ramparts Press, Palo Alto, CA. For "Sex and Politics in Pope's *Rape of the Lock,*" from *Weapons of Criticism* (1976); the essay originally appeared in *English Studies in Canada,* vol. 1, no. 1 (Spring, 1975). Massachusetts Review, vol. 16, no. 2 (Spring, 1975).

Contents

Acknowledgments

I would like to express here grateful thanks to friends, colleagues and comrades who have read and discussed with me portions of this book: John Mills, Caffyn Baxter Kelley, Paul Kelley, Robert Mandel, Alice Steen, Kaye Stockholder.

A postdoctoral leave fellowship from the Canada Council in 1975–76 enabled me to do much of the historical and political reading that informs this book. Special thanks are due to Viki Jones, Donna Shanley, Jane Harris, Bernice Farrier, and Flo McCallum of the Simon Fraser University support staff for their help in preparing the manuscript.

And especially to my sons, Nick and Lev, who have given so much without knowing it, all my appreciation and love.

1

Confessions of an ex-handkerchief head, or why this is not a feminist book

Socially, individually, in every way but biologically, woman is made, not born. So, of course, is man. Each is a cultural artifact laboriously worked up, pieced together, written and rewritten as a kind of palimpsest. Inscribed on this document, layer by layer, are other texts: scholarly disciplines, novels and poems, lyrics to popular songs, ad copy, television scripts, children's books and games and rhymes ("Sugar and spice . . . "), expectations, injunctions, permissions, and the English language itself.[1]

Woman-as-topic, then, for she is inscribed in real texts. "Writing woman" is the act of encoding certain conceptions of femininity or womanliness. But the social concept "woman" is itself a composite, as much so as every individual woman. The production of this concept, like the production of the specific individual, relies heavily on actual texts. There is a relation, therefore, between literal textual reality and the personal or social metaphor: woman-as-topic helps generate woman-as-text.

Most of the essays collected here show how certain writers have inscribed woman in their work and why, socially, they have done so in the ways they have. These ways have naturally a good deal to do with the specificity of each writer's condition: medieval or modern; male or female; English, French, Russian, or American. The "woman" in most of these essays is the one written as literary character in a fictional text. Usually "she" is offered to the contemporary audience as an exemplary figure, whether a positive one, like Chaucer's Constance or Lavrenev's Maryutka, or a negative one, like Pope's Belinda. The fictional character represents an effort to shape real woman-as-text. For me "she" also signifies a range of conditions—historical, economic, biographical, psychological—that enable "her" literary existence. (I have just committed nearly every sin possible in the bible of new criticism. So be it.)

Some of the essays also focus on women who have done the writing; hence "writing woman" as the woman who writes. Some of the authors considered here write of themselves directly and in the first person: Margery Kempe, author of the first autobiography in English, and Christine de Pisan, a fifteenth-century courtier-poet and scholar. Others write in a more generalized political or fictional mode: Rosa Luxemburg, Charlotte P. Gilman, Virginia Woolf, Marge Piercy. The two categories, writing and written about, often overlap. Gilman and Piercy certainly put forward female models in their utopian fictions, reflecting, as I argue, two distinct moments in the history of American feminism. Margery Kempe's book provides a profound commentary on, and contrast with, Chaucer's nearly contemporary fictional version of a woman rather like Margery: the Wife of Bath. Certainly much of Margery's anguish came from her inability to be what the official texts of her day (Holy Scripture, clerical opinion, civil law) said she must be. Christine's *City of Ladies* is a powerful indictment of the dominant antifeminist tradition, a haunting personal memoir about the destructive effects of that tradition, and an attempt to rewrite "woman" in a positive way.

A particular woman writes the present text, one who is composed in part of the texts she writes about: by the traditions of literature, philosophy, and politics they inscribe. In beginning with some of my own history I want to account for the special stance taken in these essays. I also intend to offer that history not simply as typical for many women of my age and profession, but as *possible,* in its general outline, for people of either sex who start from the premise that things had better change. In none of these essays had I set out to uncover what some feminists call "herstory" or to contribute to the field of women's studies. Rather, I had undertaken a consciously engaged criticism aiming to show the contextual genesis and ideological implications of certain literary works. As it turned out, much of this work centered on the figure of a female protagonist. While as a medievalist and a Marxist I had written on other topics (allegory, comedy, Marxist criticism), I confronted this one again and again in its various shape-shifting forms, whether medieval, neoclassical, or modern. The recurrence was no accident. It came from my own experience of sexism, an experience not only mine but collective and historically determined, hence as proper an object of critical attention as the literature it contemplates. Let me proceed, then, to show the connection between the two parts of the title of this introductory essay.

During the 1960s in New York, an acquaintance phoned to invite me to join a women's consciousness-raising group. We were to discuss our oppression as women, particularly as academic women, since most of us were at the time graduate students at Columbia University. I agreed to attend but added that I didn't think I'd been discriminated against as a woman at the university. My benefactor's response was to denounce me as an "Aunt Jemima handkerchief head"—a house-servant who identifies with the slaveholder rather than with the field-hands—and to withdraw the invitation.

She was right in her characterization. Nor is it wholly ironically that I refer to her as a benefactor, because it was in part moved by her anger that I began to read—and to notice and to talk. I had already read one of the early classics of the women's liberation movement, Betty Friedan's *The Feminine Mystique*. (I recalled the afternoon at Strawberry Canyon pool when the lovely wife of one of my Berkeley profs, expecting their third child, told me she thought *The Feminine Mystique* a wonderful book but her husband hated it. Even then I understood that this was no literary judgment, that the remark opened a window into their marriage.) I read more: Mary Jane Sherfey, Naomi Weisstein, Eleanor Maccoby, the innumerable little white or gray newsprint-covered pamphlets on the myth of vaginal orgasm (Ann Koedt), the politics of housework (Pat Mainardi), working women (Roxanne Dunbar). They confirmed what I had always sensed to be true, and that confirmation was valuable. But they didn't as yet affirm something new. They were right, but their lessons remained private: There must be something more definitive than shared housework, clitoral orgasm, getting a job.

I joined the Columbia chapter of NUC (New University Conference, a New Left organization of graduate students and younger faculty, modelled on the soon-to-be-defunct SDS). As part of its women's caucus (which I joined out of timidity) I helped organize a women's liberation teach-in at Columbia—possibly the first really big one in the city. It was a smashing, daylong success, attended by more than a thousand people, with child care, workshops and encounter groups, feminist theater with plays by Myrna Lamb, and lectures by virtually everyone in New York with something to say about the liberation of women, including lesbian separatists, black attorney Florynce Kennedy, Wendy Nakashima of the Progressive Labor Party, and Kate Millett, who was completing her dissertation at Columbia on the literature of sexual politics.

During this same year (1969–70) NUC was the target of an entry by Progressive Labor. Several PL members and sympathizers in NUC tried to win the group to a proletarian orientation: worker–student alliance in campus labor struggles, and participation in important off-campus labor confrontations. I think I was their only success. PL was at its best then. Its members were impressively committed, disciplined, and politically hard; certainly they made the ever-waffling New Leftists look sick. But one thing the new left rarely waffled on was anticommunism, and when PL was expelled from NUC I left with them in sympathy and in protest. Not for nothing had I as a teenager come home from school every day to watch the Army–McCarthy hearings on TV. I started to read some basic Marx and Engels, along with such elementary revolutionary history as Isaac Deutscher's biography of Leon Trotsky.

Things grated at Columbia: for instance, the fact that so many female graduate students were afraid to speak in class, to argue with a professor or a (usually male) seminar shark. Without men in classes, would it be different? It hadn't been different at Wellesley, where a class composed entirely of women ("girls," as the term was then) could be even more frustratingly silent than a mixed class. Include me among the nonspeakers then: "Why don't you talk?" a young woman teacher demanded of me in her office. It was an accusation: "People hand in A papers and never say a word in class."

We were afraid to appear competitive. It wasn't simply a matter of a male presence; it was the internalization of a way to be. It isn't a good idea to fight aggressively for your ideas, to care too much about achievement, or to be conspicuously more talkative than the rest. Not only "Why bother?"—it might also create resentment. A young male teacher complained less about the silence than about the perpetual smiles: He would take excursions to New York to see a few scowls. It was perhaps not unusual in the late 1950s, or surprising at a college whose motto, *Non ministrari sed ministrare* (not to be ministered unto but to minister), so paradoxically stresses the active voice of a verb that places female activity squarely in the nineteenth-century, maternalistic tradition of the nurturing "angel in the house."

It made me angry when a former Berkeley prof (not the one

mentioned earlier) wrote to congratulate me on the birth of my first son, praising the "true creativity" of pregnancy over the illusory creativity of writing. When one of my thesis advisors announced in seminar he'd never hire a woman because she'd cancel classes if her kid had measles. When my other advisor suggested I abandon the thesis to care for my (by that point) two infants. When the same advisor phoned the chairman of a department where I'd applied for work, to assure the latter that the burden of babies would prevent my completing the work. (I did finish on schedule, got the job, and the thesis was published by the University of Chicago Press.) In retrospect, it must have looked comical that I was seven months pregnant at my qualifying exams and again at my thesis defense a year or so later. Happily, one examiner who sat on both committees had the wit to remark that I seemed to favor the rhetorical device of *amplificatio*. Most of the comments were not so graceful.

There were also more painful personal perceptions, of fights I hadn't fought with people I loved and who loved me. I had gotten through school on a series of fellowships; my parents had cut off financial support after college, saying that graduate school was a luxury and I should find a husband to take over. Would this, I belatedly wondered, have been their response to a son wanting law or medical school? I had quit graduate school after one semester in order to remove myself from "competition" with my lover, whose grades in the courses we took together were consistently lower than mine. I had quit writing fiction about marriage because my husband "didn't want to be written about."

So it was that soon after starting work at Queens College, I and several friends—like myself faculty wives or teachers—came together for regular meetings in an informal reading and discussion group, an affinity group as we called it. (Our husbands eventually initiated a similar group, but it didn't seem to achieve the intensity or commitment that ours did.) The main benefit was, exactly as everyone says who has been through such a group, the relief of discovering, finally, that your secret anger, discontent, rebellions, and horror stories are shared by most of the women you know, that they are not the signs of insanity but of protest. I who at parties had usually wound up talking with men, found myself seeking out the company and conversation of women, repelled by the competitive fast-talk and flaunting of credentials that so often passed for conversation among university intellectuals.

As the months passed and we adjusted to our new consciousness, we spoke about our isolation and our privileged status as middle-class intellectuals. It was over that issue that the group eventually dissolved. When the others declined to walk a picket line downtown of striking telephone operators, all women and mostly black, we realized we'd gone as far as we could in consciousness raising and had arrived at a political parting of the ways. The ending struck me as paradigmatic, for even without a coherent revolutionary perspective I believed that the watershed for women's liberation was whether the self-consciousness of women could incorporate larger social issues—the institutionalized forms of work, family, and government—in the context of which the special oppression of women occurs—in short, whether our reading, support, and enlightenment could *go* somewhere.

Moving to Canada in 1970 seemed in some ways a time-machine jump ten years backwards, especially with respect to men's attitudes toward women. I heard comments there that I hadn't imagined possible any longer. Sample dialogue with new colleague at a dinner party, when he informed me proudly he'd read *The Feminine Mystique:*

Me: "What did you think of the book?"

He: "What an aggressive woman you are."

During the course of the evening this same colleague's wife, beautiful, English, and silent, herself a graduate student, began to overcome her intense shyness and to corroborate some of my observations. Whereupon another colleague jeered at us: "How common: united by dishrag and pail!" I wish I'd had Judy Grahn's wonderful poem "The Common Woman" to quote at him, but I hope I made the point effectively in prose.

I had been hired along with four or five others, all men. Though my qualifications were better than those of all the others except my husband, I was the only one in the group given a "visiting" position (i.e., at two-thirds salary, the following year supposedly to revert to a regular position). It was clearly an effort to save a few dollars in salary and benefits on the female partner in a two-person package. At the last minute the offer was changed to a full position when the chairman of the department was forced by a university women's caucus to scurry to the dean for slush funds to make up the difference. We had also received offers from a large American university with the proviso that I would never have tenure nor the vote in departmental meetings, ostensibly because the department did not want "a voting bloc."

"Have you ever been sued under Title VII?" I inquired of the university's president.

"We would never hire someone we thought would do that," was his suave reply.

It was doubtless the accumulated anger over conversations like these that I took out on an unsuspecting middle-aged gas station attendant one night. He located the gas tank, saying "There she is!" and I screamed at him for five minutes solid about the degrading sexist implications of his image.

These are experiences that might well make someone a feminist. Lillian Robinson defines feminism as "women's consciousness of being 'the other' in a male-dominated system,"[2] and I certainly qualified for that. But there is more to feminism than Robinson's definition suggests.

First off, I didn't initially radicalize around gender but around race. I was ten before I went to a school where I wasn't the only white pupil in my class. Much later, in 1964, the murder of three northern students engaged in voter registration in Mississippi—Schwerner, Cheney, and Goodman—had a decisive impact on me. Their bodies were found "mutilated," according to the press—which we readers of Faulkner recognize as a euphemism for that old southern punishment, castration. Twenty-one murderers were arrested, most of them members of the Ku Klux Klan, several of them sheriffs and police. Charges were dismissed. The episode cut straight through my dilemma about whether capitalism was reformable or not. It proved to me that any system that permitted, even encouraged, such atrocities could not be reformed but was the enemy, in an absolute way that later, when I acquired a political vocabulary, I would call "principled." I knew, later, that the Deacons for Defense and Justice were right to organize armed protection for Freedom Riders, as was Robert F. Williams with his rifle club to protect the homes of North Carolina blacks. So the race question was primary for me, and what had feminism to say about that?

Second, consciousness of one's otherness leads somewhere in practice. By 1970 I'd had a good firsthand view of the practical limitations of feminism: in NUC its anticommunism, and in my affinity group its reluctance to soil hands in real struggle by getting out of an Upper West Side living room and onto a picket line. Though this was all empirical so far, what I'd seen ran counter to my admiration for the Russian Revolution and to my prolabor impulses. I suspected that this experience wasn't *merely* empirical but susceptible of generalization.

After several years of reading and of work with two or three Left groups, I began to read the press of the Spartacist League, a Trotskyist organization. The SL made me a Marxist, and I remain a sympathizer of the organization. It is one of the distinctive contributions of the Spartacist tendency to contemporary communism to have revived the tradition of Bolshevik work among women, a tradition deliberately suppressed, with so much else, during the Stalin era, and not fully recuperated even by the revolutionary Trotskyist movement of the 1930s and 1940s. SL's orientation on the woman question is reflected in the high proportion of women in the organization and especially in its leadership collectives; in its press, which includes the quarterly journal *Women and Revolution;* in the programmatic demands and daily work of its trade-union sympathizers and supporters. Still, it wasn't the woman question per se that attracted me, but a comprehensive program wherein I recognized the continuity of the Leninist tradition and the only possible strategy to end capitalism.

It was as a guest speaker at SL forums commemorating International Women's Day (1976) that I started to research the history of feminism as an organized tendency over the last century and a quarter. It isn't a glorious history; it's a shameful one, full of evasion and betrayal—strong words, but accurate, and appropriate to the revulsion I felt on finding that these betrayals were perpetrated against women, especially the most desperately oppressed and exploited women, those most seriously in need of defense, organization, and militancy. Despite the immense courage and dedication of numerous individuals, despite the obvious supportability of some genuinely democratic demands, like suffrage or (in Germany) state care for unwed mothers, feminist "sisterhood" has been a scorpion recoiling on itself. In every country it not only has betrayed women, but continues to do so and can only do so.

Most disgraceful of them all was the American suffrage movement: deeply racist, snobbish, xenophobic, irredeemably opportunistic. Despite its early roots in the abolition movement, suffragism soon incorporated the racism endemic to American middle-class life. Colored women suffragists across the country had to form separate segregated clubs outside the national suffrage organization. Suffrage propaganda appealed to southern racism and to northern anti-immigrant prejudices: "This ignorant, bestial black or foreign man can vote, but the pure, educated, civilized white woman, your wife or sister, cannot." Indeed the movement as a whole (with very few individual exceptions) explicitly offered Congress the enfranchisement of white middle-class women as a way to preserve white supremacy in the South, since white women outnumbered blacks of both sexes. The analogous argument was made about the northern urban immigrant vote. In 1894 Carrie Chapman Catt went even further: As organizer for, and later as president of, the National American Woman Suffrage Association, she proposed to Congress that it "cut off the vote of the slums and give it to woman" in order to protect government from "the ignorant foreign vote" and from the "greed" of miners who were attempting to organize a union. Nowhere is the dead-end logic of reformist sectoralism more emblematically illustrated than in public disputes between suffragists and black leaders over which group should sacrifice its civil rights to the other. In short, the deal with Congress was that in exchange for the vote, the white Anglo-Saxon middle-class suffrage movement would close its eyes to Jim Crow (which indeed its own practices had perpetuated) and sell its black "sisters" down the river.[3]

The Canadian movement was equally unsuccessful in attracting working women. As in all countries the hostility was mutual, due on one side to the suffragists' snobbish moralism and fear of alienating middle-class support; on the other, to the class consciousness that prevented working women from uniting with those who endorsed strikebreakers for political office, enthused over prohibition, and saw the husband as the main oppressor. Trenchant criticism of the feminists also came from farm women and the farmers' organizations generally. Though they supported female suffrage and often shared the petty-bourgeois moralism and xenophobia of urban feminists, nonetheless they had a far sharper sense of political and economic reality. Canadian farm women, who worked alongside their men, felt oppressed *with* their husbands, not by them; their joint oppression, they knew, came from eastern plutocrats. Farm women opposed the Women's Party founded in 1918 by suffragists, both because of its prowar and antiunion planks and because it was based on "the antediluvian fetish of sex distinction."[4] In short, it was clear to Canadian farm and labor women that the feminists were safely in the vest pocket of big business and that feminism was not only irrelevant but hostile to the interests of urban and rural working women.

In contrast with the North American movements, the Federation of German Women's Associations (a heterogeneous coalition founded in 1894) resisted the suffrage issue until 1902 (although the socialist August Bebel had already in 1895 introduced in the Reichstag a motion for female suffrage). During World War I, while Communists like Rosa Luxemburg and Clara Zetkin led working women in opposition to the interimperialist conflict, the ultranationalist German feminists hoped, as did feminists in every belligerent country, that their ardent patriotism would be rewarded by concessions. Given the already well-established military-chauvinistic, racist-genetic, and maternalistic orientation of the German movement, Nazism offered little that was objectionable, except to a tiny pacifist tendency. When in 1933 the Nazis dissolved the federation, its leaders protested mildly, stressing the patriotic antisocialist character of their movement and its general approval of National Socialism. They then agreed to the dissolution, expressing hope for "a biological policy which supports the German family through economic and eugenic measures."[5] Many of the feminist leaders went directly into the Nazi women's organizations.

The English women's rights movement split spectacularly along the class line, dividing the famous Pankhurst family accordingly. Mrs. Emmeline Pankhurst and her eldest daughter Cristabel held fast for middle- and upper-class membership and autocratic structure in their suffrage organization, for "industrial peace," intense patriotism, and violent hatred of the Russian Revolution. Their jingoism assumed an even more obnoxious form than elsewhere, with the notorious "white feather" campaign in which suffragists pinned a "badge of cowardice" to the jackets of draft resisters and pacifists. The two younger daughters became socialist militants: Adela in Australia (though she reverted to conservatism in 1928) and Sylvia in London. Modelling herself on Rosa Luxemburg, Sylvia chose to organize working women in London's East End (as well as Welsh miners and Scottish dockworkers) and to mobilize them against the war. Mrs. Pankhurst loudly, publicly, and permanently severed all relations with her embarrassing daughter, even refusing to speak to Sylvia or visit her when the latter bore a son in 1924. (So much for "sanctity of the family" when confronted with political expediency!) Later, as a "Bolshevist," Sylvia worked with Lenin to found what she hoped would be a revolutionary party in England. By 1927, when Mrs. Pankhurst ran for Parliament as a Tory, Sylvia—though no longer a member of the Third International—could still identify herself with the socialist tradition of Robert Owen, Karl Marx, and William Morris, reaffirming her faith in "the cause of social and international fraternity."[6]

In Russia, at a time when masses of working women and men were engaged in armed battle for "bread, land, and peace," for soviets (elected councils) and a workers government, the feminist organizations hadn't moved beyond constitutional monarchy and partial female suffrage. It was the Bolsheviks whose program and achievements included abortion and divorce free and on demand, open admission to all schools, coeducation, day care, abolition of laws against homosexuality, and equal employment and equal pay for women. The collectivized industrial economy and social planning that are the legacy of 1917 form the material base to eliminate what remains of the special oppression of women in the Soviet Union—where, even under an oppressive and privileged bureaucratic caste, women have equality of education, employment, and pay, and far more access to day care and other social benefits than anywhere else in the world.[7] That the revolutionary material base hasn't led to the full liberation of women in the USSR bespeaks not the need for feminism there but for revolutionary overthrow of the bureaucracy.

And so it goes. But what of "the new feminism," "radical" or "socialist feminism"? The last phrase has always reminded me of a mythical beast out of one of my favorite childhood books, *Doctor Doolittle:* the pushme-pullyu, a horselike animal with a head at either end. The problem is that feminism and socialism do have different aims and strategies that are ultimately counterposed, even though they may unite on certain specific issues, such as support for ERA or free abortion on demand. The question is whether the bottom line is the sex line or the class line, and here even the most radical socialist-feminists wind up in trouble. Take Redstockings, certainly the left wing of American feminism in the late 1960s and early 1970s, a group that has produced some important and valuable work and has rightly deplored such class collaboration as Jane Alpert's services to the FBI and Gloria Steinem's alleged relationship with the CIA. In 1975 Kathie Sarachild, a Redstocking leader, deplored the "liberal take-over" of the radical women's movement. But there was a reason why this could happen and I believe it is found in the Redstockings' own statement of principles (1969), which says:

> We take the woman's side in everything.
> We ask not if something is "reformist," "radical," or "normal."
> We ask: is it good for women or bad for women? . . .
> We define the best interests of women as the best interests of the poorest, most insulted, most despised, most abused woman on earth.

I submit that the contradiction between the first two propositions and the last one encapsulates the contradiction of "socialist-feminism" itself: sex or class. The criterion "what is good for women" is an Achilles' heel that the cutting edge of any sharply polarized conflict pierces in an instant. Agreed, Steinem and Alpert turned their backs on exploited and oppressed women; feminism could not give them a commitment to the exploited. But neither could a manifesto that begins with "Women first." When in 1973 Alpert dismissed massacred prisoners at New York's Attica State Prison as "male supremacists" whose death was not worth mourning, she took to its furthest limit the quite respectably socialist-feminist idea that "all men are the agents of women's oppression," an idea voiced even in the Redstockings manifesto (1969): "*All men* receive economic, sexual and psychological benefits from male supremacy. *All men* have oppressed women."[8] (Italics in original.) If this is a principled position, it means I must hate the oppressor; if "all men" are the oppressor, then the logical strategy is sex war.

But when women workers are paid less than men, who benefits? Not male workers, whose wages can also be kept lower by the availability of cheap labor, and who can be placated by false feelings of superiority (much as white workers can be better exploited with the help of racism). The employer benefits. If women are oppressed in the home, whether with violence or by giving years of unpaid domestic labor, who benefits? Again the employers as a class, who prefer to keep a certain proportion of women off the jobmarket because they cannot provide full employment, and who have no intention of diverting profit to pay for the socialization of housework and childbearing.

Here is a fairly commonplace instance of how class line and sex line might come into conflict. What should recently hired women workers do about plant layoffs, to which they are especially vulnerable? Many socialist-feminists argue that men (black, Chicano, or white, with or without families), men with seniority (a hard-won gain of the labor movement), should be laid off in preference to low-seniority women. A socialist, or simply a serious trade unionist, would see this as an antiunion tactic that can only intensify sex and race divisions and instead would want to organize all workers against layoffs. In any case, laying off men instead of women doesn't end exploitation; it only shifts it. We are back to the nineteenth-century debates between suffragists and blacks about whose head should go on the block. The point is, no one's should—but only a class-based, comprehensive program can support that fight.

Sometimes sex and class criteria do coincide, as recently in Iran or Afghanistan. In Iran, it is the medieval-minded ayatollahs—who have outlawed trade unions; put women back in the veil; had homosexuals, prostitutes, and adulterers stoned to death; shut down the universities; and declared war on the entire "satanic" left—who obviously deserve only the principled opposition and hatred of any democratically minded person. For once in recent decades the Soviet Union has done something right by intervening in Afghanistan (whatever its political motives) against this same feudal-reactionary clerical establishment whose main social functions are to milk the population by taxes, maintain veil and bride price, and keep women illiterate.

Yet curiously in both these cases, where women's interest is so obvious, "socialist-feminists" have generally taken neither a socialist nor a prowoman position. Most of them hailed "the Islamic revolution" in Iran. Many even praised the return to the veil as the glorious recovery of a distinctive cultural tradition. This same heavy, dirt-laden, stifling veil—sometimes weighing thirty pounds, made of horsehair, and covering the entire body—

is that symbol of female seclusion—as Simone de Beauvoir might say, of Otherness—that in eastern Soviet areas was defiantly and joyfully ripped off by thousands of Moslem women during the 1920s.[9] As for Afghanistan, most socialist-feminists do not support the Soviet presence there. In 1981, socialist-feminists sponsored the Canadian speaking tour of Tatiana Mamonova. Mamonova is a Russian exile dissident and self-styled socialist-feminist whose claim on our attention is that she tried to persuade Russian women to persuade their men to refuse military duty in Afghanistan. It is a cheap and easy "feminism" that deplores childbirth practices in the Soviet Union but acquiesces in the devastating oppression of Muslim women. No "feminist" rhetoric can hide Mamonova's deep-rooted anticommunism, and yet the socialist-feminists gave her standing ovations. No wonder her U.S. tour was sponsored by the Ford Foundation!

Closer to home, I have observed members of the Women's Studies program at Simon Fraser University, including labor historians and self-styled socialists, gladly join their male colleagues in crossing picket lines of the predominantly female Association of University and College Employees (clerical and library staff). Perhaps their rationale was that to continue to teach their courses during the strike was a more significant prowoman gesture than respecting the picket line of underpaid working women. More concretely, perhaps the thinking was that a gesture of labor solidarity (which also happened in this case to be one of sex solidarity) might interfere with administration funding for their program.

Let me draw these anecdotal threads together. The connection is the inherent logic of sectoralism: the "us first" that inevitably comes to "some of us first" because sectoralism doesn't aim to take on the entire system but only some of its symptoms. For even the best-intentioned sectoralist, the choice sooner or later comes to dropping her less "acceptable" demands and allies for the sake of ever more limited concessions from those in power, or else dropping sectoralism for the sake of effective class struggle, whether in a local strike or a civil war abroad.

All of this is why I've been moved to write about the special oppression of women as it is manifested in literature, and why this is not a feminist book.

The essays in this book that are about a fictional female character are also about the literature of sexual politics. We needn't confine ourselves to the twentieth century in order to speak of a literature of sexual politics, for virtually every literature that is the product of a class-structured society has generated a literature of sexual politics. It is possible, then, to discuss *literatures* of sexual politics, though in extending the concept historically we will have to revise its emphasis from what is currently understood. Rather than demonstrate the existence of exploitive sexual roles and relations in literature (as Kate Millet did in her illuminating study of several modern novelists[10]), I want to look at the literary use of sexual behavior as an image of political behavior.

The sexual metaphor can work in two ways. First, the relation of man to woman can operate as a fairly direct political allegory, each sex representing a particular class or social layer as well as his or her sex in general. Hence the structure of sexual authority and submission duplicates power structures not confined to sex, a parallelism made possible by the special oppression of women. Alternatively, sexuality may operate more loosely, with varying sexual attitudes serving as an index to "corresponding" social or political attitudes. The first type requires a male and a female character in relationship; the second could use males or females only. The first is essentially allegorical in method, however realistic its style may be; the second, though equally exemplary, does not carry the same strict correlation of gender to social class or even of sexual attitude to social class. Let me illustrate.

The first type makes its appearance with the oldest extant text in Western literature, the Mesopotamian epic of Gilgamesh (c. 2500 B.C.). In an early episode the king-hero is approached by Ishtar, goddess of fertility and love. Far from being flattered by this attention, Gilgamesh rejects Ishtar with jeering accusations of promiscuity. In revenge, Ishtar has her father, the sky god

Anu, create the Bull of Heaven to destroy Gilgamesh, but the king—protégé of the sun god Shamash—and his friend Enkidu kill the bull. Scornfully they toss its wrenched-off thigh in Ishtar's face. Ishtar retires to lament with "her people, the dancing and singing girls, the prostitutes of the temple, the courtesans," while Gilgamesh calls on smiths and armorers to admire the bull's horns, which are hung in the palace as a trophy. The conflict here seems to represent a successful challenge by monarchy, with its urban/artisan/mercantile base, to the older authority of the priest-dominated, temple-centered, agriculturally and pastorally oriented cult of Ishtar.[11]

The Old Testament is full of myths of sexual politics, starting with the story of Adam and Eve, which makes woman the all-purpose rebel against duly established order. Though much in the story derives from Mesopotamian tradition, the author of the Fall wrote on behalf of the priestly ruling caste to which he evidently belonged. (He wrote probably about 1000 B.C. and is referred to by scholars as "J" because his name for God is Jahweh). In a later period (c. 740 B.C.) the prophet Hosea used his own marriage to the harlot Gomer, and his attempts to reform her, as a piece of living theater for the people of Israel, "for the land commits great harlotry by forsaking the Lord." Hosea's wife represents the Jews as a whole, whose lawful "husband" is Jahweh. The cult of Jahweh was administered, and the monarchy substantially influenced, by a priestly caste deriving its livelihood from the cash and kind devotions of the faithful. But the Jews, Hosea laments, had devoted themselves instead to the worship of various Ba'al cults, nature-cults typical of Near Eastern religion at the time, whose ceremonies included ritual copulation with temple priestesses ("prostitutes"). Marital fidelity becomes a metaphor for the harmonious maintenance of a theocratic social structure.

Christianity was able to take over the sexual metaphor and use it effectively in popular literature: Jesus as suitor of straying humanity is a commonplace in medieval religious lyric. Chaucer uses the sexual relation as a political and moral metaphor in *The*

Man of Law's Tale, where Constance's marital submission provides a timely lesson to discontented elements in fourteenth-century England. In her passive acceptance of God's will Constance is linked with Mary, while her diabolically rebellious mothers-in-law are types or figures of Eve. More explicitly allegorical is a tale I haven't written about here: the story of patient Griselda (*The Clerk's Tale*), who is both an ideally submissive wife and an ideal serf and subject in service to Walter, her overlord and husband. A less admirable figure (or so I believe Chaucer intended her) is the Wife of Bath, whose greedy ambition characterizes not only her own sexual behavior but also the economic behavior of her class, the manufacturing and mercantile petty bourgeoisie. Jehane, businesswoman-heroine of the Old French *Flore et Jehane,* offers a much more positive image of the bourgeois woman and of the class at large. The royal marriage that is Jehane's reward represents the real alliance of French kings and bourgeoisie that typified social life of the period. The *Persian Letters* (1721) of Montesquieu employs a similar literary method, showing in Usbek's relation to his harem the failure of absolute monarchy, and in the harem's revolt an admirable if unsuccessful bourgeois revolution.

The second form of literary sexual politics can be found as early as c. 800 B.C. in the *Odyssey*. Here the hero and his wife share the same ethical values, including the role of women: Penelope admires her son's good sense when, after her angry outburst to the parasitic suitors, Telemachus sends his mother to her room and advises her to leave the talking to men. The hero and his opponents, the suitors, are of the same aristocratic class. The suitors' behavior does not represent the aspirations of another class but rather an obsolescent set of social mores within the aristocracy. If Penelope remarries—as her quite honorable parents urge her to do and as society expects her to do—then her new family will inherit Odysseus's wealth and land, edging out Odysseus's son Telemachus as successor to kingship in Ithaca. Protected by the father-monarch Zeus, and by the motherless warrior Athena (who sprang fully armed from the head of Zeus),

Odysseus fights for paternal and monarchical supremacy, for the chastity of wives, for the inheritance of private property through the paternal line. The marital relation is no metaphor, but is itself the real linchpin of the "modern" system that Odysseus defends.

In Shakespeare's *Measure for Measure* the major characters are aristocrats whose sexual behavior more or less parallels their attitudes toward law and political authority. Highest on the sex-political scale is the Duke, ruler of Vienna and manipulator of the plot: He is not only chaste but the cause of chastity in others. Isabella, the heroine, is absolute in her commitment to virginity and in her acceptance of the Duke's authority, even when she perceives the latter as unjust. The legalistic rigidity of the deputy Angelo is echoed in an equally rigid denial of his own sensuality—until he is tempted by Isabella, whereupon he becomes a lecherous pervert as well as a liar, slanderer, and lawbreaker. Claudio and Julia are essentially good citizens whose single lapse—illegal premarital fornication—is mitigated by their true love and by their being legally affianced. The libertine Lucio commits slander and perjury. Lowest on the sociosexual scale is the pimp and tapster Pompey, whose cynical rationalism might be genuinely subversive if it had a larger part in the play.

Pope's *Rape of the Lock* portrays aristocratic characters whose sexual behavior represents political attitudes of which Pope was strongly critical. In *Man's Fate* André Malraux also uses sexuality as an index to political behavior: His corrupt capitalist and good revolutionary relate to women as they do to society at large (the one exploitively, the other with passionate commitment), while the "mindless" revolutionary Chen, who kills for the sake of killing, is capable of no relation with women at all.

The texts I have briefly discussed here—so varied in genre and scattered in time, without influence on one another—can scarcely be considered a tradition. Still, if literatures of sexual politics have surfaced in cultures so different, it is because they are impelled by realities common to those cultures: class structure and the special oppression of women. The actual social values they convey are varied, even contradictory: like any rhetorical device, the sexual metaphor can be used in the service of widely different political ends. Nor is socialist revolution excluded from the possibilities of the literature of sexual politics. The Chinese opera *The White-Haired Girl* (1949) epitomizes class struggle between landlords and peasants in a landlord's rape of a young peasant girl. The girl rebels and runs away to live as a fugitive in the hills. She is brought back to society by local guerillas, and in the last scene the girl and her companions condemn the landlord to death. Personal and class justice are done at once, for they are identical; the villagers sing, "We who suffered in days gone by / Shall be our own masters from now on!" More subtle but methodologically similar is Boris Lavrenev's story of the Russian civil war, "The Forty-first" (1924), in which a Red Army partisan shoots her White Guard lover. One suspects, then, that the literature of sexual politics will be with us as long as the social relations exist that make it possible. In my view it isn't feminism that will alter these relations substantively, but socialism.

Perhaps a classless society will relegate the literature of sexual politics to the status of historical curiosity—"along with Marx's *Capital* and the program of our party," as Trotsky put it. If so, it won't be done by legislative fiat but by changed tastes, possibilities, and realities. And if the literature of sexual politics disappears, there will be little to regret because the necessary accompaniment will be woman's entry into the fullest species-life—at this point a condition scarcely imaginable—both as writer and as topic.

I can't put it better than the poet Alta has done:

> The poems people need in 2072 they'll read (I hope) in 2072. & I hope a lot of the battles we're fighting now will be won, even if it means ½ our work will be irrelevant. We must work towards our own obsolescence.[12]

Flore et Jehane:
*the bourgeois woman
in medieval life
and letters*

Where, I have often wondered, is the literary heroine who is neither victim nor cheat, who does not rely on sexuality to make her mark in the world, who can succeed as a single working woman and be happy? Where is the intelligent, assertive, likable, hardworking heroine whose morality, sanity, and femininity are not called into question, whose husband (if she marries) respects her, and whose children (if she has them) lead lives of accomplished distinction? As it happens, this paragon exists, though not very accessibly. She is not the heroine of a modern utopian novel but of a little-known, anonymous, thirteenth-century prose text from the Franco-Flemish lowlands, *Li Contes dou Roi Flore et de la Bielle Jehane.* With enormous charm, *Flore et Jehane* tells a double story: that of King Florus, who is unable to have children by either of his two aristocratic wives, and that of Jehane, an impoverished knight's daughter who leaves home to earn a large fortune in business, marries King Florus, and bears him two children. The author's sympathies are clearly with his female protagonist as she accumulates the wealth that brings her to the king's attention. Most of the story narrates Jehane's exemplary (though quite adventurous) life and Horatio Alger–style success; King Florus is her reward.

It may seem paradoxical, given its plot, that *Flore et Jehane* nowhere criticizes the traditional medieval attitude toward women as expressed in the clerical antifeminist tradition.[1] In fact, nothing in the story necessarily contradicts the dominant feudal-aristocratic view of women, and in certain ways the story even confirms that view. Nonetheless, it does pose questions for the modern reader: Why is the figure of Jehane so unusual a type in European literature? Why has the author chosen a female rather than a male protagonist? What are we to make of Jehane's extreme social mobility? To what extent does the story reflect the real status of middle-class women in medieval Europe?

It is not as a "feminist scholar" that I pose these questions, nor could they be answered by a feminist, for the position of women in the Middle Ages varied enormously among classes; medieval bourgeois women gained important social and legal rights at one point and lost them at another; historically, the position of women has been no steady progression "up from slavery" but shows important advances and setbacks. Such is the testimony of *Flore et Jehane* if the *conte* is read in its full social context. But these facts cannot be accounted for by a methodology that takes sexual oppression as a prime mover of history or sees it as the inevitable product of "male ideology." I shall argue, on the contrary, that the *conte* does reflect social reality during the period of transition from feudalism to capitalism and that both the existence and uniqueness of its heroine point to changing needs of capital at different stages in its early development.

*   *   *

In itself Jehane's temperament is not unique among medieval heroines. She shares intelligence and tenacity with her contemporaneous sister Nicolette of the thirteenth-century French *chante-fable, Aucassin et Nicolette.* And, as with Jehane, Nicolette's aristocratic origin and destiny frame her sojourn in an inferior social position: Though we first meet her as a slave-girl in a noble household, she is revealed to be the kidnapped daughter of an Oriental king and eventually marries the young nobleman Aucassin. The main effort of the young couple is to avoid Nicolette's impending marriage to a *bacheler,* a university intellectual probably destined for the civil service, who *"du pain li gaaignera par honor"* (will honorably earn her bread). Despite this not unsympathetic reference to honorable employment, Nicolette's story remains confined to a courtly milieu in which no one is actually shown making money.

Jehane might be considered an ancestress of the best-known bourgeoise in medieval literature: Dame Alice, Chaucer's Wife of Bath, a petty entrepreneur in love as well as in business.[2] A five-time widow, Alice is eager to spend on young men the handsome profits netted from aged, impotent husbands by the judicious investment of her former capital in physical attraction. She has learned all too well the cardinal rules of every market, including the marriage market.

But comparison of Jehane with Alice is more instructive for the differences it reveals than for similarities. Jehane is no merchant of love; on the contrary, she is always dignified, conscious of her own worth, capable of rising to the heights of courtly manners and achieving a social status to which Alice could never seriously aspire. However attractive the modern reader may find Dame Alice's candor and vivacity, Chaucer devastates the character with ironic criticism from a dozen angles. Comparison of these characters throws into relief Chaucer's feudal-aristocratic sympathies, when we observe, by contrast with his work, how positively a bourgeoise could be portrayed. If Jehane is a forerunner of Alice, it is less in literary than in social terms, for the industry and commerce that created real prototypes of Jehane and Alice flourished earlier in the Low Countries than in England.

Despite his (or, a remote possibility, her) relatively progressive sympathies, the author of *Flore et Jehane* is no artist of stature comparable to that of the feudal-nostalgic Chaucer; nor should we expect such a connection between social partisanship and artistic capacity. Jehane does not "live" as Alice does; she is not described physically (except for a strategically located mole of temporary importance to the tortuous plot); she is given no central self-reflective monologues; she is insufficiently self-conscious to grasp our imagination as a "real" character.

Thus our author neither reveals the depths of human character nor explores major ethical issues, for, despite the verisimilitude of the story and its profusion of homely detail (which prompted earlier editors to see it as no more than *"une histoire de la vie privée"*[3]), Jehane is a symbol. Her success story is not only that of an intelligent woman but also that of a class, the newly rich *haute bourgeoisie* of merchants, commodity dealers, and financiers, whose rivalry with the ancient landed nobility brought it into a new and fruitful relation with royalty. Our story exalts hard work and thrift, investment and social mobility; its pointed satire aims at landowners and clerics; its dénouement links royalty and the new wealth. These features reflect the class attitudes and social realities of the urban patriciate of the Franco-Flemish lowlands—in the thirteenth century the most prosperous and politically advanced region in Europe.[4] The story is a parable of social change that for its central metaphor—the fertile relations between king and bourgeoisie—required a female protagonist of the middle class.[5]

Relations between this class and the king had nearly always been cordial in France, and during the thirteenth century they grew even closer. In urban centers the bourgeoisie required legal safeguards for its commercial and financial activity. It required protection from the power of local feudal lords, both lay and ecclesiastical, exemption from some taxes and the right to levy others, control of town government, and regulation of standard work conditions such as wage, price, and hours, and it required liberty of travel. These privileges only the king could grant, in the form of city charters or special decrees. He did so to his own advantage as

trician attitudes: its hostility toward landowners, lay and clerical, whose interests and indeed survival were directly threatened by the growth of the urban bourgeoisie.

Besides challenging feudal political power in the cities, the bourgeoisie challenged the economic interest of landed aristocrats. The bourgeoisie required a pool of free labor, for which it competed with landlords. The latter, in order to retain serfs and tenants on the land, were often forced to make concessions such as the commutation of feudal services in favor of wage labor. If such concessions were not made, the labor force of the manor or monastic estate might desert gradually or en masse to a town, where employment and legal freedom could be had.

Clergy were an annoyance to the bourgeoisie not only as landowners but as a specially privileged caste. Clergy enjoyed many privileges that brought them into conflict with the urban bourgeoisie: immunity from civil and criminal law, tax exemptions, the right to veto townspeople's decisions on rents and other financial matters. In many a medieval university town these and other privileges created continual town-versus-gown disputes that erupted into armed violence. Anticlerical sentiment was reinforced by the costly failure of the Crusade movement, which became more and more galling with the major defeats of the thirteenth century. And the increasingly obnoxious activities of the newly founded orders of friars, those widely satirized social parasites, added fuel to anticlerical sentiment.

Of landowners and clergy *Flore et Jehane* paints an extremely unflattering picture. There are three knights in the story. Of these, the first is irresponsible, cynical, and disloyal: Jehane's father, who has made no provision for her marriage, but simply turns her over to a social inferior, his own squire, Robert. Robert in turn is idiotically passive, clearly unworthy of his spirited wife. Immediately after the wedding he leaves on pilgrimage, abandoning his virgin bride. The third knight is outright evil: Raoul, a retainer of Jehane's father, tries to seduce and then rape Jehane in her husband's absence. Unlike the men of her class, Jehane has brains, energy, and tact. In a farcical bedroom scene she successfully defends herself from the attempted rape, but she is unable to defend herself from Raoul's lying assertion of conquest. (Here enters the aforementioned mole, for this section of the *conte* is a version of the well-known wager-motif.[8]) Hearing of his wife's supposed "infidelity" Robert immediately takes to the road again; but Jehane, disguised as a boy, follows him to Paris and offers her service as squire. Self-pitying and passive as always, Robert allows the ebullient young man to take over his life and earn him a fortune before the inevitable anagnorisis and Robert's own convenient death.

Our *conte* shows clergy to be as opportunistic and venal as knights. Two men of religion appear in the story: Raoul's confessor, and the hermit-confessor of Florus's first queen. Neither has the courage to defend a correct moral and doctrinal position; both capitulate to wealth and power, and accommodate to vice.

Thus the author shows a knighthood and clergy from whom no good can come. Admittedly, he pulls his punches by criticizing middle and lower levels of clergy and aristocracy rather than their most powerful representatives: a provincial monk and hermit rather than a cardinal, a knight rather than an earl. Given the patrician aspirations of the *haute bourgeoisie,* and its lack of national consolidation at this point, caution is to be expected: There existed as yet neither Jacobin nor Gironde. But the general point of the tale is clear enough: that the present ruling strata are so socially effete that monarchy can expect nothing valuable from them. For political stability and general social well-being, the king's best ally is his upper bourgeoisie.

On the testament of St. Louis (quoted above) the comment of the historian Georges Picot is especially appropriate for my purpose: *"Voilà les principes sur lesquels s'élévait l'alliance féconde du roi et des éléments les plus actifs de la nation."* ("These are the principles on which arose the fecund alliance of the king and the most active elements in the nation.") Though the real offspring of Florus and Jehane could not be anticipated by medieval poets, in retrospect we must acknowledge many of our own political ideas and institutions to be descended from the medieval bourgeoisie, and the bourgeois revolutions of England and France to be its true Gargantuan progeny.

As we have seen, the sex of our protagonist is dictated by the metaphor of social sterility and fertility. Monarchy must ally with the bourgeoisie in order that both may flourish; Florus must marry a woman who can conceive and bear children. Yet while Jehane's career represents the rise of her class, her story is not *only* representative. If a metaphor is to convince or persuade, it must have some degree of verisimilitude. Were there no generally recognized social model for the character of Jehane, the story could impress its audience merely as fantasy—like a tale of a talking dog or the equivalent. But such is not the treatment our heroine receives, and in fact it was the prior existence of women much like Jehane that called forth the possibility of her literary existence. The real existence of women like Jehane was due to precisely the social forces represented in her career, which thus "partakes of the reality it represents" (in Coleridge's famous phrase). The social forces symbolized in the plot had created new opportunities for women, so that on the literal plane, in social fact, Jehane was no anomaly in her time.

It was the development of mercantile capital that conferred on bourgeois women numerous legal and social advantages, the better to free new productive forces from old feudal restrictions. As markets and production expanded, more labor was required, especially during the European depopulation crisis of 1300 to 1450. In many respects the position of the medieval bourgeoise was superior to that of the aristocratic lady. I have already noted that she might be wealthier. In addition, while the aristocrat could inherit land in the absence of a male heir, she could administer and dispose of her property only while single; upon marriage, these rights and duties were assumed by the husband. But the bourgeoise could inherit even if there were a possible male heir, and even if married, she had full legal rights and obligations independent of her husband as if she were a single woman (*"femme sole"* was the legal category). She could own and run a

business or several businesses simultaneously; she could hire apprentices and initiate legal action. She could acquire an education, albeit a limited one; engage in substantial commercial or
financial activity; enter apprenticeship and practice such professions or trades as barber, apothecary, draper, grocer, tailor,
shoemaker, horse dealer, shipwright, metalworker, notary, sur-
geon, teacher, or artist, as well as the crafts and trades more
typically staffed by women, especially those pertaining to the silk
industry. By the end of the thirteenth century there were in Paris
fifteen women's guilds in those crafts wholly worked and administered by women, as well as eighty guilds of the crafts followed by
both sexes. While some guilds passed restrictive ordinances
against women, exceptions were made for the wives and daughters of male members. Clearly the impulse here was not to exclude women as such but to limit guild membership and keep
control of the industry in relatively few and familiar hands; for,
as Maurice Dobb remarks of the bourgeoisie: "To acquire political privilege was their first ambition: their second that as few as
possible should enjoy it."[9] As for the feudal–clerical conception
of woman's subordinate place and inferior strength, Georges Renard tells of the bakers of Pontoise who in 1263 attempted to
exclude women from the craft on the pretext that they were too
weak to knead bread properly with their own hands; the claim
was summarily dismissed by ordinance of *Parlement.*

Partly through the influence of the guilds on civic life women
were sometimes able to play a limited role in urban politics.
Though they generally did not hold office in urban government,
they did vote in plebiscites, as in Provins in the mid–fourteenth
century, where 12 percent of the voters were women. In
Chaucer's London women could obtain minor offices of profit,
such as inspector of commodities, and during the fourteenth and
fifteenth centuries English "silk-women" successfully lobbied
with city government and the Crown for protective price and
import legislation.[10]

This new status did not destroy feudal–clerical orthodoxy on
the woman question: New social fact existed alongside obsoles-

cent theory as it has often done before and since. At this point it was not on the level of theory that urban bourgeoisie and feudal Church confronted one another, but rather on such pragmatic issues as taxes, local administration, and territorial control. Not for another few centuries would the middle classes be sufficiently numerous and developed to counterpose an ideology expressing their own interests and, with this, ideas on marriage and family different from those of the Catholic Church and its decaying feudal social base.[11]

To some extent the working partnership of husband and wife must have modified in practice male authoritarianism in the family, but such a shift would be difficult to ascertain or measure. On the one hand, a fifteenth-century marriage manual warned husbands that "Tho sche be servant in degre / In some degre she felawe is"; on the other, women still required, at least formally, the husband's permission to travel. Diane Hughes shows that at least in Italy, where to a much greater extent than in England or France the extended family remained a coherent social unit, large family-based enterprises had the effect of tightening, not relaxing, traditional bonds of patriarchal authority; but Hughes focuses on great magnate families, not on artisans and middle bourgeois.[12]

Finally, the requirements of expanding mercantile capital did not always and necessarily conduce to the advancement of women. I have already noted the exclusionary clauses of some guild constitutions; moreover, in twelfth-century Italy women lost their ancient legal right to *tercia* (one-third the deceased husband's estate) as part of a general effort by the wealthiest families to "keep strategic urban power within the lineage group and thus preserve its political and military power."[13]

Despite such qualifications, the relative freedom of a medieval French or English bourgeoise might well have been envied by her nineteenth-century counterpart. How, then, and when did the situation change, so that by the seventeenth century a married woman could neither make a contract nor initiate legal action and had no property rights at all?

From the late fifteenth century, the Renaissance recovery from the earlier depopulation crisis, coupled with an influx of labor from villages to towns, created a surplus of labor. This was attributable partly to the decay of feudalism, partly to the extension of capital to the countryside in the form of enclosure. The already present protectionist tendencies of the guilds were intensified: not to limit the supply of labor per se, but to ensure that it was the right sort of labor. What nascent manufacture now required was less skilled, organized, independent labor and more unskilled, intensely exploitable, dependent labor. Polarization within the middle class accelerated sharply as the guilds of the bigger bourgeoisie tightened their control over the variegated processes of production. New restrictive laws were passed to drive small independent business people and artisans into the employ of the larger: laws drastically raising the guild entrance fees, requiring the execution of a costly and time-consuming "masterpiece" as a test of competency in the craft, restricting the number of apprentices a small employer could hire, and forbidding the right of assembly to worker-artisans who wished to protest such laws.

In such a climate any easily identifiable or "special" group might be victimized. The exclusion campaign was extended to foreigners, especially in England during the early years of the xenophobic sixteenth century. Country children were forbidden to apprentice in town. Women, though not the only vulnerable ones, were an easy and important target for exclusion from guilds, trades, and commercial activity. In 1461 Bristol forbade its weavers to employ their wives, daughters, or maids at the loom "lest the King's people, likely to do the King's service in his wars, should lack employment."[14] In 1490 at Kingston-upon-Hull, women were fined for weaving. And in 1511 the worsted weavers of Norwich forbade women to weave, reviving for the purpose the ancient argument that "thei bee nott of sufficient powre to werke the said worsteddes as thei owte to be wrought."[15] We have come a long way from the frustrated bakers of Pontoise!

So was created a domestic manufacturing force, male and female, adult and youth: no longer small entrepreneurs, apprentices, artisans, or business partners, but wage workers awaiting only the advent of mechanical power to complete their transformation into wage-slaves—a proletariat.[16] Deprived of the right to engage in business or pursue a profession, women were gradually reduced to economic dependency on employer and husband.

While the figure of Jehane was thus no anomaly during the high Middle Ages, it became one during the Renaissance. The surprise is not, after all, that Jehane appears in medieval literature, but that she is so isolated there. Indeed, Jehane captures a rare moment, for at the time when women like her did provide a real social model, the upper bourgeoisie was so eager to emulate the aristocratic ruling class that it preferred "courtly" romance and adventure to the depiction of its own life and struggle. And by the time the novel developed that could do justice to bourgeois life and mores, woman's social role was so depressed that a heroine like Jehane—successful on all levels—would be socially unrealistic.

I hope that the foregoing accounts for an unusual literary heroine, adducing the social facts that made her literary existence possible at one historical moment and improbable at others. If *Flore et Jehane* is in any way paradigmatic, it shows that the special oppression of women cannot be seen as the result of "male malice" or of feudal–clerical ideology, the latter itself an effect of economic and historical conditions. Although women have suffered special oppression under a variety of social systems, this oppression has varied in kind and magnitude according to the particular nature and economic needs of the society in which it has occurred. A feminist position, committed to the belief that sexual oppression is primary, cannot explain such variations. Nor can it account for advances in women's rights made during periods when no "women's struggle" existed as such.[17]

In the Middle Ages, as in our time, the special oppression of women was institutionalized in the nuclear family, validated by religion, protected by state power, and orchestrated according to the needs of production. But in the Middle Ages the social conditions for the real liberation of women did not exist any more than they did for the peasants and artisans whose continual rebellions constitute the "other side" of medieval European history. For us, those conditions do exist: Industrialization and imperialism opened the possibility for full liberation of men and women alike from exploitive relations. As in the Middle Ages, those who own sometimes find it convenient to confer a limited freedom on some women in productive labor, education, and personal life, but such gains remain limited and reversible as long as society is organized for private profit. To achieve the fullest liberation of all exploited and oppressed is the best use to which we can put our present partial freedom.

3

Womanliness in
The Man of Law's Tale

"Here is God's plenty," John Dryden affirmed of the Canterbury pilgrims. His judgment does especial justice to the variety in Chaucer's portraits of women. Dryden goes on to mention, in particular, "the mincing Lady-Prioress and the broad-speaking, gap-toothed Wife of Bath," and to these two longtime critical favorites one wants to add lithe Alison of *The Miller's Tale*, the Merchant's treacherous May, demivirtuous Dorigen, and the reluctant Emilye.

None of Chaucer's female characters, though, is as enigmatic as Constance, long-suffering heroine of *The Man of Law's Tale*. For most readers Constance is among the least attractive of Chaucer's women, sharing with patient Griselda (*The Clerk's Tale*) the repulsive masochistic qualities of extreme humility and silent endurance. Unlike Chaucer's other female characters, Constance achieves no multidimensional "reality." Since her appearance is not described, Constance exists as an agglomeration of virtues rather than as a recognizable person. Indeed Chaucer has

36

systematically reworked his nearest source (the fourteenth-century *Chronicle* of Nicholas Trivet) so as to reduce Constance's individuality, omitting, for example, the intellectual accomplishments of Trivet's bluestocking heroine.[1] Constance seems to exist in order to suffer; yet it is unclear why she suffers, certainly not to become perfect, for she is morally perfect from the start of the tale.

All this suggests that Constance is to be seen not as woman at all but rather as emblem, and while some critics have taken this view of Constance, their interpretations have not fully engaged the aesthetic problems of the tale. John Speirs sees Constance as a representation of the virtue she is named for,[2] yet the tale plainly escapes the confines of personification allegory: What would the other characters stand for? More recently, B. Huppé has identified Constance as a kind of archetypal true wife; the tale reveals "the true purpose of marriage" and also "the nature of reality by making visible the operation of God's Providence. . . ."[3] Huppé is right, I think, to focus on marriage, for the tale relates the story of Constance's two disastrous marriages. Still, marriage is not itself the theme of the tale but the image of a larger theme: It represents the relation of humanity at large to an apparently arbitrary and inscrutable God.[4]

Constance is no mere victim.[5] She is "Everywoman," who suffers because that is the human condition. Her passivity is what orthodox Christianity of the period recommended as a response to the human condition. It is this attitude toward life that makes *The Man of Law's Tale* so unattractive to the modern reader, not its narrative peculiarities. The tale represents an ethos we have learned to mistrust. We mistrust it, quite rightly, because of its social implications—implications that are present now as they were in Chaucer's time, and that continue to be exploited by some writers in their portrayal of female characters.

Constance's particular femininity serves, on the metaphysical and moral level, as an emblematic model for men and women alike. Because the tale makes a statement to and about humanity at large, its theological position becomes a social and political statement as well. To place the tale in its historical context will therefore be my aim.

Given the facts of contemporary social life in Chaucer's England, the tale would have a clear propagandistic thrust. Before taking up the politics of this medieval work of sexual politics, let us look at the sex. What is the nature of Constance's sexuality? Has she a sex life? And what is the ideological role of other women in the tale, Constance's antagonists?

In *The Man of Law's Tale,* there are three passages, one in each division of the poem, that comment on Constance's relation to a man or to men generally. All three of these passages are incongruously vulgar, yet they are neither jokes nor lapses in taste. That the incongruities are so obvious, that there are several, and that they are so symmetrically placed, argues for a deliberate rhetorical function. These passages have the effect of jarring the reader through disharmony of style, tone or content. In doing so, they direct the reader's attention to other levels of meaning.

The first of these curious passages forms part of the amplification of Constance's sorrow when she learns that she must marry the Sultan of Syria:

> The day is comen of hir departynge;
> I seye, the woful day fatal is come,
> That ther may be no lenger tariynge,
> But forthward they hem dressen, alle and some.
> Custance, that was with sorwe al overcome,
> Ful pale arist, and dresseth hire to wende;
> For wel she seeth ther is non oother ende.
>
> Allas! what wonder is it thogh she wepte,
> That shal be sent to strange nacioun
> Fro freendes that so tendrely hire kepte,
> And to be bounden under subjeccioun
> Of oon, she knoweth nat his condicioun?
> Housbondes been alle goode, and han ben yoore;
> That knowen wyves; I dar sey yow na moore.
>
> (260–73)[6]

A sudden shift in style and tone occurs in the last two lines. From the rhetorically elevated and public sorrow of the imperial court,

we descend abruptly to the cruder, more private world of husbands and wives; from sincere lamentation to coy irony; from
theatrically distanced "Allas!" to intimate direct address. And by
asserting in the last two lines what had not previously been in
doubt, Chaucer practices "deliberate mystification"[7]—one of his
favorite narrative devices. The narrator suggests that he, like the
rest of us, knows more about marriage than he can tactfully
reveal, and that the ideal wife's opinion of husbands is sadly
mistaken. Such ironies and insinuations seem more appropriate
to the Wife of Bath's world than to Constance's. But what
Chaucer accomplishes here is a double mystification, for in fact
the Sultan does appear to be a good man. He has suffered for
Constance with recognizable courtly symptoms. He falls in love
with his "princesse lointaine" sight unseen, pledges to love her
forever, threatens to die of love, and, above all, converts to
Christianity for her sake. We have no reason to suspect that the
Sultan will be other than a good husband. These lines, then, are
blatantly at odds with their rhetorical and dramatic context. The
issue is not, after all, one of husbands and marriage, but of
imposed circumstance and one's attitude toward it. Chaucer permits the narrative voice to assume the narrower, more philistine,
point of view, and in doing so he invites us to see such crudity as
unsatisfactory.

Rupture of tone and deliberate mystification appear again in
the stanzas that describe the wedding of Constance and King
Alla:

> Me list nat of the chaf, ne of the stree,
> Maken so long a tale as of the corn.
> What sholde I tellen of the roialtee
> At mariage, or which cours goth biforn;
> Who bloweth in a trumpe or in an horn?
> The fruyt of every tale is for to seye:
> They ete, and drynke, and daunce, and synge, and pleye.
>
> They goon to bedde, as it was skile and right;
> For thogh that wyves be ful hooly thynges,
> They moste take in pacience at nyght

Swiche manere necessaries as been plesynges
To folk that han ywedded hem with rynges,
And leye a lite hir hoolynesse aside,
As for the tyme,—it may no bet bitide.
(701–14)

The wedding itself is described with succinct conventionality: It is no different from any other proper royal wedding. That the narrator follows the royal couple to bed, though, seems a distinct breach of manners and literary convention, not quite voyeuristic but very nearly so, and the provocative coyness of "swiche manere necessaries" reminds us briefly of *The Merchant's Tale.* Moreover, to focus on sexuality here is to remind the reader of what he would not have wondered otherwise. We can readily accept the married Constance as a "holy thing"—until Chaucer, under pretext of reassuring us, forces us to contemplate the question of her holiness. But Chaucer's blunt reminder does not diminish his heroine's character. On the contrary, Chaucer urges us to be aware of the marital relation in all its dimensions because it is precisely in her sexual role that Constance's main virtue is best seen: the acceptance of fate and authority. This purpose is foreshadowed in the first two lines of the passage quoted: If the ceremony and feast represent only chaff or straw, and receive correspondingly brief treatment, then the grain must be what is more fully described, the wedding night.

A last incongruous note of crude sexuality occurs in the stanza in which a Roman senator (with whom Constance and her son are living incognito) describes Constance to King Alla, who has come on pilgrimage to Rome:

"But God woot," quod this senatour also,
"So vertuous a lyvere in my lyf
Ne saugh I nevere as she, ne herde of mo,
Of worldly wommen, mayde, ne of wyf.
I dar wel seyn hir hadde levere a knyf
Thurghout hir brest, than ben a womman wikke;
There is no man koude brynge hire to that prikke."
(1023–29)

The last line includes two puns that break the elevated tone of what precedes. "Man" may mean any person, or it may mean specifically a male; "prikke" may be a point (degree, situation, condition), or it may be the male genital. The senator's description, then, like the two examples already cited, is an oddly cynical, nearly lecherous reminder of the world of real men and women. Like the others it seems at odds with the story itself, for it effectively reduces moral virtue to sexual abstinence, though we have seen Constance's virtue to be far superior to simple physical chastity. Again the abrupt descent into crudity reminds us how limited would be the view of Constance as a "real" woman, of her trials merely as adventures, or of her passive nature as an exclusively feminine virtue.

Constance is defined not only by her own virtue, but by contrast with women who are her opposites. The three passages cited above show Constance to be a humble woman who seeks no influence, who does not complain about her role but submits willingly to the authority of father, husband, and God. Another sort of woman appears in the tale: proud, subversive, and jealous. This is the nature of the two women responsible for Constance's suffering: her mothers-in-law, the Sultaness and Donegild. Both are characterized in apostrophe:

> O Sowdanesse, roote of iniquitee!
> Virago, thou Semyrame the secounde!
> O serpent under femynynytee,
> Lik to the serpent depe in helle ybounde!
> O feyned womman, al that may confounde
> Vertu and innocence, thurgh thy malice,
> Is bred in thee, as nest of every vice!
> (358–64) Unto thy malice and thy tirannye!
>   And therfore to the feend I thee resigne;
>   Lat hym enditen of thy traitorie!
> Fy, mannysh, fy!—o nay, by God, I lye—

> Fy, feendlych spirit, for I dar wel telle,
> Thogh thou heere walke, thy spirit is in
> helle!
> (778–84)

Unlike Constance, the older women seek power and do not hesitate to abuse power to protect private interests. In striving to maintain their own authority both the Sultaness and Donegild inflict suffering on Constance, thereby flouting superior authorities. Both commit an offense against their sons, who love Constance—a breach of maternal obligation. Both attempt to destroy a marriage, the sacrament binding Constance to her husband. Both women rebel against the royal will, for both sons are kings; and both violate the principle of *caritas* (charity, or selfless love of one's fellows) in their malice toward Constance. Most important, Constance's mothers-in-law have rejected the will of God as it is manifested in the conversions of the two kings and especially in the miracle performed at Alla's court. So unnatural are Donegild and the Sultaness that they are addressed not simply as bad women, but as not truly women at all: "virago," "serpent under femininity," "feigned woman," "mannish," "fiendly spirit." In passing the limits of morality they have lost their sexual identity, for were they truly women they could not behave so viciously.

Indeed, the female antagonists have virtually forfeited human, as well as sexual, identity; they are tools and types of Satan, and as such are associated with the Fall of man—an event that Chaucer notes (367–68) was traditionally attributed to the baneful influence of woman. Constance, on the other hand, is associated with redemption. In stress she always appeals to Christ; like Mary, she suffers passively. Eve and Mary, opposed exemplars of feminine conduct, appear in Constance's prayer when she is exiled from England:

> "Mooder," quod she, "and mayde bright, Marie,
> Sooth is that thurgh wommanes eggement
> Mankynde was lorn, and damned ay to dye,
> For which thy child was on a croys yrent.

> Thy blisful eyen sawe al his torment;
> Thanne is ther no comparison bitwene
> Thy wo and any wo man may sustene.
>
> "Thow sawe thy child yslayn bifore thyne yen,
> And yet now lyveth my litel child, parfay!
> Now, lady bright, to whom alle woful cryen,
> Thow glorie of wommanhede, thow faire may,
> Thow haven of refut, brighte sterre of day,
> Rewe on my child, that of thy gentilesse,
> Rewest on every reweful in distresse."
>
>   (841–54)

Eve's ambitious refusal to accept her assigned role was responsible for universal damnation, while Mary, accepting God's will both in bearing Jesus and in watching him die, contributed to salvation. Constance claims that there can be no comparison between Mary's suffering and that of other human beings. But surely her saying so encourages us to make exactly that comparison, especially in view of the Madonna-like image of Constance at the moment when this prayer is uttered, holding her baby and abandoned by the world. As Eve's fault recurs in the Sultaness and Donegild, so Mary's virtue is exemplified in Constance. The characters of Mary and Eve live symbolically in Constance and her antagonists and, further, in each of us as possible attitudes toward circumstance. Constance's femininity, then, is not merely that of home and hearth; like that of the patient Griselda, it is the image of a metaphysical stance. Through time and circumstance Constance remains the exemplary sufferer.

With Alla's rediscovery of Constance at Rome, and the couple's return to England, the story seems to have ended happily. Husband and wife are reunited "in joye and in quiete" (1131).

> But litel while it lasteth, I yow heete,
> Joye of this world, for tyme wol nat abyde;
> Fro day to nyght it changeth as the tyde.
>
> Who lyved euere in swich delit o day
> That hym ne moeved outher conscience,
> Or ire, or talent, or som kynnes affray,

> Envye, or pride, or passion, or offence?
> I ne seye but for this ende this sentence,
> That litel while in joye or in plesance
> Lasteth the blisse of Alla with Custance.
> (1132–41)

The event that intrudes on their happiness is the death of Alla, for which Constance "hath ful greet hevynesse" (1145). The reader may wonder why Chaucer, having brought his heroine to a deserved happy ending that rounds off the tale so neatly, now bothers to undercut that ending by visiting on Constance yet another misfortune. The point, I think, is that even the saintly or exemplary character is not finally exempt from the cycle of woe that has been Constance's lot. No virtue suffices to free one from the mutability of circumstance, for, given the uncertainty of life, virtue is always tested and must always be renewed. Unlike Constance's other trials, that of her husband's death is not the work of demonic antagonist, but of time and nature, to which we are all subject.

Constance now returns to her father's court in Rome, where she "heryeth God an hundred thousand sythe" (1155), and lives out her life "In vertu and in hooly almus-dede" (1156). The last lines of the tale place the earthly cycle of fortune in ultimate perspective:

> Now Jhesu Crist, that of his myght may sende
> Joye after wo, governe us in his grace,
> And kepe us alle that been in this place! Amen
> (1160–62)

More than simply another example of the pious commendation that often ends a medieval poem, this, like the ending of *Troilus and Criseyde,* is part of the symbolic action of the story. The final prayer reminds us once again that there is only one source of everlasting joy. Although the means is symbolic action rather than logical argument, the message of Chaucer's tale is the same as that of Boethius's tract:

> . . . God, byholdere and forwytere of alle thingis, duelleth above, and the present eternite of his sighte renneth alwey with the diverse

qualite of our dedes, dispensynge and ordeynynge medes to gode
men and tormentz to wikkide men. Ne in ydel ne in veyn ne ben
ther put in God hope and preyeris that ne mowen nat ben unspedful
ne withouten effect whan they been ryghtful.[8]

In *The Man of Law's Tale,* then, delineation of female character conveys the moral dialectic of the poem. It is unlikely,
though, that the reader who dislikes Constance as a woman will
be pleased with her as an emblem of human submission, for he or
she will sense the topical or historical uses of that emblem.
Chaucer is notoriously silent about the important social movements of his day, and most conspicuously silent about the great
rebellion in 1381 of thousands of laborers and artisans. The rebellion was no isolated event but climaxed a long series of protests
against oppressive taxes and labor laws; even after 1381 rebellions continued on the local level. To Chaucer's courtly patrons,
employers and friends, the tale of Constance (written probably
about 1390) must have been a welcome reaffirmation of the hier-
archical values that had been so recently and so sharply attacked.
In rejecting Eve's faults, and in praising acceptance of one's lot,
the tale would have had timely application.

As for the rebels, they, too, were alert to the propagandistic
uses of Christian myth, and their use of it also reflects their class
consciousness. They, too, could adduce Eve as an archetypal
female model, but to a very different end from that of the courtly
poet. Here, according to Froissart's version of John Ball's famous
sermon, is their view of Eve:

> Ah! ye good people, the matters goeth not well to pass in England,
> nor shall not do till everything be common, and that there be no
> villeins nor gentlemen, but that we may be all united together, and
> that the lords be no greater masters than we be. What have we
> deserved, or why should we be kept thus in servage? We be all
> come from one father and one mother, Adam and Eve: whereby
> can they say or show that they be greater lords than we be, saying
> that they cause us to win and labor for that they dispend?[9]

Universal mother and symbol of egalitarian democracy, this Eve
is far different from the archetypal sinner of *The Man of Law's*

Tale. It is not the peasant's Eve whom God caused to "brynge us in servage"—into servitude, spiritual for all, but for many social as well. The Eve of the rebellious peasants represented not their slavery but their freedom, not the source of feudal hierarchy, but a golden age of social equality that feudalism had turned to lead. This is the Eve of the oppressed. She reappears five centuries later in a very different social context, but still as an image of primordial and desired equality, in the verse preface to *Women and Economics* (1898) by the American feminist Charlotte P. Gilman:

> In dark and early ages, through the primal forests faring,
> Ere the soul came shining into prehistoric night,
> Two fold man was equal; they were comrades dear and daring,
> Living wild and free together in unreasoning delight.

As literary figures, Mary and Eve, Constance and Donegild of *The Man of Law's Tale,* are with us still. One thinks, for instance, of Hawthorne's or of Henry Miller's novels about stereotypically submissive or stereotypically willful women. More recently we have observed the evolution of Constance into the equally emblematic, and emblematically named, antiheroine of *The Story of O,* whose political meaning is made explicit in an attached essay entitled "A Slave's Revolt." The commentator's point is that slaves love their master and cannot do without him. Here, praise of suffering has reached its furthest point, and the value of O is to have shown us what a modern Constance might look like. These models of submission will remain the stuff of our literature as long as the social conflict exists that calls them into being. One hopes that they will eventually become historical curiosities, along with that social conflict, and along with the real-life Constances and O's of both sexes that have been created by it.

4

Slaying Python: marriage and misogyny in a Chaucerian text

A woman is murdered by a man who loves her. This act of brutal misogynistic violence is the center of two Chaucerian narratives. In both of them a breach of female chastity motivates the crime, which is preventive in one case, in the other punitive. Both narratives recoil from confronting the crime; instead, they displace attention to other topics, clearly trivial as compared with the murder.

I am writing, of course, of the Physician's and Manciple's tales, those oddly free-floating fragments in *The Canterbury Tales*.[1] To strip the stories to skeletal form, as I have just done, is to see them as two versions of the same story: It is as if the poet returns to the scene of the crime, the better to repeat it. If *The Physician's Tale* digresses on woman's relation to nature, *The Manciple's Tale* both raises that topic rhetorically and illustrates it dramatically in the "natural lust" of Phebus's wife. If *The Physician's Tale* digresses on the control of young women, *The Manci-*

ple's Tale again transforms rhetoric into action, showing an ultimately homicidal version of the impulse to control women. The protagonist-murderer is much more fully characterized in *The Manciple's Tale;* he is given a past, a personality, and dialogue with someone other than his victim. In line with increased complexity, the murder in *The Manciple's Tale* is an impulsive act, followed by the perpetrator's self-lacerating repentance.

It is as the more developed version of the story that *The Manciple's Tale* interests me here. An arsenal of linguistic resources is deployed in the tale, in a dazzling display of tactical variety implementing the strategy of misogyny—a strategy, I will argue, at once personal and cultural. At stake is not so much the "meaning" of the tale as its energies and movements, particularly the movement of displacement, whether by sarcasm, apostrophe, metonymy, metaphor, or rearrangement of source material. In what has been called "the relentless pursuit of displaced desire"[2] I have used various tactics. These may well offend medievalists, since medieval criticism, more than that of any other period, has resisted the salutary, if rough, ministrations of contemporary methods. I have rehabilitated the poet's biography. I have read a psychoanalytic subtext in the tale, using Freud's theory of pregenital libido organization. I have inserted individual misogyny into the cultural context of Christian doctrine and of classical myth, foregrounding the productive and reproductive economics represented in the myth. And I have interspersed my argument with fragments from certain contemporary texts, not all of them artistic creations. If this is not the tale some critics are accustomed to read, so much the better—so much the more necessary this reading.

What I offer, then, is a deliberately and necessarily eclectic meditation on the tale, a reading that, like its object, is at once personal and cultural in its motivation and its anger.

Animal Love

It happens in many analyses that as one approaches their end new recollections emerge which have hitherto been kept carefully con-

cealed. Or it may be that on one occasion some unpretentious remark is thrown out in an indifferent tone of voice as though it were superfluous; that then on another occasion something further is added, which begins to make the physician prick his ears, and that at last he comes to recognize this despised fragment of a meaning as the key to the weightiest secrets that the patient's neurosis has veiled.

Sigmund Freud, "The Wolf Man," chap. 8

> A she-wolf hath also a vileyns kynde.
> The lewedeste wolf that she may fynde,
> Or leest of reputacioun, wol she take,
> In tyme whan hir lust to han a make.
> Alle thise ensamples speke I by thise men
> That been untrewe, and nothyng by wommen.
> For men han evere a likerous appetit
> On lower thyng to parfourne hire delit
> Than on hir wyves, be they never so faire,
> Ne never so trewe, ne so debonaire.
> Flessh is so newefangel, with meschaunce,
> That we ne konne in nothyng han plesaunce
> That sowneth into vertu any while.
>
> (183–95)

The passage immediately above, spoken by the narrator of *The Manciple's Tale,* requires a double excavation: first, to locate sarcasm within the literal sense; then to locate a literal truth beneath the sarcasm. Of whom are these exempla predicated? Men, says the narrator, but rhetoric and plot belie this assertion, showing that the exempla actually apply to women, who are like animals in their lust and newfangledness. At another level, though, the sarcasm vanishes. The words become literally true, for the narrator asserts what we recognize, and what Chaucer's audience evidently recognized, as a truth about many men: that they tend to feel sexually attracted to women beneath them in social rank and moral or intellectual capacity, while for their virtuous peers they feel respect but not desire.

It is an attitude that, at least according to Freud's testimony, survived to prevail as the dominant neurosis among middle-class

European men of the nineteenth and twentieth centuries; it is by no means extinct today. Here is Freud's version of the phenomenon, less moralistic than the Manciple's:

> Two currents whose union is necessary to ensure a completely normal attitude in love have, in the cases we are considering, failed to combine. These two may be distinguished as the *affectionate* and the *sensual* current. . . . The whole sphere of love in such people remains divided in the two directions personified in art as sacred and profane (or animal) love. Where they love they do not desire and where they desire they cannot love. They seek objects which they do not need to love, in order to keep their sensuality away from the objects they love. . . . As soon as the condition of debasement is fulfilled, sensuality can be freely expressed, and important sexual capacities and a high degree of pleasure can develop. . . . We have reduced psychical impotence to the failure of the affectionate and the sensual currents in love to combine, and this developmental inhibition has in turn been explained as being due to the influences of strong childhood fixations and of later frustration in reality through the intervention of the barrier against incest. [Italics in original.][3]

It is certainly a vision of debased "animal love" that occupies the consciousness of the narrator of *The Manciple's Tale,* a preoccupation anticipated in the recurrent animal imagery of the exchanges among Manciple, Cook, and Host: "Fy, stynkyng swyn!" (40), "I trowe that ye dronken han wyn ape" (44), "He wole . . . / Reclayme thee and brynge thee to lure" (71–72), "So myghte he lightly brynge me in the snare. / Yet hadde I levere payen for the mare" (77–78). There is also the Cook's horse, which its drunken rider can barely guide and from which he is in constant danger of falling. The tale itself virtually swarms with animal life. Phebus is slayer of "Phitoun, the serpent;" the crow is compared with jay, swan and nightingale (130–38); the lover is described as not worth "the montance of a gnat" (255). In a series of exempla, women are compared with birds who prefer worms to the dainties of captivity, with cats who prefer a mouse to milk, with a she-wolf who accepts any mate in heat (163–86).

The narrator isn't alone in his reductive vision of woman, for Phebus himself has set the stage. A jealous husband, Phebus oppresses his wife with dehumanizing possessiveness. The degrading reality of his attitude is revealed in the damning verbal parallelism that introduces captive crow and captive wife:

> Now hadde this Phebus in his hous a crowe
> Which in a cage he fostred many a day. . . .
> (130–31)

> Now hadde this Phebus in his hous a wyf
> Which that he lovede moore than his lyf. . . .
> (139–40)

Phebus does all he can, day and night, to please his wife, yet his effort seems primarily sexual and primarily for his own gratification: "for his manhede and his governaunce" (157–58). "Plesaunce," "embrace" and "labor" appear in the passage, and the phrase "to spille labor" contains, I would suggest, a play on the spilling of semen. But despite diurnal and nocturnal labors, Phebus cannot satisfy his wife, for women's natural promiscuity is not to be restrained by husbandly effort. So asserts the narrator:

> But God it woot, ther may no man embrace
> As to destreyne a thyng which that nature
> Hath natureelly set in a creature.
> (160–62)

It is a portrait of sexual ineffectiveness within an ambivalent relationship. Phebus desires where he cannot satisfy, loves where he cannot trust, and fears what he loves. His is certainly a case of split affect, albeit not along the identical lines that Freud posits or that the Manciple confesses on behalf of men in general.

Of a piece with Freud's theory of split affect, though, is the narrator's digression on the word *lemman* (205–39). The ostensible purpose of this digression is to justify the use of *lemman* to denote the wife's lover: Yet the justification is unnecessary, for the word is an ordinary one, common in medieval popular lyric, and neither obscene nor pejorative. The passage ends by degrading women across the board: Lady or wench, "Men layn that oon as lowe as lith that oother" (222). The Colonel's lady and Judy O'Grady are sisters under the skin because they are slits, sexual objects, animals. Thus, the passage moves from false prudish gallantry to brutal degradation. That sort of oscillation is what we also encounter in Phebus's attitude toward his wife: from loving her "moore than his lyf" (140) to killing her on the spot, from uxorious obsession to homicidal rage, then back again to sentimentality: "O deere wyf! . . . /that were to me so sad and eek so trewe, . . . /Ful giltelees, that dorste I swere, ywys!" (274–77).

At the higher stage of the pregenital sadistic-anal organization, the striving after the object appears in the form of an impulse to mastery, in which injury or annihilation of the object is a matter of indifference. This form and preliminary stage of love is hardly to be distinguished from hate in its behavior toward the object.
Sigmund Freud, "Instincts and Their Vicissitudes" (1915)

The narrator lacks rhetorical balance. He apologizes for the innocuous *lemman* but not for the genuinely crude *swyve* (256); he dispatches the wife in a single line (265) and winds up the tale as if it were primarily about a crow. If we may see Phebus as the narrator's fictional projection, it isn't surprising that he shows a similar lack of proportion. I want to argue that such imbalance is what the tale is fundamentally "about": a condition of unintegrated or unbalanced sensuality as expressed in relations with women and attitudes toward women.[4] It is here that I would locate the source of its misogyny.

It is time, then, to address the question of author and narrator, for insofar as I see the tale as misogynistic, rather than as a cautionary exposé of misogyny, to the extent that I refuse the author/narrator distinction, to that extent I implicate the author. Is it legitimate to hold the poet responsible for the attitudes of his characters?

There are reasons, of course, not to do so. We have no hard extrapoetic evidence of Chaucer's real opinions; art is not the direct transcription of life, and, as Talbot Donaldson has shown,

even the narrator called "Chaucer" is not necessarily the poet.[5]
This distinction is an important gauge of Chaucer's aesthetic so-
phistication, on which depends the interpretation of many passages, including one in *The Manciple's Tale* (223–34) where the
narrator extends his sexual exempla into the social sphere. Surely
those are opinions that Chaucer didn't consciously share. Rather,
he shows the dangerously subversive social consequences of be-
lieving language to be "only" language, verbal difference
"merely" verbal, *flatus vocis*. And since the social examples are
wrong, and work analogically to the sexual, the latter, too, are
wrong in Chaucer's view. The Manciple's cynical misogyny is part
of Chaucer's indirect ironic critique of his narrator; so are the
disproportion in the tale and its evasion of its own central moral
issue. Chaucer has given us too many charming and sympathetic
female characters to be considered a misogynist at any level.
Moreover, the greatness of spirit displayed elsewhere, as well as
the elevated Christian sentiments that Chaucer obviously en-
dorses, all argue against anything narrow or brutal in his work.

With some of these arguments I agree—to a point. But here is
another way of looking at the evidence.

A murder is committed. The perpetrator is a character within a
fiction within a fiction. It is possible to see the character as a
projection of the fictional narrator's desires or flawed personality: a possibility not limited to *The Manciple's Tale*. Many critics
agree, for example, that the Loathly Hag's happy fate in *The
Wife of Bath's Tale* can be seen as the narrator's fictional realization of her own desire to regain youth, beauty, and a rich young
husband. The same may be seen, too, in *The Merchant's Tale*,
where the series of boxes within boxes includes a third term:
Justinus and Placebo personify the components of January's psy-
chomachia, and January is a projection of the Merchant's disillu-
sion and marital failure. In such cases, what prevents us from
extending the series a step further, to include the author?

The distinction between poet and narrator has, like Newtonian
physics, a circumscribed validity: The latter works for a given
range of phenomena, but outside that range another physics—

Heisenbergian or Einsteinian—is required. So here: If we wish to disengage from the story a psychoanalytic or cultural subtext, to locate the unsaid, then the boundary between poet and narrator becomes less distinct. Indeed, that distinction itself might be seen as a displacement of attention from poet to character.

Nor is such effacement of boundary the invention of modern criticism; it is part of Chaucer's own practice. At what point does the narrator of *The Parson's Tale* become the poet himself, retracting some of his works and praying for personal salvation? No change of voice, no crossing of the boundary is explicitly signalled. Similarly with the *Troilus:* somehow, with no verbal indication, the naive and gullible narrator is transfigured into the world-weary sophisticate who orchestrates the pain-ridden final stanzas and dedicates the entire work, in his own authentic poet's voice, to his historically real friends. So that it may at a given point be either true or not true, or both, to assert that Chaucer "is" or "is not" his narrator.

For [the metaphysician] a thing either exists or does not exist; a thing cannot at the same time be both itself and something else. Positive and negative absolutely exclude one another; cause and effect stand in rigid antithesis one to the other.

At first sight this mode of thinking seems to us very luminous, because it is that of so-called sound common sense. Only sound common sense, respectable fellow that he is in the homely realm of his own four walls, has very wonderful adventures directly he ventures out into the wide world of research.

Frederick Engels, *Socialism: Utopian and Scientific*

"Mathematical axioms are not axioms of general truth. What is true of relation—of form and quantity—is often grossly false in regard to morals, for example. In this latter science it is very usually untrue that the aggregated parts are equal to the whole. In chemistry also the axiom fails. In the consideration of motive it fails; for two motives, each of a given value, have not, necessarily,

*a value when united, equal to the sum of their values apart. There
are numerous other mathematical truths which are only truths
within the limits of relation. . . . I mean to say," continued Du-
pin, while I merely laughed at his last observations, "that if the
Minister had been no more than a mathematician, the Prefect
would have been under no necessity of giving me this check. I
knew him, however, as both mathematician and poet, and my
measures were adapted to his capacity, with reference to the circumstances by which he was surrounded."*

Edgar Allan Poe, *The Purloined Letter*

Certainly Chaucer indicates his narrators' inadequacies in numerous ways throughout *The Canterbury Tales;* doubtless he would
disapprove morally and intellectually of murder, even the murder
of an adulterous wife. At the same time, poets are well known,
even notorious, for not having one-track minds; they are known
to reveal in their work disjunction and inconsistency. On the
level of fantasy or wish fulfillment, Blake may not have made a
mistake about Milton. Art isn't simply the transcription of life,
but it is partly that, and it is partly the creative figuration of fear
and desire as well.

In keeping with the two positions I have just laid out—maintaining versus effacing the author/narrator distinction—Chaucer's
handling of his source for *The Manciple's Tale* can be interpreted
in two ways. One is represented by J. B. Severs, who tends to
efface the distinction with statements like this: "Chaucer is not
only unsympathetic but deeply antagonistic to Phebus' wife. He
blackens her character and turns the reader's sympathies against
her at every opportunity."[6] Severs' inference was drawn from the
alteration of sources; other changes not mentioned by Severs also
help intensify the misogynistic thrust of the tale.

Item: whereas in Ovid and other texts the woman is named
Coronis, Chaucer deprives her of the individuality of a name as
of any other characterization. She is a flat, anonymous, stereo-
typical figure, "The Adulterous Wife," no more an individual
than an animal is. Her only identity is that of being possessed.

WRITING WOMAN : 56

Item: Whereas in Ovid, Coronis is Apollo's mistress, Chaucer makes her his wife. Therefore, she is no longer a free agent but, restricted by a range of obligations and expectations and laws, becomes adulteress and sinner. The previously gratuitous murder becomes a punishment, harsh but not necessarily unjust.

Item: Whereas Ovid offers no characterization of Coronis's other lover, Chaucer makes him "A man of litel reputacioun" (199). This detail shows the wife to be indiscriminate in lust, confirming her affinity with the animals mentioned in the exempla preceding the revelation of her adultery.

Beside reducing the reader's sympathy for the woman, such changes make it far more difficult to condemn the man. To follow out Severs' view is to posit latent sympathy for the husband on Chaucer's part: his acceptance of Phebus's motive if not of his act.

Now one might propose instead—to maintain the author/narrator distinction—that these changes "render the moral issues more complex" than in the sources, where sympathy is heavily weighted for Coronis. The aesthetic aim would be accordingly to recreate in and for the reader a justice–mercy debate centering on the question of justifiable homicide of an adulterous wife. (This might not be a completely grotesque issue in, say, Spain, although it would certainly be obsolete in late-medieval England.) In such a debate the mercy side would be so glaringly self-evident as to require no elaboration in the tale itself, any more than *The Prioress's Tale* requires explicit defense of the Jews in order to show the illogic of anti-Semitism. Chaucer would be saying something like this: "The sources make it too easy to condemn the man. I want to make it more difficult because some people (not me, of course) think he would be justified in killing his wife. They are the ones I propose to tempt by making their error easy to fall into. Hence the correct response will require not only moral struggle; it will require even resistance to my text."

Attractive as this alibi may be, I believe that it sidesteps too much: Chaucer's repetition of the murder motif, the pervasive psychoanalytic content of the tale, cultural factors conducive to misogyny, Chaucer's own life. So I propose another view, a return to the obvious, if you will: that this repeated story does actually emanate from Chaucer, "representing"—in whatever mediated fashion we like to think of it—his attitudes and fantasies.

The plot thickens when we turn to Chaucer's biography. My reading of the tale will stand without biographical support. Nonetheless it doesn't strike me as pure coincidence that the life offers material tending to invite some extension of the tale's misogyny to its author. I refer to the *raptus* of 1380 and to the poet's marriage with Philippa Payne de Roet: two controversial and often-ignored episodes that it is perhaps time to restore to our understanding of Chaucer.

In a legal document dated May 1380, one Cecily Chaumpaigne releases to Chaucer her right of legal action against him in connection with her *raptus*. Was the offense a sexual assault committed by Chaucer during one of his wife's frequent absences? (Philippa was at the time, as she often was, in attendance in the household of her patron, John of Gaunt.) Or was it, as Chaucerians have usually preferred to believe, the abduction of a rich heiress and ward for the purpose of marriage, with Chaucer acting on behalf of an unknown principal? The opinion of two legal historians who have written on the case is that by the later fourteenth century, *raptus* meant unequivocally a sexual assault. They agree that contemporary legal practice as well as various extant documents make it clear the case *could not* have been one of abduction.[7] Given these conclusions, and given that our historical "knowledge" often depends upon evidence far less detailed and convincing than what is available here, it appears to me a case of willful ignorance to claim, with F. N. Robinson and others, that "the circumstances of the Chaumpaigne case and Chaucer's connection with them, still remain unknown"[8] and to leave it at that.

A similar deliberate agnosticism surrounds the central arena of Chaucer's relation to women (his marriage), maintaining it as perpetually mysterious. As with the *raptus* case, we have a detailed study by an expert in a special field: there law; here heraldry. A close heraldic study of the tomb of Thomas Chaucer,

> For God would never have created any, I do not say angel, but even man, whose future wickedness he foreknew, unless He had equally known to what uses in behalf of the good He could turn him, thus embellishing the course of the ages, as it were an exquisite poem set off with antitheses. For what are called antitheses are among the most elegant of the ornaments of speech. They might be called in Latin "oppositions." . . . As, then, these oppositions of contraries lend beauty to the language, so the beauty of the course of this world is achieved by the opposition of contraries, arranged, as it were, by an eloquence not of words but of things. This is quite plainly stated in the Book of Ecclesiasticus, in this way: "God is set against evil, and life against death: so is the sinner against the godly. So look upon all the works of the Most High, and these are two and two, one against another."[13]

Scarcely surprising, then, that desire is split into *caritas* and *cupiditas:*

> For there is also a love wherein we love that which we ought not to love: and this love is hated by him who loves that wherewith he loves what ought to be loved. For it is quite possible for both to exist in one man. And this co-existence is good for a man, to the end that this love which conduces to our living well may grow, and the other, which leads us to evil may decrease, until our whole life be perfectly healed and transmuted into good. For if we were beasts, we would love the fleshly and sensual life, and this would be our sufficient good. . . . [14]

This philosophical version of split affect remains in essence if not in rhetoric culturally dominant into our own day. The well-known "whore–madonna" syndrome accompanies it, for how obvious it is to perceive women, among the works of the Most High, set like all other phenomena "two and two, one against the other": Eve or Mary, sinner or saint, wife or prostitute, good girl or bad. But the polarity of woman is inevitably subsumed in a larger binary structure, that of woman and man, so that it is only a short step to the sort of reductive consciousness we have already observed with the Manciple. Here are two other versions of it, an earlier and a later:

> What is the difference? Whether it is in a wife or a mother, it is still Eve (the temptress) that we must beware of in any woman.[15]

> I always believed there was good girls and bad girls. This was a
> strong belief my father taught me. I had to learn the hard way that
> all women are alike.[16]

What is surprising about *The Manciple's Tale* is the consistency with which it inscribes both a Christian and an ancient Greek version of a struggle between "lower" and "higher" powers that inevitably takes the form of misogyny. The Greek version of the struggle is carried, in our text, in the story of Python, who for that reason is the symbolic center of this chapter. Let us return to the text, then, to follow in it the traces of Python.

The story of Python's death at the hands of Phebus opens our tale:

> Whan Phebus dwelled heere in this erthe adoun,
> As olde bookes maken mencioun,
> He was the mooste lusty bachiler
> In al this world, and eek the best archer.
> He slow Phitoun, the serpent, as he lay
> Slepynge agayn the soone upon a daye;
> And many another noble worthy dede
> He with his bowe wroghte, as men may rede.
>
> (105–12)

To have included the story of Python as part of the characterization of Phebus is one of Chaucer's most striking innovations, for the two episodes are connected in none of the sources. It is a felicitous juxtaposition. In Ovid, Python is one of the assorted monstrous creatures spawned from earth after the great flood has receded. The postdiluvian race fear Python, whose coils cover the hillside, so that Apollo, conquering hero of the new life, empties his quiver into the chthonic beast. The episode characterizes Phebus in his aggressive aspect, hence anticipates the murder of Coronis; serpent and wife are killed with the same weapon, Phebus's bow.

Chaucer offers no explanation for the slaying of Python, nor need he do so: Christian myth and iconography provide the reason. In Genesis the serpent is the primordial agent of evil and of

disobedience to God's command; the exegetic tradition interpreted the serpent as type and figure of Satan; Christian hagiography relates that St. George slew the dragon, the latter usually
figured as a serpent. So for a Christian audience Phebus's victory
over Python establishes him as a crusading hero of orthodox
morality. We do not need to know why or whether Python deserved to die: Python deserves to die because it is a serpent.[17]

Nor can the episode fail to affect the reader's response to the
rest of the narrative, for although Chaucer designates Python as
"he," the Christian iconographic tradition equates serpent and
woman. Eve was the tool of Satan and the serpent's human
agent. In some medieval paintings of the Fall the serpent itself is
given a woman's face; the serpent becomes the metonymic projection of Eve's pride, ambition, autonomy, and will to knowledge—in short, of her desire. Chaucer, too, makes the woman/
serpent connection in *The Man of Law's Tale,* apostrophizing the
wicked Sultaness as "serpent under femynynytee, / Lik to the
serpent depe in helle ybounde!" (360–61). So the slaying of Python, even so briefly referred to, would have for the medieval
reader rich moral and theological associations. As an introduction to *The Manciple's Tale* it anticipates the series of exempla
comparing women to animals, prepares us to sympathize with the
murderer rather than his victim, and invites us to interpret the
murder as the just (if harsh) punishment of a breach of Christian
morality.[18]

Underlying this intersection of classical and Christian myth is a
more fundamental cultural revision, not unique to the Judaeo-
Christian tradition but inscribed in the classical myth itself and
extending back into pre-Olympian Greece. To follow the history
of Python, so long antedating Ovid, is to approach the cultural
roots of misogyny.

Who, then, or what was Python? "Pytho" is an archaic name
for the site that later came to be known as Delphi. One scholar
traces the name to the Phoenician/Hebrew *puth/poth* (pit, fissure,
vulva), deriving it from a word for the deep chasm that is a
prominent geographical feature of the place.[19] The original deity

of the site was Gaea, the neolithic/Bronze Age chthonic nature-goddess typical of Mediterranean cultures, who was Earth herself, with her dark powers of fertility and death. The snake, Python, was the sacred cult animal at Pytho; according to some ancient representations, it slept curled in the *omphalos* (navel) or sanctuary-mound that was thought to mark the center of the world and was tended by the *pythia* or priestess of the shrine. Eventually the cult of Gaea was displaced by that of Apollo, tribal god of the northern Dorians who transformed the shrine and spread Apolline worship through the Peleponnesus. Whether the process was peaceful succession (as Aeschylus would have it in the prologue to *Eumenides*) or actual military conflict is unknown. Since the great migratory waves occurred over a millennium (c. 2200–1100 B.C.), doubtless both occurred: The earlier period, to about 1800, was apparently one of gradual penetration and settlement, followed by a phase of violent disruption by the Dorians among others. My main interest here, though, is in what Jane Harrison calls "the relation between Earth and Apollo and their ultimate hostility as figured in the slaying of the Python."[20] In what would this hostility consist?

The confrontation projected in the myth is nothing less than that between two competing social and ideological orders. Gaea-worship was grounded in a society collective and agrarian in its economic base, totemistic in its thought and ritual. It was a society perhaps matrilineal (though almost certainly not matriarchal), in which women played a central social role. Women's function as producer of future tribe members participated in the great procreative mysteries of mother Earth, with sexual union a temporal version of cosmic generation and the agricultural cycle: the sacred marriage of Earth and Sky, Gaea and Ouranos. The totem animal—bull, goat, serpent—was a *daimon* embodying natural forces. As in most totemistic societies, the snake represented both regenerative and funerary aspects of earth: an umbilical cord occupying the world-*omphalos* and linking humanity to its primal mother; an intermediary to the realm of the dead in their earth-sanctuary, hence, to the individual and collective past; a magical capacity for annual self-renewal, like the earth, hence, repository of the way or wisdom of nature itself.

With Apollo and the sky-god Olympians there was introduced an entirely different set of conceptions of nature, woman, and the human community. The tribes worshipping these sky gods were pastoral and nomadic in their economic base, military and patriarchal in their social organization.[21] The Olympian community was a monarchy and a patriarchal family, repressive and authoritarian. It was a constantly quarreling family, its members driven by jealous rivalry and sexual possessiveness. With the Olympians a great abyss opens on either side of humanity, separating us from nature on one side, godhead on the other. No longer is divinity inherent in nature; it transcends nature and humanity as well. To "descend" to the level of animals is foolish or insane; to aspire to the condition of the gods is hubris. Moreover, whereas the *daimon* eternally dies and is reborn, the Olympian is immortal:

> All this, all life and that which is life and reality—Change and Movement—the Olympian renounces. Instead he chooses Deathlessness and Immutability—a seeming Immortality which is really the denial of life, for life is change.[22]

Thus Python becomes, eventually, all that is dark and monstrous—might we add "menstruous"? It becomes the shameful, the repressible: the coiled mass emitted from earth's interior, the diffuse, the promiscuous and perverse. And Apollo? He is hero of the new order whose mythic function is precisely to repress the old: sun god, light to Python's dark; god of the arrow, straight to her sinuosity; god of poetry, lyric, and mathematics, of the individual voice and of predictable, numerical structure, the phallogocentric god.[23] The pre-Ovidian myth of their encounter renders the contrast suprahistorical, collapsing a millenium of invasion, infiltration, and adaptation into a single momentous confrontation.

With the historical background in mind, we can see that, more than an ironic anticipation of its central act, the killing of Python that opens *The Manciple's Tale* is the double of that act, linked metonymically with the murder of Coronis by common agent, metaphorically as another representation of the destruction of female autonomy and free sexuality. In killing the real female, Phebus obliterates the externalized "cause" of his own passions: the rage and frustration, the obsessive love composed in part of infantile dependency. He also eliminates the "cause" of his inability to satisfy. Since he twice tries to cut off aspects of himself, the logic of Phebus's passion leads from sadism to partial masochism—from murder to a symbolic self-castration that in turn is symbolic suicide:

> This is th'effect, ther is namoore to sayn;
> For sorwe of which he brak his mynstralcie,
> Bothe harpe, and lute, and gyterne, and sautrie;
> And eek he brak his arwes and his bowe. . . .
> "Allas, that I was wrought! why nere I deed? . . .
> Allas! for sorwe I wol myselven slee!"
> (266–91)

Again unique to Chaucer is the physical destruction of Phebus's iconographic attributes, for in the sources and analogues Phebus only curses his weapons and himself.

Phebus destroys his instruments. (We recall that "sely instrumentz" is the phrase the Wife of Bath uses of the human genitals [132, and also 149]). These instruments define him uniquely as god of lyric poetry and of war, enabling his intervention in the world and representing his distinctive power/virtue/virility. Further, to destroy the instruments that provide the accompaniment to poetic recitation is metonymically to destroy his own special linguistic function. Short of suicide, Phebus cannot destroy his own nonpoetic speech, but for this he finds another surrogate in the crow, whom he condemns now not to loss of voice but to loss of language as speech and as song (294–97). Henceforth the crow can neither project desire nor intelligibly assert itself as conscious subject. It remains a living creature, but deprived of its only distinctively human function.

Our text presents a chain of acts of real or symbolic violence:

the slaying of Python, the possessive claustration of a wife, the murder of a wife, the breaking of musical instruments and weapons, a suicide wish, the removal of a bird's ability to speak and to sing. These acts of violence are to some extent versions of one another: supplementary efforts to suppress a certain mode of imaginative or instinctual self-assertion whether vocally or sensually expressed. In my third and last section I will concentrate on the crow as the final link in this signifying chain.

The Crow

In various circumstances, in circumstances of heated and passionate argument, we can all understand that a man might murder his wife, but my God, it's difficult to understand that you would actually falsify her dental charts.
                    Judge Guignard to Cyril Belshaw, *The Vancouver Sun*
                                                    (December 3, 1980)

I have just offered an interpretation of the crow as a surrogate object for Phebus's self-punishment. Yet the crow can and must be read in other ways, for it is a polysemous signifier. This is as it should be, since the crow is a nodal point, incorporating several strands in a narrative whose subject is contradictory: the range of conflicting impulses that transform, impede, or repress one another, constituting in their ensemble something we call "sexuality."

What is the crow punished for? Why does the crow's punishment generate a rhetorical coda that displaces the human actors from the text's narrative center? How does this coda—a long apostrophe by the narrator to his youthful self in his mother's voice—relate to the rest of the tale? No determinism of sources will suffice here, for we know that Chaucer's artistic method left him quite free to perform radical alterations in accordance with his own purpose. In any case, the argument from sources only defers the question, for we would then need to investigate the function of a given feature in the source itself, understanding that it might differ radically from ur-text to literary descendants. Let us turn, then, to the crow.

Objectively the crow is a voyeur, silently witnessing an adulterous love-making scene. He must be a habitual voyeur, for his cage hangs in the bedroom and he must have had ample opportunity to observe the married couple at play. Two details are noteworthy here: first, that despite the crow's ability to speak, it "biheeld hire werk, and seyde never a word" (241); second, that despite the crow's ability to speak, the woman leaves its cage hanging in her room. It is as if woman and crow form an active/passive pair, exhibitionist and skoptophiliac, each subject and object at once: not so much complicit as complementary or even at some level identical. (I will return shortly to the notion of the crow as the woman's double and to the pregenital phase of infantile sexuality with which Freud associates both voyeurism and the sadistic desire for control.) The crow witnesses a scene in which he cannot participate, as if he were a child spying on the coitus of adults. The crow is impotent as a sexual being, and his only experience must be vicarious. Only visually can he appropriate, only verbally can he duplicate, the pleasure of full human genital sexuality. (We can scarcely avoid noting parenthetically how similar is this position to that of the typically Chaucerian poet-narrator of the dream-visions and the *Troilus,* perpetually observing others in the service of love but never himself involved.) What the crow witnesses is the forbidden: not simply adulterous betrayal but active sexuality and the genitals. Yet the crow is not punished for seeing the forbidden but for speaking it; not for visual violation of the genital taboo but for verbal violation of social standards; not for trespassing into knowledge of free sexuality but for revealing this to the possessive male who fears precisely that knowledge ("For al thy waityng, blered is thyn ye," taunts the tactless crow [252]). In short, the infantile transgression becomes an adult offense. Such displacement becomes virtually the rhetorical method of choice in the second part of the tale.

Related to voyeurism is the crow's function as a critical watching faculty or conscience figure, whose function is familiar in

folktale, where a crime is often witnessed and eventually revealed by a bird.[24] It falls to the crow to speak against un-
checked libido, in the service of repressive social institutions,
especially marriage and orthodox religion, bulwarks of female
chastity. Now it is not necessarily the case in medieval literature
that to reveal adultery is a good thing. Those who would reveal
to King Mark the love of Tristan and Isolde are shown to be
malicious curmudgeons. The *Roman de la Rose* constantly in-
veighs against gossips, prudes, and hypocrites who might en-
danger an affair. In Malory's *Morte d'Arthur* the self-interested
intervention of Agravayne and Mordred forces Arthur to renounce his genial toleration of Guinevere's long-term romance
with Lancelot, with massively disruptive social consequences.
These works offer a useful foil to the Chaucerian text wherein
the crow, Phebus's lieutenant or agent-in-repression, speaks
with the voice of parents, church, and state—and is ultimately
confirmed in that role. For if the informer's voice is reduced to
a mere croak, it retains nonetheless a double truth-value, pre-
dictive and commemorative: It will "crie agayn tempest and
rayn, / In tokenynge that thurgh thee my wyf is slayn" (300–
301). Moreover, the effaced linguistic function is immediately
replaced with the admonitory speech of an even more explicit
authority/conscience figure: the narrator's mother. Conscience is
of course a self-criticizing faculty, the introjection of what we
have been taught by social institutions, including mothers.
Whose conscience, then, does the crow represent if not that of a
composite textual personality whose libido is Coronis and whose
effective daylight ego-component is Phebus?

But the crow is also a double for the woman. Here again,
Chaucer's alterations are important. In all the sources and analogues there are two birds, crow (Latin *cornix;* OF *cornille*) and
raven (Latin *corvus,* OF *corbiaus*). The latter is Apollo's pet and
witnesses the adultery; the former attempts unsuccessfully to prevent the revelation. Chaucer has economically conflated the two
birds in one; it is the "wrong" one actually, but the one whose
name is virtually identical phonetically with the woman's name—

which, however, he has suppressed. (The deterrent advice formerly put in the crow's mouth before the revelation Chaucer defers until afterward, to be spoken by the narrator's mother. The associative chain thus goes Coronis/*cornix*/mother, and I shall take up the role of the mother further on.) We may also note that the Middle English nouns for bird and woman are homonymic: bridde/bridde, and that several verbal details that in one source, *The Seven Sages of Rome,* are related to the wife, Chaucer transfers to the crow. I have already mentioned that bird and woman are possessed by the same man, and have cited the syntactically identical lines that introduce crow and wife. Both creatures "betray" Phebus and are punished by him, and the animal exempla encourage us to see Coronis as having an animal nature. To this we may add the traditional iconography of birds as symbols of lusty libido (e.g., "so priketh hem nature in hir corages" [*General Prologue,* 11]).

It is this cluster of metonymic and metaphoric relations of woman and bird that permits the major displacement in the text: the diversion of attention from murder to gossip for the last fifty lines of the poem. Coronis is repressed, but *cornix* remains. It is a cover-up in which the Manciple and Chaucer are not without accomplices among contemporary critics. For some it is convenient to ignore the awkward fact of murder as the affective center of the narrative. Others ignore the crime in writing about it, that is, by accepting its displacement as the real point.[25] One would like to ask these gentlemen to look again, for the color change of a crow matters less than the murder of a wife. The text offers a tale of *crime passionnel* disguised as an etiological fable (why the crow is black) in turn disguised as a moral homily (the importance of discretion).

With the hope of seeing justice done one turns to feminist scholarship, to find there a rather cleverer version of the same thing: a curiously inverted version of the conventional desire to recuperate Chaucer for the great liberal tradition by reading him as a would-be women's liberationist frustrated only (only!) by historical limitations. One feminist Chaucerian, even while noting the polarity in Chaucer's portrayals of women, summarizes the case as follows:

> [Chaucer] means to be woman's friend, insofar as he can be, and it is this painfully honest effort, this unwillingness to be satisfied with the formulas of his age, which we as feminists can honor in him.[26]

Such a view reveals an ahistorical voluntarism: the assumption that somehow the individual can escape from history. I would argue to the contrary that the contradictions in Chaucer's portrayal of women do not transcend but repeat the contradictions already present in his own culture. Misogyny in Chaucer's day or our own will not necessarily be clothed in Theophrastian rhetoric, as any of us know who work in a university. Nor will misogyny always be most meaningfully carried at the relatively superficial level of dramatic character (e.g., is the Wife of Bath a "good" or a "bad" character?). The misogynistic stance includes sexuality, sensuality, desire, and assertion, together with what thwarts these impulses. It is carried, as I have tried to show here, at many levels of signification, in all the tactics available to language to reveal or repress: what Paul de Man calls "the distinctive privilege of language to be able to hide meaning behind a misleading sign, as when we hide rage or hatred behind a smile."[27]

The distortion of a text is not unlike a murder. The difficulty lies not in the execution of the deed but in the doing away with the traces. One could wish to give the word "distortion" the double meaning to which it has a right, although it is no longer used in this sense. It should mean not only "to change the appearance of," but also "to wrench apart," "to put in another place." That is why in so many textual distortions we may count on finding the suppressed and abnegated material hidden away somewhere, though in an altered shape and torn out of its original connection.
Sigmund Freud, *Moses and Monotheism*, part 2, sec. 6

If the last section of the poem is a massive displacement, an effort to divert attention from the subversive knowledge of free sexuality and its ultimately homicidal control, it nonetheless points to what it seeks to repress. How does the latent content of the work make itself known in the conclusion of the tale?

The initial displacement that we observe is literal and spatial: the transfer of literary material from an early to a later point in the text. If, as in Ovid or the *Ovide Moralisé,* we encounter the advice against gossip before the murder, then we are less likely to sympathize with the informer crow, for he is correctly warned in advance by another bird what will probably happen and arrogantly disdains the warning. Chaucer removes the advice from its definitive introductory position, with two results. First, its absence forces into narrative prominence the marital relation, displacing the topic of verbal discretion. Second, deferral damages the credibility of advice that now appears only as an afterthought. So that the thematic or affective displacement—the sense of incongruity with which we finally receive the advice—is created by the author's literal displacement of source material.

Next in the structure of displacement is the rhetorical device through which the displacement is accomplished: the apostrophe to himself that the narrator places in his mother's mouth. It is a double "turning away" (Greek *apostrephein,* to turn away), for both subject and object are dramatically absent: the mother who gives, and the childish self who receives, the advice. "To apostrophize is to will a state of affairs, to attempt to call it into being by asking inanimate objects [or absent individuals—S.D.] to bend themselves to your desire. . . . [Apostrophe] displaces the temporal pattern of actual loss."[28] The desire rhetorically accomplished here is to reestablish the lost intimacy of the mother–child relationship—the same that Phebus, with obsessive infantile determination, had sought with Coronis and failed to find. And it is a double restoration, for the real (perhaps dead) mother is brought to life, or at least made present through the repetition of her words, while the murdered substitute-mother is resurrected in the wished-for nurturing role. Language is the real possibility of control.

The restored mother seems to appear in her nurturing, protective aspect, counselling worldly (if opportunistic) wisdom for her son's success. Yet there is a curious ambiguity to this apparently nurturing role, for the advice is actually repressive in its denial of oral satisfaction. The words "tongue," "teeth," and "lips" occur no fewer than eleven times in forty-eight lines (314–62), "tongue" nine times, so that the tongue comes to possess, as it were, a life of its own. But it is a life to be rigidly controlled, for the tongue is a dangerous organ, a weapon: it is "wikked," "worse than a feend," it is "walled . . . with teeth and lippes," it is like a "swerd" that "forkutteth and forkerveth / An arm a-two." The message here is: "Do not use your oral apparatus impulsively or instinctually; control it!" The latent content of the passage evokes what small children experience at the hands—or, more accurately, at the breasts—of their mothers, those powerful sources of satisfaction and frustration.

To return to the level of rhetoric: The mother's own use of language is as ambivalent as her role, apparently helpful but in fact ironically confirming her warning about the destructive power of language. It is evidently she from whom the Manciple learned the brutal tale he has just told. "Thenk on the crow" is the phrase with which she frames her advice, a phrase whose obverse is "Do not think of the wife." From a mother, then, comes the story of a wife murdered in revenge for adultery, together with its concluding moral: Both the misogynistic act and its rhetorical evasion were her lessons. She has ironically practiced what she preached, or rather preached and practiced in the same speech, demonstrating as well as describing the power of language to distort, dissimulate, distract.

We know that the mouth is the infantile source of narcissistic pleasure. The infant's cries control its world and its mother; feeding brings erotic pleasure encompassing the infant's entire physical being. Yet at the pregenital phase of libido development, desire ("love") is not distinct from the desire to control—in order to survive as well as to get pleasure. Hence, it cannot help but have a sadistic component. Freud characterizes this period by "the impulse to mastery, which easily passes over into cruelty."[29]

The diffuse nature of "pleasure" at this phase, its "polymorphous perversity," includes such forms as voyeurism and anality, sadism and oral eroticism.

It is not only in *The Manciple's Tale* that Chaucer presents a cluster of images and actions evoking the components of pregenital libido organization. In *The Miller's Tale,* a rather intense orality is the dominant mode of Absolon's wooing. He serenades young Alison and sends food (3377–80), anticipates a kiss (3678–83), sweetens his breath (3690–93), addresses Alison as something edible (3698–99), confesses, "I moorne as dooth a lamb after the tete" (3704) and "I may nat ete na moore than a mayde" (3707). He gets no tit, however, but "hir naked ers" to kiss, reciprocating this mild anal/oral/exhibitionistic sadism with a more painful act of anal sadism intended for Alison (!) but finally perpetrated on handy Nicholas. Another instance of the pregenital cluster occurs in *The Prioresse's Tale,* whose narrator opens with a prologue praising the intuitive piety of infants "on the brest soukynge," reduces herself rhetorically to "a child of twelf month oold, or lesse," then proceeds to narrate a perfervid tale of throats cut, shithouses, hanging and drawing with wild horses, together with a child-hero's devotion to an all-healing, miracle-working virgin mother.

If the infant controls its world through oral exercise (cries and smiles that produce the satisfaction of being fed), it is the power of words, rather than the unarticulated cry, that gives control to adults. The idea of verbal influence is always fearfully present to Chaucer. Interesting, then, that the mother ends with an injunction extending beyond gossip to verbal assertion in general:

> Thyng that is seyd is seyd, and forth it gooth,
> Though hym repente, or be hym nevere so looth.
> He is his thral to whom that he hath sayd
> A tale of which he is now yvele apayd.
> My sone, be war, and be noon auctour newe
> Of tidynges, wheither they been false or trewe.
> (355–60)

These lines recall the last portion of *The House of Fame,* where truth and falsehood and tidings are also linked, posing for writers the problem repeatedly confonted in the body of that poem: how to use traditional material whose heterogeneity virtually guarantees the presence of falsehood mingled with truth. There, no ending is possible. Here, the ending advises "litel speche" (327), silence except to speak of God (329–31), and not simply "speak no evil" but "speak nothing unknown (new) at all, neither false nor true." This is nihilistic counsel in its implications, potentially antiart, and hinting at anxieties more fully crystallized in the Retraction. Chaucer is too much the poet to renounce all of his work, but he is enough of a Christian to abjure at least the "tale(s) of which he is now yvele apayd."

In narrating his tale, the Manciple has violated his mother's injunction. The social structure of pilgrimage and game requires him to tell a tale, but were he to obey his mother he would have to tell something very like *The Parson's Tale.* The poet, though, seems to have the maternal advice more at heart, for he has given the mother a speech whose austere aesthetics are afterward displayed in *The Parson's Tale* and acted on in the Retraction. In this respect the mother is conscience not only to the narrator, who cannot satisfy her (he can tell only one tale) but to the poet, who can (he can tell an infinite variety).

What, then, is the power of language? For Chaucer it is to write both Manciple and Pardoner, Miller and Retraction, to body forth bawdry and moralism, produce his fantasies and renounce them. He can have it both ways, for the poet's control of language and audience is in turn controlled—or should be—by the maternal/clerical/scriptural injunctions we encounter in this last section of *The Canterbury Tales.* For the medieval Christian, the liberating act is willful submission to the superior term in a power structure, and the liberating word is not ours but His.

I find myself now in the awkward position of Chaucer at the end of *The House of Fame:* how to end, when the writing itself denies the possibility of a neat ending? A psychoanalytic interpretation or a cultural interpretation of literature should produce anything but a monolithic conclusion, for their objects—human drives, human societies—are characterized by flux and self-contradiction. In a sense, one would like the Chaucerian corpus to be a mere literary fossil, for that would mean its contradictions were irrelevant to us—had been resolved. But in fact, what animated the work hasn't died out yet, so that there are still dinosaurs among Chaucer critics and—more important, as some of my contemporary quotations show—at large: Some of them are judges, others criminals. Chaucer's craft, and craftiness, are, as usual, impressive; his values, one hopes, will not be with us always.

5

Sexual economics, Chaucer's *Wife of Bath*, and The Book of Margery Kempe

Few individuals in the Middle Ages occupy our attention as com-
mandingly as two women—one fictional, one real—from the decline of that era. One is Chaucer's Dame Alice, the Wife of Bath;
the other is Margery Kempe, the fifteenth-century gentlewoman
from Lynn, author of the first autobiography in English. Both
women were curiously "modern," inasmuch as both were of the
middle class; both travelled extensively in Europe and the Middle
East; both were of an independent and robust nature; both preferred the autobiographical mode; and both were deeply concerned with sexuality, though from different perspectives: the
one to enjoy, the other to renounce.

Chaucer's portrayal of the Wife of Bath shows on acute
awareness of what I am here calling "sexual economics": the

psychological effects of economic necessity, specifically upon sexual mores. The Wife of Bath belongs to the petty bourgeoisie; she is a small-time entrepreneur in the textile trade which, already by the thirteenth century, had come to dominate the English economy and its international trade. From her suburb of St. Michael's juxta-Bathon, Dame Alice is in no position to rival the great textile magnates of her time; she remains a middle-sized fish in a small pond, though, as Chaucer remarks with some irony:

> Of clooth-makyng she hadde swich an haunt,
> She passed hem of Ypres and of Gaunt.
> (*General Prologue*, 447–48)[1]

The theme that Chaucer develops in Dame Alice's revelation of her marital history is that her sexuality is as capitalistic as her trade. For her, God's commandment "to wexe and multiplye" (28) bears fruit not in children but in profit: marriage settlements and land inheritances from her husbands, together with everything she can wring from them by nagging and manipulation. The old image of copulation as the marriage debt Alice wrenches round to her own point of view by asserting that her husband must be "bothe my dettour and my thral" (155), adding the notion of an exploitive social relationship. She goes on to claim the profit motive as the basis for marital harmony:

> But sith I hadde hem hoolly in myn hond,
> And sith they hadde me yeven al hir lond,
> What sholde I taken keep hem for to plese,
> But it were for my profit and myn ese?
> (211–14)

The cynical conclusion to which Alice's experience leads is also phrased in the imagery of commerce:

> Wynne whoso may, for al is for to selle;
> With empty hand men may none haukes lure.
> For wynnyng wolde I al his lust endure,
> And make me a feyned appetit. . . .
> (414–17)

Her strategy in marriage is based on the economic principle of supply and demand:

> Forbede us thyng, and that desiren we;
> Preesse on us faste, and thanne wol we fle.
> With daunger oute we al oure chaffare;
> Greet prees at market maketh deere ware,
> And to greet cheep is holde at litel prys:
> This knoweth every womman that is wys.
>
> (519–24)

Thus the Wife of Bath has thoroughly internalized the economic function of the bourgeoisie in reducing quintessentially human activity—love and sexuality—to commercial enterprise. She understands that as a woman she is both merchant and commodity: her youth and beauty the initial capital investment, and her age—the depreciation of the commodity—a condition against which she must accumulate profit as rapidly and therefore as exploitatively as possible.

In evaluating the Wife of Bath, however, we must also recognize the degree to which such internalization of capitalist method is a defensive strategy against the special oppression of women in a society whose sex and marriage mores were thoroughly inhumane. Alice can inherit land and engage in business, but she can exercise no control over the disposition of her body. Her first marriage to a rich but impotent old dotard took place when she was twelve: Not Alice but her parents or guardians would have invested this choice piece of sexual capital for the sake of social standing and a profitable settlement—just as we see the Miller of *The Reeve's Tale* expecting an advantageous match for his virginal Malkin, until the goods are damaged by Alain the clerk. The potential horror of a January–May match Chaucer graphically details in *The Merchant's Tale;* nor was it, in Chaucer's time and later, by any means an uncommon practice for girls (and, less frequently, boys) to be wed at an early age. It was not only parents who profited from the marriage of their offspring but also the legal guardian, who held the custody or wardship of the marriageable person in return for a fee or tax upon marriage: a form of feudal privilege conferrable by the king. In 1375 Chaucer, as king's esquire, was granted custody of the lands and marriage of the heirs of Edmund de Staplegate, himself heir of a wealthy Canterbury merchant; the grant was worth £10 in its time (probably close to $25,000 today). Thus Chaucer himself, as well as many of his friends involved in similar transactions, made substantial profit on the marriage market.[2]

In fact, Alice's alternatives were few and unattractive, for outside the convent there was little room in medieval Europe for the single woman. Religious, social, and parental authority combined to urge acceptance of a profitable match, however repulsive personally. From one point of view, therefore, it is the Wife of Bath's personal triumph to have adapted with such success to the institutions of her day: to have found pleasure and even, toward the end of her life, some peace of mind. This is not, of course, the last word on Dame Alice. From the doctrinal point of view she is spiritually impoverished, and Chaucer's condemnation of her sexual economics represents in small his critique of the competitive, accumulative practices of the medieval bourgeoisie at large.

In real life, though, such triumphant adaptation to the reality principle can scarcely have been the rule. Medieval society took its toll, whether in murder, infanticide, suicide, insanity, or daily misery, as surely as modern society continues to do. Unfortunately, the realities of sexual economics are usually such as to bankrupt the investor, who is also commodity. Margery Kempe, as much as Alice of Bath, is of the bourgeoisie, but Margery's internalization of her class ethos brings no profit and large loss. Not five husbands but only one; not happily childless but perennially pregnant (she had fourteen offspring); not flinging herself into a life of venerian hedonism, but guilt-ridden and full of ambivalence about sex, fascinated by and loathing it at once; not rejoicing in the permissive behests of a kindly god, but sacrificing herself to the continual remonstrances of a strict, authoritarian Jesus, with visions, crying fits, and trances. In order to understand the differences between the fictional and the real versions of sexual economics, we will need to know something about Margery Kempe's specific environment and also about the general development of capitalism in the fifteenth century.

Let us begin with the specifics, by placing Margery Kempe in her social milieu. The exact dates of her birth and death are not known, but they can be safely estimated at about 1373 and 1438.[3] Her home was Lynn, Norfolk—Bishop's Lynn, as the city was called, after its ecclesiastical overlord, the Bishop of Norwich.[4] Because of its strategic location at the mouth of the Ouse River, and its function as the only port for the trade of seven shires (especially the Scandinavian trade), Lynn had by the thirteenth century established itself as one of the richest and most important commercial cities in England. It was also one of the staple towns for wool, that is, one of certain few designated towns where wool could be officially weighed, taxed, and shipped.

These two distinctive features, an ecclesiastical overlord and a thriving commercial base, meant that in Lynn, class struggle took on an even sharper and more protracted character than in most other English towns. For the effort of the upper bourgeoisie to gain political control of the city and establish its independence of the feudal aristocracy was met by more than the usual resistance. As A. S. Green points out:

> Prelates of the Church professed to rule with a double title, not only as feudal lords of the soil, but as guardians of the patrimony of St. Peter, holding property in trust for a great spiritual corporation. . . . Leaning on supernatural support for deliverance from all perils, it could the better refuse to discuss bargains suggested by mere political expediency.[5]

Such spiritually sanctioned intransigence led to many confrontations, both legal and physical. It is possible that as a child Margery witnessed the riotous expulsion of the bishop in 1377 by the armed populace of Lynn.[6]

It is important that we not misjudge Margery by viewing her through eighteenth-century spectacles. During the eighteenth century, such individualistic religious enthusiasm as Margery's was practiced largely by the lower-middle-class and proletarian members of dissenting sects. Though we may see Margery as a forerunner of later developments, she remained nonetheless an orthodox Catholic and member of the upper bourgeoisie of Lynn. Her father, John Brunham, was, she tells us, "mayor five times of that worshipful borough, and alderman also many years."[7] Brunham's yearlong terms as mayor ran from September 29, 1370–71, 1377–78, 1378–79, 1385–86, and 1391–92. He was elected from and by a governing body of twenty-four jurats, all named for life terms from the guild merchant, or professional association of the wealthiest merchants of the town; in Lynn it was called the High Guild of the Trinity. When he was not mayor, and sometimes even concurrently, Brunham served in other important public offices: as coroner, justice of the peace, member of Parliament, and chamberlain (one of four burgesses elected annually as financial officers of the city). Margery's husband also belonged to the upper ranks of the bourgeoisie who, by their wealth, qualified for the name of burgess (in contrast to the lower bourgeoisie and artisans who, as *inferiores,* were excluded from municipal government). Though John Kempe was not as consistently in the public eye as Brunham, he was also one of the first citizens of Lynn and was elected chamberlain in 1394.

In a passage that recalls the Wife of Bath's status-conscious love of finery (*General Prologue,* 448–52), Margery recounts "her pride and pompous array" as a daughter of what Henri Pirenne has called "the urban patriciate":

> for she wore gold pipes on her head, and her hoods, with the tippets, were slashed. Her cloaks also were slashed and laid with divers colors between the slashes, so that they should be the more staring to men's sight, and herself the more worshipped. (p. 12)

To become even richer—"for pure covetousness and to maintain her pride," as the author puts it—Margery went into business for herself: first brewing, "and was one of the greatest brewers in the town for three years or four, till she lost much money" (p. 13), then into grinding corn, with two horses and a hired employee, until that enterprise failed as well. Yet these ventures by no means impoverished Margery. She remained a rich woman despite her business losses, more solvent than her husband apparently, for when Margery asked her husband to remain chaste he countered by asking her to pay his debts (p. 31). Still later, the records of Lynn give notice of a Margeria Kempe being admitted to the Trinity Guild.

In brief, then, Margery Kempe was what the Wife of Bath would have liked to be: socially prominent and well-to-do, a member of one of the most prominent families in one of England's richest towns. It is with a grain of salt, then, that we must take R. W. Chambers' somewhat patronizing remarks about "poor Margery,"[8] even if we do not take "poor" in its economic sense. Yet, of course, there is a kernel of truth in Chambers' epithet, inasmuch as what he was responding to—and what I suspect we respond to even more sympathetically—is the quality of personal agony in Margery's book. Margery's spiritual autobiography is, according to Chambers, disappointing and even "from certain points of view, painful." It is not a book of devotion; we are constantly aware of Margery in relation to her society; and it is the peculiar quality of her religious experience—unsatisfying for Chambers, fascinating for us—that it is so inadequate an instrument of transcendence.

We learn nothing of Margery's childhood—an omission to be regretted by psychoanalytic critics and social historians alike. The book opens with the fact of Margery's marriage at the age of twenty. Her first pregnancy occurred "within a short time, as nature would." Both pregnancy and labor were difficult, and during the pregnancy she was "ever hindered by her enemy, the devil," so that she often did penance by fasting and prayer. After the birth of her child she "went out of her mind," because of fear of damnation, for a period of eight months, during which time she suffered diabolical hallucinations. She was kept from suicide only by being bound night and day. Her remission came spontaneously with a vision of Jesus who, clad in a mantle of purple silk, sat by her bed and said, "Daughter, why hast thou forsaken me and I forsook never thee?" (p. 11).

The next twenty-five years were an amalgam of worldly and

religious experience; her business ventures, her prideful array, the temptation to adultery with a close friend who rejected her after he had made the initial advance, the bearing of fourteen children, and several serious illnesses including dysentery. Interspersed with these worldly concerns were visions of paradise; conversations with Mary and Jesus and SS. Peter, Paul, and Catherine; auditory, olfactory, and other sensory hallucinations with religious import; diabolical fantasies of men (including priests) showing her their genitals; revulsion against "fleshly communing" with her husband and repeated efforts to persuade him to abstain from sexual intercourse; travels to local and foreign shrines; and, in Jerusalem, the onset of what came to be her best-known trait, her "crying," the uncontrollable sobbing and shouting that overcame her at moments of religious intensity, especially through pain and sorrow in contemplation of the Passion of Christ.

Eventually John Kempe was won over to the chaste life and took up separate residence in order to avoid gossip. In old age John fell downstairs in his own house, suffering a head injury that left him senile and incontinent. With characteristic split attention to physical detail and spiritual values, Margery describes their pathetic last years together:

> Then she took home her husband with her and kept him years after, as long as he lived, and had full much labour with him; for in his last days he turned childish again, and lacked reason, so that he could not do his own easement by going to a seat, or else he would not, but, as a child, voided his natural digestion in his linen clothes, where he sat by the fire or at the table, whichever it were; he would spare no place.
>
> And therefore was her labour much the more in washing and wringing, and her costage in firing; and it hindered her full much from contemplation, so that many times she would have loathed her labour, save she bethought herself how she, in her young age, had full many delectable thoughts, fleshly lusts, and inordinate loves to his person.

It is easy enough to say, then, that the remarkable *Book of Margery Kempe* gives us a social reality that Chaucer could neither observe firsthand nor sympathize with if he saw. As a man, as a devout Catholic, as a highly placed civil servant and courtier, as a poet in the continental courtly tradition, he could scarcely be expected to see the bourgeois woman in other than the conventional doctrinal and literary terms. Chaucer shows us one version of the internalization of mercantile capitalism, the commodification of sexuality, but his neat schema is far too simple. The analogy between sexual and economic realms is engaging, in part because of its simplicity, and it helps Chaucer to expose what from the courtly point of view constitute the "vices" of the bourgeoisie. Yet Margery's story shows that the bourgeois woman was far less likely to be a successful entrepreneur in her domestic life than she was to be an exploited worker; as Friedrich Engels remarked, "Within the family the husband is the bourgeois and the wife represents the proletariat."[9] Of course, Margery is far from being literally a proletarian, but the function of Engels' metaphor is to call attention to the special oppression of women in class-structured society. It may be difficult to see Margery as an oppressed person when she is wealthy and seems to hold her own so well. Nonetheless I want to suggest that her book is precisely a document of the special oppression of women in early capitalist society. Despite her class position, and to some extent because of it, Margery is exposed to and has internalized the most damaging aspects of bourgeois society.

This is not to negate the significance or validity of other approaches to the book. Hope Emily Allen, first editor of the text, showed its indebtedness to the continental tradition of "feminine mysticism," especially to the works of St. Bridget of Sweden (who died in 1373 and was canonized in 1391, and whose chapel Margery visits in Rome), and Blessed Dorothea of Prussia.[10] Admittedly this tradition offered Margery a vocabulary and a form for the expression of her own experience, but it offers no understanding of the genesis of that experience. Nor is a psychoanalytic approach fully adequate to the task of explaining Margery and her book. Everyone agrees that she was "neurotic"; Allen's diagnosis emphasizes hysteria, and to this we may add postpartum psychosis, wish-fulfillment, infantile regression, and reaction formation as obvious neurotic syndromes revealed in the book. Yet because psychoanalysis generally omits the social factor in the development of neurosis, suspending the individual in artificial isolation, it cannot provide a real understanding of neurosis, which is not, after all, an answer but the very thing to be explained. Both source study and psychoanalytic criticism must be supplemented with a methodology that places the individual in a social context and also provides as full as possible a definition of "social context." By placing Margery Kempe in time, place, and class, I have merely provided some of the data necessary to such an effort. I have not gone beyond the phenomena of history to the laws of history, nor have I dealt with the question of how Margery's internalization of the ethos of early capitalism is manifested in her book. I now want to focus on three aspects of the book that help us to address those problems. They are the author's constant awareness of money, her perception of herself as property, and the alienated quality of her relationships.

The transition from feudalism to capitalism during the later Middle Ages was the transition from an economy based on use value to one based on exchange value. The feudal manor produced goods (mainly agricultural) that were used or else exchanged for other goods. Feudal dues were generally paid in labor or in kind, and the manor's surplus was used by its producers or its owners. In such an economy money was not a prime necessity, and while it was never wholly absent in the earlier Middle Ages, it played a very limited role in the economy of Europe. The development of industry and of mercantile capitalism meant that goods were no longer being produced for immediate use, but rather for sale in domestic and foreign markets; they were to be exchanged not for other goods but for money. Money could be accumulated then reinvested for profit or lent at interest; large fortunes could be rapidly made; the big bourgeoisie could subsidize kings and impoverished aristocrats, buy titles and estates, and successfully compete with the feudal aristocracy for political power. Serfs and villeins left the manor to become free workers and artisans in the towns; those remaining began to demand the commutation of feudal dues and taxes and the establishment of money wages—in other words the abolition of feudalism, as in the English rebellion of 1381, the Bohemian Taborite rising of 1420, and the Peasant Wars in Germany during the first part of the sixteenth century. It was a lengthy process, which Marx and Engels characterize in their famous sentences from the *Communist Manifesto:*

> The bourgeoisie, wherever it has got the upper hand, has put an end to all feudal, patriarchal, idyllic relations. It has pitilessly torn asunder the motley feudal ties that bound man to his "natural superiors," and has left remaining no other nexus between man and man than naked self-interest, than callous "cash payment."[11]

With Margery Kempe, one is kept constantly aware of the "cash nexus"; it pervades her consciousness as it pervaded her world, part of every human endeavor and confrontation. No one is immune from money consciousness. From lowest to highest we see everyone pinching pennies, whether his own or someone else's: even the Archbishop of York squabbles over the fee to be paid Margery's escort (p. 167). Jesus denounces such concern for lucre (p. 209), but it is nonetheless the backdrop to Margery's religious devotion. The economics of pilgrimage is laid before us almost as prominently as its spiritual motivation. Thus we learn of the public financial settlement that Margery made before embarking for the Holy Land; of her expenditures for food, wine, bedding, lodging, and transportation; of the groat she paid a Saracen to bring her to the Mount where Jesus fasted forty days; of wage negotiations with the humpbacked Irishman who became Margery's servant. We hear continually of her fear of being robbed and her anxiety at being delayed in Rome because of insufficient funds, and are as relieved as she when gold finally arrives—proof that God is with her. With account-book scrupulosity Margery registers every gift, whether alms, cloth for a dress, or payment for her stories. Perhaps the most revealing single passage is the conversation in which Margery asks Jesus to be her executor:

Lord, after thou hast forgiven me my sin, I make thee mine executor of all the good works that Thou workest in me. In praying, in
thinking, in weeping, in going on pilgrimage, in fasting, or in speaking any good words, it is fully my will, that Thou give Master N.
[Margery's confessor] half of it to the increase of his merit, as if he
did them himself. And the other half, Lord, spread on Thy friends
and Thine enemies, and on my friends and mine enemies, for I will
have but Thyself for my share.

Daughter, I shall be a true executor to thee and fulfill all thy will;
and for the great charity that thou hast to comfort thy fellow thou
shalt have double reward in heaven. (pp. 26–27)

It is a spiritual economics as schematic as anything produced by
the Puritans: good deeds and prayer the commodity, transferable
and administered by Jesus (with the legal/psychological pun on
"will"), invested in Master N. and other projects, and producing
an enviable profit in heaven of 100 percent.

Yet despite this profound awareness of money, with Margery
we are far from the aristocratic acceptance of wealth as a natural
thing, or from the aristocratic virtue of largesse and the continual
circulation of goods that is so prominent a feature of the courtly
romance. On the contrary, the dominant tone of her concern is
anxiety: the fear of loss of money or goods and the fear of being
unable to provide for herself. This anxiety reflects not only Margery's personal experience of business failure but also that of her
class, whose fortunes depended on speculation and investment
and were therefore always subject to loss. This anxiety appears
especially in her ambivalent attitude toward poverty. Margery
views poverty as a spiritually glorifying condition, and she yearns
in the Franciscan manner to imitate the poverty of Jesus. Yet
once she is moneyless, moving among the common people of
Rome without the security and social advantages conferred by
wealth, she is deeply frightened.

And indeed this was the paradox of wealth for the medieval
woman: that it created and destroyed at once. The creative
power of money is that it compensates for the deficiencies of
nature: The ugly person can buy a beautiful mate; the stupid
person can buy intelligent employees; the bad person is honored

for his or her social position.[12] Thus money creates socially, and Margery is created a valuable piece of property, a good match for the burgess John Kempe and with a social position entirely unrelated to her desires or talents. Yet it is precisely as a piece of valuable property that Margery is most profoundly destroyed, for she can never attain full humanity while she has no power to dispose of herself as she pleases. Like any medieval woman, Margery is born the property of her father; on her marriage this right is transferred to her husband. While she is owned by someone else, she remains alienated from herself—and I am using the verb *alienate* here in its original sense: to transfer the rights of ownership to another person.

Early in the book, Margery recounts an incident that poignantly reveals her understanding of this impotence. After her first vision of paradise, she urges her husband to continence. Yet having no right of property over her own body, Margery must endure legal rape when persuasion fails:

> She said to her husband, "I may not deny you my body, but the love of my heart and my affections are withdrawn from all earthly creatures and set only in God."
> He would have his will and she obeyed, with great weeping and sorrowing that she might not live chaste. . . . Her husband said it was good to do so, but he might not yet. He would when God willed. And so he used her as he had done before. He would not spare her. (p. 16)

Like the Wife of Bath, Margery is free to own property, run a business, and enter a guild, but she is not free to dispose of her person. Oppressed within her class, she participates in the economic advantages of the class but not in the full range of personal freedom extended to the bourgeois man. The incident recounted above reminds us that rape—*raptus*—sometimes means theft: here, the theft of one's person. It is not, of course, only Margery's husband who is guilty of this most fundamental form of theft, but the laws of religion and society that gave a husband authority over that piece of valuable property, his wife. And it is not only Margery who is victimized by these laws, but John as well, who is forced into the unpleasant choice of abusing his wife or abusing himself. For he cannot be divorced; neither can he find a normal sex life elsewhere. Luckily for Margery, though, her husband was the complete bourgeois: more committed to his needs than to those of his wife, but even more committed to financial than to physical necessity. Thus, when Margery offers to pay his debts, John finally agrees to let her take the vow of chastity (p. 32). In this way Margery, like any serf, buys manumission from her lord: the human property whose service she removes has its price.

Margery is as alienated from spiritual selfhood as she is from physical, for without her husband's consent she cannot obey the urging of her soul to go on pilgrimage. Luckily John Kempe grants his wife permission to go. Her confessor, too, has the right to deny permission and is angry that she does not ask. Yet even in her travels, Margery has only jumped out of the frying pan into the fire, for she is as plagued with fear of rape throughout her journey as she is with fear of theft; indeed, on one occasion she is threatened with rape and only narrowly manages to dissuade her assaulter.

The alternatives were few in medieval society for the woman who resented the alienation of self. One was violence against the most immediate oppressor, the husband, and it has recently been suggested that the Wife of Bath availed herself of this alternative in disposing of her fourth husband.[13]

We may read a thinly veiled death-wish against her husband when Margery has a vision in which Christ promises to slay him.[14] But more often the internalization of oppression led to self-inflicted punishment, which, as mortification of the flesh, brought the social advantage of ecclesiastical approval. Thus, in the Middle English translation of the *Vita* of the French mystic Marie d'Oignies, we read, "And for she [Marie] hadde not openly power of hir owne body, she bare prively under hir smok a fulle sharpe corde, with the whiche she was girded ful harde."[15] Margery, too, internalizes the special oppression of women through self-inflicted punishment: Not only is she continually obsessed with the desire to die, but she practices fasting, waking, and other forms of asceticism, and also wears a hair shirt under her clothes every day for several years.

With substantial limitation on her personal freedom, the medieval bourgeoise remained far more dependent than her husband on personal relationships for a sense of fulfillment. Yet even in this realm Margery seems to find little to sustain her. Her children are never mentioned as a source of stability, security, or comfort, with the exception of one son whom Margery converts from a profligate life. Likewise, there is no reference to Margery's relation with her parents. It is through her marriage that we get some sense of what "normal" family relations were like. Though Margery wore a hair shirt for several years, her husband never knew about it, even though, as the author emphasizes, "she lay by him every night in his bed and wore the haircloth every day, and bore children in the time" (p. 17). Plainly, the absence of intimacy and communication seems as awful to Margery as it does to us.

Now John Kempe was not a cruel or an evil man, nor does Margery accuse him of monstrosity: He neither beat her nor had her put away as insane nor denounced her publicly. He was distressed by his wife's eccentricity, though more, it seems, because it interfered with his sex life than for any other reason. Yet considering the measures at his disposal and the social standards of the time, John Kempe was a fairly reasonable man. He was, of course, a very busy man, extremely concerned with profit and loss, getting and spending, office and status; we have already seen that while he could not be persuaded to live chastely, he could be bribed to do so. A busy man, too, was Margery's father, five times mayor of Lynn, and doubtless no less money-minded than John Kempe. Even the clergy emerge from Margery's moral account-book as busy, ambitious, and often greedy. This, then, is the normal world in which Margery moves. Its normalcy is grotesque, not unlike our own, and its relationships are often deformed and dehumanized. In such a world, Jesus is the only male authority figure who is neither busy nor ambitious but always available and ready to love. Thus Jesus becomes ideal father, promising "all manner of love that thou covetest," and ideal husband as well, united with Margery in mystical marriage (p. 112) and demanding only virtue.

Though Karl Marx knew nothing of Margery Kempe, his remarks on religion read as if tailor-made for her:

> Religious distress is at the same time the *expression* of real distress and the *protest* against real distress. Religion is the sigh of the oppressed creature, the heart of a heartless world, just as it is the spirit of a spiritless situation. It is the opium of the people.[16]

Religion is Margery's way of asserting her ownership of herself, of overcoming alienation while simultaneously providing the most poignant testimony to that alienation. It is also her way of projecting into mental reality the loving relationships so fervently desired and so glaringly absent from her domestic life. One could also say that Margery discovered a way to use the system against the system—a way to leave home, travel, establish a name for herself, and meanwhile remain both chaste and respectable. Religion became her way of combatting the special oppression of women, which she in no way understood as oppression, though she suffered and rebelled against its experiential weight.

Compared with Margery Kempe, the Wife of Bath capitulated, consenting to the abuse of her sexuality but turning it to personal profit. Hers is the bureaucratic mentality, and it is she who, with her ethos of "making it in a man's world" and "beating the man at his own game," seems familiar enough to us now. But even Alice cannot really beat the man at his own game, nor can Margery really opt out of an abhorrent social system, and neither capitulation nor abstention recommends itself as a viable alternative to us. Instead, as Marx goes on to say immediately after the lines I have quoted above,

> The abolition of . . . the illusory happiness of the people is required for their real happiness. The demand to give up the illusions about its condition is the demand to give up a condition which needs illusions.

It is not the bourgeoisie that can, or ever could, create "real happiness" for women any more than it can or could for society at large. What we see in Chaucer's Wife of Bath and in Margery Kempe are two strategies doomed to failure precisely because the capitalism they internalized was still immature. The social conditions did not yet exist for the emancipation of women any more than for the emancipation of the English rural and urban workers whose strategy in 1381 could also only lose. Factory labor, the industrial revolution, finance capital, and imperialism—these laid the basis for the full emancipation of women and men from exploitive relations of production and property. They created the worldwide proletariat that can replace the institutions of bourgeois society with those of socialism. We no longer have to make the choices that Margery Kempe did. Significant personal freedom is available to us, in education, productive labor, and sexuality. To be sure, our freedom is far from complete, nor can it be complete while exploitive relations of property and production continue to exist. But we are able now to address ourselves to the problem of full and genuine liberation, and to do so is the most important task we are freed for. To undertake that task moves us from the world of religion to that of politics: the struggle to destroy "a condition which needs illusions" and to create one in which illusions have no place.

6

Sex and politics
in Pope's
Rape of the Lock

Although Pope's *Rape of the Lock* is not an openly partisan piece, it has nonetheless a politics that differs little from that of Pope's other work. The politics of *The Rape of the Lock* is expressed in two major ways: in the sexual attitudes of its characters and in the narrator's comments. Sexual behavior functions in the poem as an analogue to political behavior. In Belinda and the Baron we observe attitudes that, limited to themselves, have only private consequences, but practiced generally, have important public meaning as well. In criticizing Belinda and the Baron, Pope criticizes the social class that behaves politically as they do personally. That larger perspective appears in various passages of commentary, scattered through the poem and ranging in tone from solemn sincerity to sharpest irony. Through these passages the poem achieves its fullest meaning, for in them Pope expands his canvas from "high society" to society at large.

In defining the politics of *The Rape of the Lock,* I will begin by placing the poem in its social context. Here I use the word "social" to mean both the larger political situation, and the more immediate personal dispute which called forth *The Rape of the Lock.* A reading of the poem follows, one that shows how Pope's version of sexual politics both reflects his general political attitude and shares its limitations. While my conclusions will not surprise, they do represent a critical approach that has not been fully exercised on this best-known and most engaging of Pope's works.

The subject of *The Rape of the Lock* is love among the nobility. The poem was commissioned in 1711 by Pope's friend John Caryll, a wealthy squire. Its purpose was to reconcile two great Catholic landowning families whose quarrel began when Robert, seventh Lord Petre, a relative of Caryll, snipped a lock of Miss Arabella Fermor's hair.

Pope himself by this time had become part of the high society he wrote about, although he was the son of a Catholic linen-merchant and inherited only a modest legacy from his father. Yet the poet's combination of literary genius and political tact won him the appreciation of noble patrons of both political parties, while the fortune he earned from his writing enabled him to remain financially independent of them. Pope cultivated the acquaintance of the rich and famous, and among his friends counted some of the most powerful and distinguished figures of the age. They included George Granville, Baron Lansdowne, the Tory electoral manager who requested that Pope revise his pastoral *Windsor Forest* into a celebration of the Tory Peace of Utrecht and the glories of Anne's regime; John Arbuthnot, Queen Anne's physician; Henry St. John, Viscount Bolingbroke, secretary of state to Queen Anne, and Pope's lifelong friend to whom the *Essay on Man* is addressed; James Craggs, secretary at war and secretary of state under George I; Bishop William Warburton, preacher to Lincoln's Inn, chaplain to King George II, and Pope's literary executor. Pope was all his life distinguished by what his biographer Samuel Johnson called "voracity of fame," and lived to have his desire amply fulfilled.

What can we learn about *The Rape of the Lock* from Pope's personal response to the central figure in the aristocratic feud he had been asked to mediate? The question seems to violate the most sacred precept of criticism, in disregarding the distinction between Pope's personal opinions and his poetry, or between life and art in general. Yet in the case of *The Rape of the Lock,* the connection between life and art is unusually close, and few of Pope's contemporaries failed to make that connection. Moreover, there is no fixed aesthetic distance between the artist and his art. With Chaucer it is sometimes a mistake to confuse narrator with poet, whereas with Pope that identification is rarely wrong, and with a poet like Sylvia Plath, say, personal and poetic voices are virtually identical. Given the special circumstances in which *The Rape of the Lock* was composed, and given the usual particularity of Pope's poetry, an acquaintance with Pope's real opinions can only illuminate the work of art in which he explores at leisure the moral and social questions raised by an apparently trivial event.

In a famous essay, Cleanth Brooks has argued that Pope felt quite fully his heroine's charm, and that we are intended to feel it too.[1] In emphasizing what he considers to be the ambivalence of Belinda's character and of Pope's attitude toward her, Brooks inflates the psychological dimension of the poem at the expense of its prominent social themes. I shall argue that Pope is far from being ambivalent about his heroine or her real model, and that his attitude toward both is more hostile than the polite critic might wish it to be. The complexity of tone in the poem comes, in my view, not from the character of Belinda, then, but from the nature of the society she inhabits.

In the autumn of 1714 Pope wrote a congratulatory letter to Fermor after her marriage. The letter is a model of stiffly elegant courtesy, far different in tone from what Pope was capable of writing to women he liked. But let us hear Pope when he is writing to one such woman, his intimate friend Martha Blount, on the subject of Fermor's marriage:

> My Acquaintance runs so much in an Anti-Catholic channel, that it was but tother day I heard of Mrs Fermor's being Actually, directly, and consummatively, married. I wonder how the guilty Couple and their Accessories at Whiteknights look, stare, or simper, since that grand Secret came out which they so well concealed before. They concealed it as well as a Barber does his Utensils when he goes to trim upon a Sunday and his Towels hang out all the way: Or as well as a Fryer concealed a little Wench, whom he was carrying under his Habit to Mr Collingwood's Convent: Pray Father (sayd one in the street to him) what's that under your Arm. A saddle for one of the Brothers to ride with, quoth the Fryer. Then Father (cryd he) take care and shorten the stirrups—For the Girls Legs hung out—[2]

This letter suggests that Arabella Fermor had good reason to fear the gossip to which *The Rape of the Lock* exposed her and that Pope's attitude toward her, when he was not writing for the public, consisted of a somewhat prurient contempt.

That the Fermors were not wholly pleased with Pope's effort is hardly surprising, and in a letter to Caryll (November 8, 1712), Pope disingenuously remarks that "the celebrated lady herself is offended, and, which is stranger, not at herself, but me." Pope managed to appease the lady and clear her name by attaching to the 1714 edition of the poem an unctuously flattering dedication, in which he assures Arabella that "the character of Belinda . . . resembles you in nothing but in Beauty." Yet such flattery rings hollow next to Pope's patronizing explanation of the machinery of the poem: "I know how disagreeable it is," he begins, "to make use of hard words before a Lady. . . ." One is reminded of the portrait of Atticus in the *Epistle* to Dr. Arbuthnot; for *The Rape of the Lock,* with its prefatory letter, shows how well Pope himself could "Damn with faint praise, assent with civil leer, / And without sneering, teach the rest to sneer."[3]

Pope's letter to Martha Blount shows him well armed against the charm of even such a famous beauty as Arabella Fermor. His additions to *The Rape of the Lock* beyond its original 334 lines confirm the harshness of his judgment of Belinda. The additions include the machinery of the Sylphs, through which the deficiencies in Belinda's character are more fully exposed. They also

include some of the most cuttingly ironical and damaging lines in
the poem, many sexual innuendoes, and the important "touch-
stone" speech of Clarissa, whose "good sense" Belinda rejects.

All this suggests, then, that the complexity of *The Rape of the
Lock* is not located in character. The source of complexity in the
work is rather to be located in those passages that deal with
Belinda's social world. Here Pope's attitude is necessarily ambig-
uous, for his attitude toward the ruling class he wrote about was
as divided as that class itself.

Competition among different ruling-class interests is a constant
feature of social history. In Pope's time it was expressed in the
contest of the Whig and Tory parties to control national policy.
As the party representing mainly landowning interests, the Tories
disliked the War of the Spanish Succession, which had dragged
on since 1702. They preferred in general a policy of peaceful
isolation, for the cost of expansion and war fell most heavily on
them. The Whigs, composed mainly of merchants, financiers,
army men, lawyers, and other professionals, stood for an aggressive foreign policy: it was they who lent money to the government, supplied war materials, and would profit from the total
defeat of England's commercial rivals. The period 1710–14 was
the peak of Tory power, for in the general elections of 1710 the
Tories on a peace platform had gained control of Commons.
They concluded the Peace of Utrecht in 1713, which—despite
compromises to which the Whigs were opposed—established
Britain as a major colonial and commercial empire. Although the
House of Lords, dominated by Whigs, opposed the treaty, Queen
Anne obligingly created twelve new peers to provide the neces-
sary Tory majority.

It was always Pope's boast, particularly in his letters, to have
remained independent of both parties. Indeed, his dislike of
party politics was shared by others, even by Queen Anne, who
in 1705 wrote to her treasurer Godolphin, "I dread falling into
the hands of either party. . . . Do all you can to keep me out of
the power of the merciless men of both parties." It was shared,
too, by Lord Halifax, who astutely remarked that any party is a

conspiracy against the rest of the nation. Yet neither Anne's fear nor Halifax's disdain prevented their playing a political role, and Pope's financial independence should not be confused with neutrality. *Windsor Forest* was a service to the Tories; so was the later satirical campaign against the Whig gentry and the ministry of Walpole. As a Catholic, moreover, Pope would naturally incline more toward the high-church (and sometimes Jacobite) Tories than toward the Protestant Whigs under whose anti-Papist laws Pope and his family had been deprived of civil rights.[4]

I hope to show in what follows that *The Rape of the Lock* presents, on the one hand, Pope's general commitment to aristocratic and repressive values and, on the other, his distaste for the crude profiteering, the blatant display, and the moral superficiality of an increasingly influential part of England's ruling class. Belinda and the Baron are at fault, in Pope's view, in failing to maintain an aristocratic code of conduct, and in holding their sexual attitudes up to criticism Pope exposes the social attitudes of the upper bourgeoisie. Of course, Pope's political criticism must remain limited by his acceptance of an aristocratic norm, for the aristocracy had an economic base quite as crudely exploitative as that of the commercial bourgeoisie. Because of this the poem can offer no serious alternative to the false sexual values it exposes or to the political attitudes to which they correspond.

Belinda's foremost trait is self-centeredness. This quality Pope conveys partly through narrative action, partly through rhetoric. Ironic hyperbole is obvious from the start: Belinda is said to inspire the poem, like a Muse; in her soft bosom, as in Juno's (*Aeneid* I.11) "dwells such mighty Rage"; her eyes, more than suns, "must eclipse the Day." These phrases parody the conventions of epic and of Petrarchan love poetry; they also parody Belinda's sense of her own importance.

We first see Belinda asleep and dreaming: an appropriate introduction to a woman whose entire life has the narcissistic quality of dream, and whose consciousness is so limited that even awake she seems asleep. The content of Belinda's dream is no different from that of her waking life: flirtation and egotism. She dreams of "A youth more glittering than a birth-night beau" who whispers in her ear—not words of love, but of self-love:

> Fairest of Mortals, thou distinguish'd Care
> Of thousand bright Inhabitants of Air!
> If e'er one Vision touch'd thy infant Thought,
> Of all the Nurse and all the Priest have taught,
> Of airy Elves by Moonlight Shadows seen,
> The silver Token, and the circled Green,
> Or Virgins visited by Angel-pow'rs,
> With Golden Crowns and Wreaths of heav'nly Flow'rs,
> Hear and believe! thy own Importance know,
> Nor bound thy narrow Views to Things below.
>
> (I.27–36)[5]

Does "thy infant Thought" mean "your mind when you were a child" or "your innocent mind" or "your immature mind"? The reference to nurse's fairy tales implies the first, that to religious instruction the second, and the argument itself the third; for we find that the long conditional clause supports the naive conviction of self-importance. The startling juxtaposition of elves and the Annunciation ("Virgins visited by Angel-pow'rs") further suggests the limitations of a mind in which fairy tale and theological mystery are scrambled without discrimination.

The young man in Belinda's dream reveals himself to be none other than Ariel, her guardian Sylph. It is his special duty to protect Belinda, for

> . . . whoever fair and chaste,
> Rejects Mankind, is by some *Sylph* embrac'd.
>
> (I.67–68)

The condition will prove Belinda's undoing, for later, at the moment when the Baron prepares to snip her lock, the Sylphs perceive that Belinda's mind is on a man, and their protection is suspended. That moment need occasion no surprise, for we have already seen that Belinda's thoughts are not wholly chaste. Some thought or impulse "ev'n in Slumber caus'd her Cheek to glow"

(I.24), and on waking she receives a billet-doux which is "no sooner read, / But all the Vision vanish'd from thy Head" (I.119–20).

The narcissistic dream is soon translated into action when we see Belinda at her dressing-table, at once priestess and goddess in "the sacred Rites of Pride" (I.128). The attack on pride and vanity was a common topic in eighteenth-century literature, and one to which Pope, drawing on the Catholic tradition of the seven deadly sins, could contribute with special fervor. It is a constant theme in his own work as well. In May 1711, just before Pope began work on *The Rape of the Lock,* the *Essay on Criticism* appeared; there Pope had castigated pride as the main cause of "erring judgment," as "the never-failing vice of fools," as the enemy of wit, sense, and reason.[6] He meant, of course, literary judgment and literary sense, but he meant a good deal more, and his strictures on pride are not likely to have been forgotten so soon either by the poet or by his audience.

At her dressing-table, Belinda is surrounded by exotic ornaments, the result of Britain's booming commercial expansion:

> Unnumber'd Treasures ope at once, and here
> The various Off'rings of the World appear;
> From each she nicely culls with curious Toil,
> And decks the Goddess with the glitt'ring Spoil.
> This casket *India's* glowing Gems unlocks,
> And all *Arabia* breathes from yonder Box.
> The Tortoise here and Elephant unite,
> Transform'd to *Combs,* the speckled and the white.
>   (I.129–36)

It is as if England's luxury trade existed to bedeck Belinda with its "glitt'ring Spoil." Indeed at this moment Belinda is the very symbol of commercial Britannia, her self-absorption the image of the colonial nation's will to absorb into itself the world's wealth. Pope himself suggests an analogy between Belinda and Britannia in Ariel's second description of the Sylphs and their work. Some, says Ariel, guide the planets; others watch over nature and human affairs:

> Others on Earth o'er human Race preside,
> Watch all their Ways, and all their Actions guide:
> Of these the Chief the Care of Nations own,
> And guard with Arms Divine the *British Throne.*
>   (II.87–90)

To gloss these lines, as Warburton did, as "a mere piece of raillery" would be to ignore the complexity of Pope's political attitudes. Britannia, like Belinda, is "hedged round with divinity." For Belinda it is, as the poem shows, rather an unreliable divinity. For Britannia, though, Pope had recently found such divinity a useful rhetorical device. In *Windsor Forest,* Pan, Pomona, and Ceres lavish gifts upon England, and Queen Anne is "As bright a Goddess, and as chaste a Queen" as Diana. Pope was far from being as critical of the British throne as he was of Belinda's dressing-table, even though he could scarcely avoid perceiving certain similarities.

A similar ambivalence appears if we compare the dressing-table scene with Father Thames's speech to the assembled rivers in *Windsor Forest.* Anticipating the commercial advantages of the Tory peace, Thames says,

> For me the balm shall bleed, and amber flow,
> The coral redden and the ruby glow,
> The pearly shell its lucid globe infold,
> And Phoebus warm the ripening ore to gold.[7]

It is as self-serving a vision as Belinda's, yet it can hardly be interpreted ironically unless we see *Windsor Forest* as an exercise in pure servility. More likely, I think, is that Pope was not in principle opposed to colonial expansion or to the profit accruing from it—indeed, he invested in the Tory South Seas Company—but that he despised the profit motive in its cruder manifestations, along with the less discriminating taste he tended to associate with the mercantile Whigs. We may see Belinda, then, as an aristocrat whose main fault is that she behaves like a bourgeoise. She is a silly aristocrat who, like Arabella Fermor, needs to be laughed into a serious aristocrat.

Having seen Belinda in private, we see her next, in canto II, in public, a powerful figure and the object of general admiration:

> Not with more Glories, in th'Etherial Plain,
> The Sun first rises o'er the purpled Main,
> Than issuing forth, the Rival of his Beams
> Lanch'd on the Bosom of the Silver *Thames*.
> Fair Nymphs, and well-drest Youths around her shone,
> But ev'ry Eye was fix'd on her alone.
> On her white Breast a sparkling *Cross* she wore,
> Which *Jews* might kiss, and Infidels adore.
> Her lively Looks a sprightly Mind disclose,
> Quick as her Eyes, and as unfix'd as those:
> Favours to none, to all she Smiles extends,
> Oft she rejects, but never once offends.
> Bright as the Sun, her Eyes the Gazers strike,
> And, like the Sun, they shine on all alike.
>
> (II.1–14)

Purple and silver, imperial colors, are associated with Belinda here; her jewelled cross and impartial gaze intensify the impression of power. The devotion revealed by the cross is of course to Belinda's own public image rather than to more orthodox objects of worship; perhaps that is why Jews and infidels might so readily kiss and adore it.

> Yet graceful Ease, and Sweetness void of Pride,
> Might hide her Faults, if *Belles* had Faults to hide:
> If to her share some Female Errors fall,
> Look on her Face, and you'll forget 'em all.
>
> (II.15–18)

So Pope concludes his description, with cutting irony. His letter to Martha Blount hinted strongly that Belle Fermor did have faults to hide, and we have already seen Belinda busy with the "Rites of Pride." The equivocal "might" and "if" help to make the point that ease and sweetness may serve the same purpose as rouge. Equally ironic is the advice in the last two lines, for to respond to Belinda solely on the basis of her appearance would be to commit another 'female error" of superficiality, of the sort already judged in canto I.

Belinda's lock is now described in a passage whose imagery suggests the predatory element in her self-presentation:

> This Nymph, to the destruction of Mankind,
> Nourish'd two Locks, which graceful hung behind
> In equal Curls, and well conspir'd to deck
> With shining Ringlets the smooth Iv'ry Neck.
> Love in these Labyrinths his Slaves detains,
> And mighty Hearts are held in slender Chains.
> With hairy Sprindges we the Birds betray,
> Slight Lines of hair surprize the Finny Prey,
> Fair Tresses Man's Imperial Race insnare,
> And Beauty draws us with a single hair.
>
> (II. 19–28)

She has got herself up to hunt, to prey, to capture, and her object is not love itself but the social status that comes from being admired. We begin, then, to see susceptible mankind more as victim than aggressor, or, more accurately, we are invited to see the Baron, like Belinda herself, as aggressor and victim at once.

At this point Pope introduces the Baron, whose response to Belinda's beauty can be no surprise:

> Th'adventrous *Baron* the bright Locks admir'd;
> He saw, he wish'd, and to the Prize aspir'd.
>
> (II.29–30)

Belinda expects him, after all, to see and to wish, perhaps even to aspire. That the Baron acts on his wish is only a consequence, then, of the false values to which both are committed. The Baron, like Belinda, commits the fault of behaving like a bourgeois. His motive is acquisition and profit, although not of money: He hopes to get the symbols of sexual victory however he can and to flaunt them to increase his status among competitors. His altar is as much a monument to masculine self-importance as Belinda's was to feminine narcissism, and on it lie the obsolete sacrifices to his image of self-respecting virility:

> There lay three Garters, half a Pair of Gloves;
> And all the Trophies of his former Loves.
>
> (II.39–40)

Determined to add another trophy to his collection, the ruthless Baron will use any means to augment his status:

> Resolv'd to win, he meditates the way,
> By Force to ravish, or by Fraud betray;
> For when Success a Lover's Toil attends,
> Few ask, if Fraud or Force attain'd his Ends.
>
> (II.31–34)

That the Baron and Belinda so readily reduce themselves and each other to objects or tools—that their game is one that dehumanizes—is a facet of their consciousness that Pope can duplicate in his rhetoric. The animal and hunt imagery already cited helps to do this, and the poet further expresses the reductive consciousness of his characters in the brilliant use of such devices as zeugma and parallel construction. Ariel, for example, anticipating disaster, does not know

> Whether the Nymph shall break *Diana's* Law,
> Or some frail *China* Jar receive a Flaw;
> Or stain her Honour, or her new Brocade;
> Forget her Pray'rs, or miss a Masquerade;
> Or lose her Heart, or Necklace, at a Ball,
> Or whether Heav'n has doom'd that *Shock* must fall.
>
> (II.105–10)

Later, when the lock has been cut,

> Not louder Shrieks to pitying Heav'n are cast,
> When Husbands, or when Lap-dogs breathe their last. . . .
>
> (III.157–58)

"But now secure the painted Vessel glides": Belinda's barge, to be sure, and Belinda herself. So in temporary confidence she moves, while her Sylphs tremble "for the Birth of Fate."

The third and central canto of the poem, in which the climactic "rape" occurs, is the most explicitly political of all. Its opening lines set the scene at Hampton Court Palace, establish the real grandeur of the place, and delicately expose the very diminished grandeur of its current personnel:

> Close by those meads, for ever crown'd with Flow'rs,
> Where *Thames* with Pride surveys his rising Tow'rs,
> There stands a Structure of Majestick Frame,
> Which from the neighb'ring *Hampton* takes its Name.
> Here *Britain's* Statesmen oft the Fall foredoom
> Of Foreign Tyrants, and of Nymphs at home;
> Here Thou, great *Anna!* whom three Realms obey,
> Dost sometimes Counsel take—and sometimes *Tea*. . . .
> One speaks the Glory of the *British Queen,*
> And one describes a charming *Indian Screen;*
> A third interprets Motions, Looks, and Eyes;
> At ev'ry Word a Reputation dies.
>
> (III. 1–16)

The target here is not, of course, Queen Anne or the institutional
aspect of government. The first four lines convey a genuine so-
lemnity, and "for ever crown'd with flowers" suggests a perma-
nence transcending that of the public gardens at Hampton Court.
England's past and future, the history that has been made and
will be made on those meads and in that structure: Surely this is
the source of Thames's pride and Pope's seriousness here. His
tone changes abruptly, though, when he speaks of the present
inhabitants of the court. (It is not entirely irrelevant to note that
Anne was rarely at Hampton—she preferred Windsor and Ken-
sington—but that it was a favorite gathering place for noblemen
and wits.) The damaging zeugma and rhyme aim instead at the
warped consciousness of courtiers: a consciousness that permits
them to discuss queens and screens in the same tone, as it permits
Belinda's friends to bewail the death of husbands and lapdogs
with the same loud shrieks.

Place has been specified; now time is specified as well, and it is
defined in terms of the larger social world:

> Mean while declining from the Noon of Day,
> The Sun obliquely shoots his burning Ray;
> The hungry Judges soon the Sentence sign,
> And Wretches hang that Jury-men may Dine;
> The Merchant from th'*Exchange* returns in Peace,
> And the long Labours of the *Toilette* cease. . . .
>
> (III.19–24)

Not surprisingly, the inhabitants of this larger world exhibit the same irresponsibility as do those of the court. Society at large is not merely a backdrop against which the trivial and not-so-trivial dramas of court life were played, nor is the sole purpose of the passage to remind us that girls like Belinda are as carefully shielded from social reality as they are from the sun's "burning Ray." The work of judges, jurymen, and merchants is precisely that on which court life depends, and Pope shows us here—as he has shown us all along, whether directly or by allusion—the social fabric to which a serious aristocrat must acknowledge responsibility. Yet this does not exhaust the complexity of the passage either. Why does Pope offer such an unflattering view of a social order in which he does believe? And just how unflattering a view is it?

Pope shows a social order whose members at various levels have abandoned their obligations to it. In doing this he suggests the graver consequences of such abdication, for while the Baron and Belinda can do no lasting harm in their limited circle, their selfishness writ large can do a great deal of harm indeed. No doubt Pope would deplore the miscarriages of justice that resulted from the irresponsibility of judges and jurymen. What he seems not to see is that wretches hanged not only so that jurymen could dine, but so that they could exist as a class, along with the wealthy landlords, financiers, and merchants who in Parliament made capital offenses of housebreaking, robbery, vagrancy, and the coining of base metal. Such property laws increased in savagery until, by 1740, "for stealing a handkerchief worth one shilling, so long as it was removed privily from the person, children could be hanged by the neck until dead."[8] These are the laws that an aristocracy made and jurymen only enforced; they represent the habitual response of a ruling class to the protests of those whom it exploits. Pope has little to say about the multitudinous poor, except to criticize a too-open contempt for them (in *Moral Essay III*, 99–106), and, to note, in *An Essay on Man*, that "The rich is happy in the plenty giv'n, / The poor contents him with the care of Heav'n."[9] Social criticism in the passage cited is limited, then, to an obvious and superficial form of injustice, and, moreover, to injustice committed by members of the middle class. Once again the aristocracy is left, as a class, intact, its legal crimes unmentioned and its brutality ignored.

Nor is the passage on society without implications for the theme of sexual attitudes. We begin to see that Belinda's presentation of herself as an object originates in her society's reduction of all value to money value, all life to commodity. Indeed, we can hardly avoid concluding that the reductive consciousness that Pope parodies originates in the economic process by which that society exists. The wretches who hang, being numerous and easily reproduced, have little commodity value. Belinda, like any wealthy young girl, has commodity value in cash and land settlements on her marriage, and in influential family connections. Her beauty, like that of an estate or a Chinese vase, makes her a more valuable acquisition. The effect of economic reality is observable in contemporary poems written on belles of the day, for these poems have more in them of appraisal than of praise. Noteworthy in the following "compliment" to Arabella Fermor are real-estate imagery and an attitude of cool scrutiny that belie the poet's purely verbal raptures:

> Thus Farmer's [Fermor's] Neck with easie Motion turns;
> The Purpling Flood in Circling Currents runs:
> Her Snowey Breasts those lovely Mounts arise,
> And with surprizing Pleasure seize our Eyes,
> Between these Hills flows Heliconian Dew,
> Which makes the Poet's Raptures ever new. . . . [10]

So Belinda has learned to see herself as society sees her, and to compete for the rewards that society grants. Only in *Moral Essay II* does Pope glance at the social causes of feminine self-display. Women, he writes, are ruled by two passions: "The Love of Pleasure, and the Love of Sway." The first is given by nature, the second by experience, and "by Man's oppression curst, / They seek the second not to lose the first."[11] The relation of means to ends here is disputable, and it is reversed a few lines later. But the tantalizing glimpse of social reality disappears; "Man's oppression" plays no further role in Pope's treatment of women in the *Moral Essay,* and we are left with a parade of power-hungry, pleasure-hungry caricatures. I do not find, then, that the passage cited above displays any such "totality of view" as Cleanth Brooks claims for it. On the contrary, Pope's loyalty to the ruling class he wrote for must limit his social criticism quite narrowly, just as his sexist assumptions preclude any real alternative to Belinda's mode of existence.

Belinda now sits down to a game of ombre (Spanish, *hombre*) with the Baron and another young lady. The politics of sex is advanced here through the pervasive sexual and military images of the episode, which allow us to see the card-game as a symbol of more complicated and important contests. It represents first the war of sexes in which Belinda habitually participates, and which will shortly erupt into armed skirmish. It also represents the "Spanish game" recently settled to Britain's advantage in the Peace of Utrecht. Belinda wins the game of cards, but her exultation is brief. Clarissa offers the Baron a pair of sewing scissors, and

> The Peer now spreads the glitt'ring *Forfex* wide,
> T'inclose the Lock; now joins it, to divide. . . .
> The meeting Points the sacred Hair dissever
> From the fair Head, for ever and for ever!
> (III. 147–54)

At this point the two meanings of "rape" come into play, for *raptus* is both the theft of property and the abduction and violation of a woman. The rapacious Baron has taken from Belinda what is most intimately her own property. Pope would have us see that Belinda encouraged such a violation by displaying herself as nothing more than a desirable piece of property; he does not suggest that women display themselves as objects when society makes it worth their while to do so.

The Baron's theft constitutes, in Pope's view, a double offense, for in showing the acquisitive fervor of a bourgeois, he stoops to stealing from a fellow aristocrat. Minor as it is, the theft is a breach of class trust, and the Baron requires, like Belinda, to be laughed into good sense. But the modern critic may inquire whether the Baron does not behave, after all, like an aristocrat. His class existed, in a sense, by theft. Their wealth—the rents, fines, and taxes produced and paid by the laborers of England—was the fruit of theft on a national scale, and the development of British colonialism only expanded that *raptus* worldwide. The rape of the lock is the smallest possible theft in a society founded on legal theft, and Pope's acceptance of the latter will always provide a *terminus ad quem* for his criticism of wayward aristocrats.

Canto IV describes Belinda's sulking spell, and takes us through the fantastic landscape of the Cave of Spleen. Spleen is a fashionable aristocratic malaise and a specifically feminine complaint, for Spleen "rule[s] the Sex to Fifty from Fifteen." Pope suggests through the imagery of Spleen's Cave that the complaint may well be due to sexual frustration; there "maids turn'd Bottels call aloud for Corks." Belinda's friend Thalestris only increases her despondency with a vision of shameful gossip and isolation. Belinda is no longer a marketable commodity; thought to be unchaste, she will attract neither wealthy admirers nor friends. The superficiality of Belinda's concern with the appearance of honor is devastatingly exposed in the sexual innuendo of the last couplet of the canto:

> "Oh hadst thou, Cruel! been content to seize
> Hairs less in sight, or any Hairs but these!"
> (IV.176–77)

Canto V opens with the speech of Clarissa, sole representative of good sense in the poem. There is no doubt that her speech— imitated from that of Sarpedon in *The Iliad* (XII.371 ff.) and specially added in 1717—offers a fairly reliable version of Pope's opinion in the matter. Pope's own note to the 1736 edition describes Clarissa as "a new Character introduced . . . to open more clearly the MORAL of the Poem." Unlike Belinda and Thalestris, Clarissa does not speak to the adamant and unrepentant Baron, "For who can move when fair *Belinda* fails?" Instead Clarissa addresses Belinda, much as Pope himself had done when, in his dedicatory letter to *The Rape of the Lock,* he urged Arabella Fermor, along with other young ladies, to self-knowledge and to "good sense and good humour enough to laugh not only at their sex's little unguarded follies, but at their own." Like Pope, Clarissa does not dispute the whole process of self-presentation at the core of Belinda's character. Neither does she question the importance that society attaches to physical beauty, nor the luxurious life-style in which belles are "deck'd with all that Land and Sea afford." She merely asks, without answering, why all this is done, and advises the addition of good sense to physical beauty, for

> "How vain are all these Glories, all our Pains,
> Unless good Sense preserve what Beauty gains. . . ."
> (V.15–16)

In what does this good sense consist? Clarissa urges Belinda to make a virtue of necessity:

> "But since, alas! frail Beauty must decay,
> Curl'd or uncurl'd, since Locks will turn to grey,
> Since painted, or not painted, all shall fade,
> And she who scorns a Man, must die a Maid;
> What then remains, but well our Pow'r to use,
> And keep good Humour still whate'er we lose?"
> (V.25–30)

The substance of Clarissa's speech is repeated in *Moral Essay II,* in Pope's portrait of the woman of sense. There, in a passage recalling the imagery of *The Rape of the Lock,* Pope describes the woman who

> Charms by accepting, by submitting sways,
> Yet has her humour most, when she obeys;
> Let Fops or Fortune fly which way they will;
> Disdains all loss of Tickets, or Codille;
> Spleen, Vapours, or Smallpox, above them all
> And Mistress of herself, though China fall.[12]

Clarissa's sentiments also anticipate in small the advice Pope would later give, on a metaphysical scale, in the *Essay on Man:*

> Submit—In this, or any other sphere,
> Secure to be as blest as thou canst bear. . . . [13]

It is useful advice for a ruling class to offer those whom it exploits. It is equally useful to the chauvinized Clarissa, for she counsels good humor in a theft to which she was accessory (III.127–30). The opportunism of Clarissa's position becomes even clearer when she remarks that "she who scorns a man, must die a maid." This, we discover, is the answer to the questions posed earlier: The right use of beauty is not to tease a man, but to catch a man; a husband is "what Beauty gains." So that while Clarissa rightly deplores Belinda's "airs, and flights, and screams, and scolding," she, with Pope, is unable to address herself to the larger situation that calls forth such mannerisms.

Clarissa's advice is rejected, although for other reasons (one hopes) than it would be rejected now. The battle of sexes begins in earnest, with Belinda's attempt to get back her lock. But the lock,

> . . . obtain'd with Guilt, and kept with Pain,
> In ev'ry place is sought, but sought in vain. . . .
> (V.109–10)

The lock is translated to heaven in the shape of a comet (*comes,* hair) that will serve, according to the ironical prediction, to foretell historical events:

> This *Partridge* soon shall view in cloudless Skies,
> When next he looks thro' *Galileo's* eyes;
> And hence th'Egregious Wizard shall foredoom
> The Fate of *Louis,* and the Fall of *Rome.*
> (V.137–40)

"John Partridge," read's Pope's note to these lines, "was a ridiculous Stargazer, who in his almanacs every year never failed to predict the downfall of the Pope, and the King of France. . . . " Had Partridge lived two generations later, part at least of his prediction would have come true when in 1789 the grandson of Louis XIV was deposed and later beheaded by the new national assembly of citizens. Perhaps the events of the French Revolution could have been foretold, although not from comets, and not by one who believed, as Pope did, that the existing social order duplicated a cosmic order and that both were "right!" But to some in the eighteenth century, the bourgeois revolutions of America and France were as welcome[14] as the socialist revolutions of China and Cuba have been to many in our own time. For modern revolutionary movements, the target is precisely the cluster of values represented in *The Rape of the Lock:* sexism, together with the economic structure that supports it.[15]

7

Red Rosa:
bread and roses

Now Red Rosa is also gone,
Where she lies is quite unknown.
Because she told the poor the truth,
The rich have hunted her down.
　　　　　Bertolt Brecht, "Grabschrift 1919"

A woman, a Jew, and a Pole—it sounds like the beginning of a bad joke. Rosa Luxemburg was all three, but as a revolutionary Communist she transcends definition by sex, religion, or nationality.

Franz Mehring, the colleague and first biographer of Marx, called Luxemburg "the best brain after Marx." When Lenin paid homage to Luxemburg in 1922, three years after her death at the hands of German police, he told "a good old Russian fable":

> "Eagles may at times fly lower than hens, but hens can never rise to the height of eagles." . . . In spite of her mistakes, Rosa Luxemburg was and remains for us an eagle. Not only will Communists all

over the world cherish her memory, but her biography and her *complete* works . . . will serve as useful manuals in training many generations of Communists all over the world. [Italics in original.][1]

Yet six years later, Communist party stalwarts were denouncing Rosa Luxemburg's work as "opportunist deviation" and even as a "syphilis bacillus" infecting the German proletariat. During Stalin's regime she was linked with Leon Trotsky as a heretic and deviant from "official" Bolshevik doctrine. Today in East Germany Luxemburg's reputation has begun to revive in a limited way, although her antibureaucratic stance and uncompromising rejection of all opportunism still make party bureaucracies uncomfortable. Brecht's "Ballad of Red Rosa" does not appear in his official *Collected Works.*

In the West there has been a slow but steady revival of interest in Rosa Luxemburg. Several anthologies have appeared; many of her pamphlets are now available in new editions; the important early biography by her comrade Paul Froelich has been reissued; there are new editions of her letters; and her doctoral dissertation is now available in its first English translation.[2]

Even this output is far from complete, for Luxemburg was an enormously prolific writer: of pamphlets, newspaper articles, theoretical works, speeches, and letters. Much of this material remains unpublished or untranslated, and some was destroyed when Luxemburg's Berlin apartment was ransacked after her murder. Her major work has been taken up by a mixed audience of anarchists, surrealists, spontaneists, feminists, vanguard-party theoreticians, revolutionary groupuscules, and disillusioned ex-leftists (I intend no equations here, nor any blanket evaluation). Obviously their motives differ, as consequently does their understanding of Luxemburg's contribution to Marxist theory. Luxemburg's work and her life are full of apparent paradox (like history itself, or like Marxist theory), and it's in part the inadequate understanding of such paradox that permits such a wide range of interpretation of her ideas. It isn't my purpose here to analyze Luxemburg's contribution to Marxist economics, and I am not convinced it is primarily as an economist that she is most usefully seen. As Luxemburg herself noted, the reader of her economic work must "thoroughly master political economy in general and Marxian economics in particular. And how many such mortals are there today? Not a half-dozen. From this standpoint my works really are luxury items and could be printed on handmade paper."[3] Nonetheless I want to explore some of the meaning of this immensely powerful figure from our revolutionary past and to suggest some of her importance for our revolutionary future.

She was born in 1871, the same year as Lenin and the year of the Paris Commune whose short life did so much to show the world revolutionary movement what proletarian democracy could and ought to be. Her family—like the families of Marx, Engels, Lenin, and Trotsky—was cultured and of comfortable means, though far from wealthy. A star pupil in high school, Rosa was denied the traditional gold medal for excellence "because of her oppositional attitude toward authority." In 1889, when Rosa was nineteen, her involvement in Warsaw with the Proletariat party and with the new Polish Workers' League was discovered by the czarist police. It was an offense that carried the punishment of imprisonment or exile to Siberia; so, hidden under straw in a peasant's cart, Rosa Luxemburg left Poland. She escaped to Zurich, a major center of intellectual life and of international socialist activity.

In Zurich Luxemburg made enduring friends and enemies. Among her enemies was Georgii Plekhanov, leader of the Russian exile group and "grand old man" of the revolutionary movement abroad; for personal and political reasons Plekhanov was antagonistic to Luxemburg and her friends. And, most important, Luxemburg met Leo Jogiches, the young Polish revolutionary who was her lover for many years and her lifelong comrade in the Polish socialist movement.

The dissertation with which Rosa Luxemburg earned her doctorate was a study of the industrial development of Poland during the nineteenth century. It was a pioneering effort, still used by modern historians in the field, which became an important part of Luxemburg's argument against the claims of the Polish nationalist movement for independence from Russia. The dissertation demonstrated that Poland's economic growth depended on the Russian market, so that separation would lead to economic chaos. Further, the ideological emphasis on patriotic nationalism would divert the Polish proletariat from class struggle and the struggle for socialism, thus benefiting the bourgeoisie. Luxemburg's position, then, was that Polish Communists should lend no support to the movement for national independence in Poland.

This stance was one of the mistakes that Lenin mentioned in his eulogy of Luxemburg, for the Bolsheviks consistently supported the right of oppressed nations to self-determination, while at the same time recognizing the reactionary nature of nationalism—"national egoism," in Lenin's phrase—and the equally retrograde influence of such mystical trends as pan-Islamism. Luxemburg's mistakes here were several. She confused support for national liberation with capitulation to nationalism. And, in her zeal to avoid the reformist mistake of limitation to democratic demands, she recoiled to the opposite (ultraleft) extreme of rejecting the democratic demand—rather than, as Lenin urged in his writings on the question, taking up the democratic demand for national liberation, supporting it, and combining it with the struggle for socialism. Stalin's analogy to the religion question is helpful: the Bolsheviks will defend freedom of religion, while simultaneously agitating against religion as an ideology hostile to the interests of the proletariat. Similarly, the revolutionary party will support the right of nations to self-determination while agitating for its own program. The Bolshevik position implied neither (as Trotsky put it) "an evangel of separation" nor political support to the bourgeoisie of a colonial country, even if that bourgeoisie were waging a struggle for national independence. Here the key principle is the organizational and propagandistic independence of Communists within the movement: to support militarily the struggle for national liberation, while simultaneously exposing and opposing the colonial bourgeoisie and pushing the struggle toward socialist revolution.

It was partly through her polemics against Polish independence and her leadership of the Polish group that the young Rosa Luxemburg established her reputation as an important member of the international socialist movement. On completing her degree in 1898, she decided, against the advice of Jogiches, to continue her revolutionary career in Germany. The specific reasons for her decision are not known, but it must have been clear that Germany, with its rapidly growing (though already internally divided) Socialist party, its developed capitalist economy, and its well-organized working class, offered the serious prospect of socialist revolution in the near future. It was in Germany that Luxemburg developed into one of the most formidable and creative leaders of world socialism, both a brilliant theoretician and a militant strategist. She sustained that position until she was arrested and murdered by army officers during the abortive German revolution of 1918–19, when working-class militancy made her leadership (and that of her comrade Karl Liebknecht, who died with her) a serious and immediate threat to the government. She and Liebknecht were arrested in Berlin on January 15, 1919, beaten, and shot; Jogiches met the same fate two months later. Luxemburg's body was dumped into a canal, not to be recovered for another four months. In Goebbels' bookburning of 1933 her works were thrown into the fire along with those of Marx and Engels, Wilhelm Reich, and the rest of Europe's greatest artists, scientists, and revolutionaries.

The central struggle in Rosa Luxemburg's political life in Germany was the struggle against reformist revisionism, that is, against the abandonment of socialist revolution and class struggle in favor of legal and parliamentary reforms. Until World War I, "social democracy" had been the general name for scientific or Marxian socialism as distinct from other currents such as Fourierist or Owenite utopian socialism. Thus Lenin's party was the Russian Social Democratic Workers' party. What set scientific socialism apart from other programs for social change was, first, the dialectical and materialist understanding of history and of capitalist social relations (relations of production, together with the class structure and political institutions that followed from these relations of production). Second, the understanding of the revolutionary tendency of the working class because of its position in capitalist society as the productive but exploited class. Third, understanding the necessity of revolution in order to expropriate the capitalist ruling class, smash the bourgeois state, and establish new, genuinely democratic forms of social life.

Reformist revisionism began its major theoretical development in the European socialist movement in the work of the German social democrat and pacifist Eduard Bernstein who, even while revising the most basic economic and political premises of Marxist theory, continued to pose as a sincere socialist. Briefly, Bernstein's argument runs as follows. By means of various adaptive mechanisms such as the credit system, improved communications, and employers' organizations (cartels, trusts), capitalism can avoid the recurrent crises that Marxist economics sees as inevitable. Thus capitalism becomes flexible enough to satisfy everyone, including the proletariat. In addition, the trade union activity of the organized working class will gradually improve its lot to the point where "the trade union struggle . . . will lead to a progressively more extensive control over the conditions of production," while through legislation the capitalist "will be reduced in time to the role of a simple administrator."[4] Class struggle can thus be eliminated by parliamentary reforms, and capitalism can survive indefinitely. The net effect of enough reforms would be socialism: No revolution required.

The best short exposure of this sleight-of-hand is still Rosa Luxemburg's polemic against Bernstein, *Reform or Revolution,* first published in 1899. The pamphlet examines the economic assumptions and the practical political consequences of revisionism, counterposing the correct Marxist analysis of the question. It shows, for example, how credit and cartels, far from suppressing the anarchy of capitalism, intensify and precipitate its crises. In particular they "aggravate the antagonism existing between the mode of production and exchange by sharpening the struggle between the producer and the consumer"—a principle whose concrete operation affects us now in the artificially inflated prices of housing, food, and other consumer commodities, and in such carefully engineered "shortages" as the mid-1970s oil crisis. Nor will the trade-union movement lead steadily to a proletarian paradise, for as capitalism proceeds through its decadent phase the demand for labor power will increase more slowly than the supply. Moreover, losses suffered on the world market will be compensated by reduction of wages. So that unemployment and falling wages (real wages, if not nominal wages) can be expected, and the trade-union movement will find its effort to protect the proletariat doubly difficult. Some of these problems are taken up in more detail by Lenin in *Imperialism, the Latest Stage of Capitalism.*[5]

This is not to say that revolutionary communism minimizes the importance of reform struggles, of safeguarding the gains made by the organized working class, or of defending all democratic rights. Indeed, as Luxemburg notes in her introduction to *Reform or Revolution,* it is only in Bernstein's work that one finds for the first time any opposition between the two indissolubly linked aspects of socialism. In fact, she writes, "the daily struggle for reforms . . . and for democratic institutions, offers to the Social-Democracy the only means of engaging in the proletarian class war and working in the direction of the final goal—the conquest of political power and the suppression of wage-labor. [For Social Democracy] the struggle for reforms is its means; the social revolution, its aim."[6] The difference from revisionism, then, is that revisionism declares the stated aim of socialism to be impossible, unknowable, or unimportant: "The final goal, no matter what it is, is nothing; the movement is everything." Yet since, as Luxemburg notes, "there can be no socialist movement without a socialist aim, [Bernstein] ends by renouncing the movement" as well.[7] It remains painfully familiar; one thinks of Herbert Marcuse's advice in *Counter-Revolution and Revolt* to young revolutionaries: to abandon mass action and "labor fetishism" and retreat to the universities.[8]

Perhaps the worst practical consequence of the growing influence of revisionism in the German Social Democratic party (SPD) was its inability to deal correctly with the outbreak of World War I. In 1914 the SPD, along with socialist parties of other countries, went patriotically in support of the national war effort, instead of refusing to participate in a war among imperialist nations. When the SPD voted war credits to the government, its theoretical and practical bankruptcy became as obvious to many as they had been for some time already to Rosa Luxemburg. "Social democrat" has since remained the term for those who want to reform capitalism rather than destroy it. Such reformists allied with the bourgeoisie to protect interests now their own. Indeed, it was with the complicity of an SPD government (to which power had been handed over in November 1918) that Luxemburg and Liebknecht were arrested and killed.

Obviously, the collapse of German social democracy cannot be laid entirely at the feet of Bernstein. In the introduction to his edition of Luxemburg's political writings, Robert Looker points out that "a stress on the insidious influence of revisionism . . . mistakes symptoms for causes."[9] Looker is surely correct in citing as important contributing factors the history of the German labor movement and the history of the SPD from the nineteenth century on. Still, the 1899 controversy with Bernstein and the 1914 abdication of a proletarian class line were symptoms of the same disease: opportunism. As Luxemburg wrote in "Either/Or," a Spartacus League pamphlet of 1916, "The proud old cry, 'Proletarians of all countries, unite!' has been transformed on the battlefield into the command, 'Proletarians of all countries, cut each other's throats!'"[10] And the Marxist principle that all written history is the history of the class struggle, now had "except in time of war" added to it ("Rebuilding the International," 1915). This was the demise of the Second International, as Lenin, Luxemburg, and other revolutionary socialists recognized. At the Zimmerwald Conference (September 1915) the foundations of the Third International were laid, though not until 1919 was it officially established.

In spite of their shock and outrage at the party's defection, Luxemburg and other comrades were not paralyzed. Those who were committed to Marxian economics, to dialectical materialism, and to revolution formed an opposition faction within the party, the Spartakusbund (Spartacus League), named after the famous leader of a Roman slave revolt. Some four years later the group would become the Communist party of Germany (KPD) and, in 1919, affiliate with the Third International. In the intervening years their tasks were to oppose the revisionist party leadership especially around the war issue, to propagandize among the masses for a correct line, and to organize actions against the war—as best they could without too blatantly breaching party discipline. The opposition conference of March 1916 showed impressive support in key industrial areas and in the party youth: a solidarity squandered by the faction leadership's firm decision to remain inside the party as long as possible. Their reason was to not abandon the party masses to the reformist leadership. The eventual effect—visible in the tragic defeat of the so-called Spartacus uprising of 1918–19—was to do exactly that, in failing to build the unambiguous and distinct revolutionary organization that in the critical moment could have provided the leadership abdicated by social democracy.

What was Rosa Luxemburg's experience as a woman leader of the SPD? In an ideal world, an ideal party, the question would be irrelevant. But since neither the world nor the party was perfect, gender was a factor both in inner-party life and in the party's external work around "the woman question."

For twenty-five years this pioneering work was led by Rosa's good friend Clara Zetkin, who did more than anyone to produce a synthesis of Marxian theory, political principle, and organizational practice on the woman question, a synthesis imitated by the Bolsheviks before and after they came to power. Until 1908, women in most parts of the Habsburg empire were forbidden by law to join a political party. Since the SPD could not recruit women directly, at a time when millions of women were joining

so strongly that I have no special corner of my heart reserved for the ghetto.[15]

Doubtless Rosa Luxemburg considered her (ultraleft) position on national independence to be of a piece with this view, and the Bolsheviks' insistence on the democratic right of nations to self-determination a diversionary concession to backward popular sentiment, a concession to the immediate needs of a portion of the oppressed. And similarly with the oppression of women.

In 1908 a new law granted women the right of association. Female membership in the SPD rose dramatically as the party both recruited directly and integrated the women's groups: Between 1908 and 1914 about 150,000 women joined. Though it would be simplistic to claim that all the new female recruits were more radical than the leadership, it is certain that *Gleichheit,* under Zetkin's leadership, was a powerful instrument of opposition propaganda, especially after the war broke out in 1914. Zetkin was with the Spartacists, the most radical of the opposition factions, whose antiwar propaganda (contradicting the official national, patriotic party line) won an enthusiastic hearing among proletarian women. But the revisionist leadership did not for long tolerate this state of affairs: Zetkin was forced out of her position in 1916, and the new majority-loyal *Gleichheit* editorialized:

> Women are more influenced than men by their emotions. In this lies their strength and also their weakness. In this case, the strength is a passionate opposition to war. . . . Their weakness is that, due to emotionalism, they are more susceptible to the erroneous view that majority socialists favored war.[16]

Perhaps the most startling revelation in Luxemburg's letters is the stubbornness with which she created and clung to a private world, a sense of herself apart from political life. Her painting, her carefully classified collection of dried plants, her intense sympathy for the pain of animals and insects, her love for music and literature, her close friendships with women comrades, the poignant vignettes of ordinary life observed from prison—these testify to a many-sided personality that is most evident in Rosa's

letters to Hans Diefenbach: "I still don't know what will become
of me for, as you know, I too am a land of boundless
possibilities."[17] It was a sense of self that did not contradict her
political commitment but complemented and confirmed it, as she
could write with utter candor to a woman friend and comrade:

> Inwardly, I feel so much more at home in a plot of garden like the
> one here . . . than at one of our party congresses. Surely I can tell
> you this, since you will not immediately suspect me of betraying
> socialism! You know that, in spite of it all, I really hope to die at my
> post, in a street fight or in prison.
>   But, my innermost self belongs more to my titmice than to the
> "comrades." And not because I find a restful refuge in nature like
> so many morally bankrupt politicians. On the contrary, in nature,
> too . . . I find so much that is cruel that I suffer very much.[18]

Precisely this strong, unerring sense of self gave Luxemburg
her fierce tenacity in struggle; certainly it is what she drew on for
her unique power as a writer and speaker:

> When people write, they forget . . . to dig deeply into themselves
> and to feel the whole import and truth of what they are writing. I
> believe that every time, every day, in every article you must feel
> your way through it, and then fresh words—coming from the heart
> and going to the heart—would occur to express the old familiar
> thing. But you get so used to a truth that you rattle off the deepest
> and greatest things as if they were the "Our Father." I firmly in-
> tend, when I write, never to forget to be enthusiastic about what I
> write and to commune with myself.[19]

And it was surely this sense of self that enabled Luxemburg to
survive so wonderfully intact the long sojourn in prison that left
her sick and gray-haired but never touched her revolutionary will
or her lifelong conviction that "Being a *Mensch* [person] is the
main thing! And that means to be firm, lucid and cheerful."[20] It
is in a letter from prison that she reconstructs a domestic scene
overheard from a neighboring tenement, a scene whose imagery
repeats the roses in my title and seems to evoke the beauty she
never lost sight of as the ultimate goal. It is night; a little girl is
stubbornly singing a nursery song despite orders to go to bed:

In this jumping rhythm of the nursery song, in the bubbling laughter, there was so much carefree and victorious lust for life that the whole dark, mouldy building of the police presidium seemed enveloped in a coat of silvery mist; it was as if, all of a sudden, my malodorous cell smelled of falling dark-red roses. Thus, wherever we are we can gather up a little happiness from the street, and we are reminded again that life is beautiful and rich.[21]

In 1916 Rosa Luxemburg was again arrested (taken into "protective custody"), and it was in prison that she heard the news of the Bolshevik revolution in Russia. "For three years Europe has been like a musty room," she wrote in May 1917, "almost suffocating those living in it. Now all at once a window has been flung open, a fresh, invigorating gust of air is blowing in, and everyone in the room is breathing deeply of it."[22] This was her enthusiastic welcome to long-awaited revolution, in the famous essay "The Old Mole." It seemed that the old mole, revolutionary history, having gone underground for the time in Germany, had now surfaced in Russia. Its reappearance there would and must herald similar events in Germany, not only by force of example, but because, as the Bolshevik leaders knew all too well, the success and even survival of their revolution depended on the rapid development of revolutions in other countries. They confronted the dangers of military invasion, economic strangulation, political compromises: These meant either more European revolutions in a fairly short time, or a worldwide setback for the international socialist movement as well as for the Russian Revolution itself. Naturally, the notion of "socialism in one country," Stalin's invention, was never considered a realistic solution; nor is it dialectically possible—hence it has no basis in the Marxist-Leninist tradition. Rather it represents both an absolute failure to understand the dialectic of revolutionary process, and a most opportunistic attempt to transform the concessions and defeats of the Russian Revolution into iron principle and virtue. Without denying that some of these concessions may have been necessary for the survival of the new state, one has nonetheless to call a spade a spade. As Luxemburg acknowledged (in September 1918), even while (again incorrectly) denouncing the Treaty of Brest-Litovsk, "Admittedly Lenin and his friends deluded neither themselves nor others about the facts. They admitted their capitulation. Unfortunately they did deceive themselves in hoping to purchase a genuine respite at the price of capitulation. . . . "[23] Such a deceptive slogan as "socialism in one country" could not have been and was not seriously entertained by the victorious Bolsheviks in 1917, though the idea (if not the explicit wording) was put forth by some Mensheviks and revisionists. "Imperialism or socialism! War or revolution! There is no third way!"—that was Luxemburg's battle cry.[24]

The proletarian rising of November 1918 to January 1919 seemed to fulfill these hopes. As a participant in what he calls "the German Revolution," Paul Froelich writes with vividness and pace of mass risings in Berlin and other major cities, of workers' councils, of the revolutionary alliance of sailors and factory workers, of the kaiser's abdication, and the proclamation by Karl Liebknecht of the Socialist Republic of Germany.[25]

But, having shown its head all too briefly the old mole disappeared in Germany with the defeat of the November rising. As Luxemburg foresaw it might, it soon went underground in Russia, too, after Lenin's death, and it is a favorite speculation among Luxemburg's biographers what her position might have been had she lived through the periods of the Third (Stalinist) and Fourth (Trotskyist) Internationals.

Luxemburg's criticism of the Bolshevik party has been a thorny question on the left. Her position, and Lenin's too, has often been caricatured and oversimplified, as in Bertram D. Wolfe's introduction to his edition of two Luxemburg tracts.[26] Wolfe went so far as to publish Luxemburg's 1904 piece "Organizational Questions of the Russian Social Democracy" under the theatrical and misleading title given it by a later publisher: "Leninism or Marxism?"—as if a revolutionary of Luxemburg's caliber would formulate the problem so mechanically. It seems to me that Luxemburg never understood as profoundly as Lenin did two things: first, the necessity for "iron discipline" within a vanguard party so that the party can be a unified fighting force and avoid the tragic capitulation of the Second International, and second, the unpleasant necessity to make certain compromises, such as the Brest-Litovsk peace treaty or the New Economic Policy, to ensure the immediate survival of the Russian Revolution so that genuine socialism could be built. Lenin was always painfully aware of the differences between dictatorship of the proletariat as it existed under his leadership and full socialism: It is a constantly recurrent theme in his writings of the 1920s.

It is important to bear in mind and as far as possible to duplicate the very finely balanced dialectical sensibility that permits support and criticism to exist simultaneously, in all their complexity, without taking the easy way out by a crudely mechanical solution (whether fanatical enthusiasm or outraged rejection). The Bolsheviks existed, for the moment, "under the conditions of bitter compulsion and necessity in the midst of the roaring whirlpool of events."[27] In such circumstances, Luxemburg reiterates time and again, one does not expect perfection. Yet Rosa Luxemburg is also thinking of the long run, always pressing ahead to the long-range implications, the possibilities. As Georg Lukacs remarks, "She constantly opposes to the exigencies of the moment the principles of future stages of the revolution."[28] Some may view the idea of perfection as a luxury that few revolutionaries can afford. I suggest that Rosa Luxemburg saw it as a costly necessity and tool of the trade, without which there is no long-range criterion for specific situations—worse, no principled guide to practical action, hence no ability to predict or control events, and hence passivity and virtually certain defeat. Is this utopian? Only if we extend the "no place" of utopia into "never": It depends on your sense of possibility. At the same time, the vision of perfection can lead, and it sometimes led Luxemburg, into ultraleft, hence incorrect, positions.

Operating, then, from the sense of maximum possibility, Luxemburg wrote "The Russian Revolution." Fourteen years earlier, in 1904, she had published in *Iskra,* the Bolshevik theoretical journal, a review of *One Step Forward, Two Steps Back,* "written by Lenin, an outstanding member of the *Iskra* group." There she had argued that the militant centralism of the Bolshevik tendency would paralyze the party, rendering it incapable of accomplishing its historic tasks." In 1918 the success of the Russian Revolution forced Luxemburg to revise at least part of her earlier judgment. In "The Russian Revolution" she addressed herself to the Bolsheviks in power. On one hand she eulogized their clear-sightedness and discipline:

> The Bolshevik tendency performs the historic service of having proclaimed from the very beginning, and having followed with iron consistency, those tactics which alone could save democracy and drive the revolution ahead. All power exclusively in the hands of the worker and peasant masses, in the hands of the soviets—this was indeed the only way out of the difficulty into which the revolution had gotten; this was the sword stroke with which they cut the Gordian knot, freed the revolution from a narrow blind-alley and opened up for it an untrammeled path into the free and open fields.
>
> The party of Lenin was thus the only one in Russia which grasped the true interest of the revolution in that first period. It was the element that drove the revolution forward, and thus it was the only party which really carried on a socialist policy.
>
> . . . The "golden mean" cannot be maintained in any revolution. The law of its nature demands a quick decision: either the locomotive drives forward full steam ahead to the most extreme point of the historical ascent, or it rolls back of its own weight again to the starting point at the bottom. . . . This makes clear the miserable role of the Russian Mensheviks . . . etc., who had enormous influence on the masses at the beginning, but, after their prolonged wavering and after they had fought with both hands and feet against taking over power and responsibility, were driven ignobly off the stage.[29]

Now, after the Chilean coup of September 1973, our generation can add to this that those who hesitate to take full power are driven brutally off the stage, along with thousands of revolutionary workers who sacrifice their lives in the process.

Besides praising, Luxemburg criticized Bolshevik land reform as inadequate and tending to create a conservative stratum of landowning peasants. She also protested the suspension of certain democratic rights, especially for the opponents of soviet rule:

WRITING WOMAN : *130*

Such interference with free public life and political debate would certainly, she said, cut the party off from its vital roots in the masses and turn it into an authoritarian bureaucracy. In both cases she was right theoretically but wrong practically—defeated, I would suggest, by that characteristic vision of perfection that enabled her to ignore the exigencies of the particular moment. Indeed, one could argue that her criticism was inconsistent, inasmuch as the compromise land reform did constitute one of Lenin's efforts to halt bureaucratic degeneration by satisfying, through temporary measures, a relatively backward part of the population who would otherwise have to be dealt with by force and bureaucracy.

The bureaucratic degeneration of the Russian Revolution after Lenin's death in 1924 does not necessarily prove, as Froelich claims, that Luxemburg was prophetically correct in all her criticism of the Bolsheviks. Such a claim omits the necessary scrupulous analysis of world events, of the Russian situation at any given moment, and of the individuals involved. Certainly to use her work in support of an antivanguard or "spontaneist" position, as some groups and individuals have recently done, is dishonest and crude in the extreme. Moreover, it ignores the importance of correct leadership, which Luxemburg stressed throughout her life and which, after all, provided the impetus for her struggle against revisionism in the party. What was required was a leadership both disciplined enough and flexible enough to work with the spontaneous energies of the masses, to prepare the masses for the assumption of state power, and to direct its spontaneous energies toward that goal. This, like so many other Marxist positions, appears paradoxical to the fragmented or mechanical consciousness; as a dialectical appreciation of reality, however, it is, I believe, correct.

Froelich's book has had several incarnations before its latest one, having been published in Paris (1939), London (1940), and Frankfort (1967). It is an extremely thorough political biography by a close associate of Luxemburg, for, with her, Froelich led the revolutionary Spartacus League, participated in the 1918 rising, and helped found the KPD. With clarity and detail Froelich sets out the historical and political context in which Luxemburg lived and worked.

As a biography, though, Froelich's book presents an almost one-dimensional view of its subject, and that dimension is the political. One gets no sense from Froelich's pages of the passion and inner conflict that emerge from Luxemburg's correspondence. All of the personal material is collected in a single chapter, where Froelich briefly documents Luxemburg's love for music, poetry, and botany, her talent for painting, her romantic streak, and the intensity of her personal relations. Yet by confining this material to one chapter, Froelich sets it apart from her political life and trivializes it.

Froelich never alludes to sexual relations, not even the tempestuous long-term (and often long-distance) union with her comrade Leo Jogiches, whom she met in Zurich and with whom she founded the Social Democracy of the Kingdom of Poland. To Jogiches Rosa wrote nearly a thousand letters over a period of twenty years, intense letters full of ardent self-revelation as well as history in the making. Froelich does not mention Jogiches' extreme possessive jealousy (which had both a sexual and a professionally rivalrous component), nor the breakup of their relationship over Jogiches' friendship with another woman, nor Rosa's romantic rebound affair with Konstantin, the twenty-two-year-old son of her close friend and comrade Clara Zetkin, nor the last love of her life, Hans Diefenbach. Her expensive tastes and love of luxury, her sarcasm often at the expense of friends, her craving for privacy and order, her desire to have a baby, her stubborn determination to "haggle for a daily portion" of personal happiness—all these traits are omitted.

For these reasons it is not Froelich but J. P. Nettl's splendid two-volume biography (1966) that presents the recognizable human being, the political woman rather than the political machine. Partly the lacunae in Froelich's biography can be explained, as the author himself points out in his preface, by the loss or inaccessibility of a good deal of material, particularly correspondence and manuscripts: There is simply a lot that Froelich did not know. Beyond this, though, one senses that Froelich wanted us to concentrate on the important historical and political issues without being distracted by mere curiosity. Though such an approach is not always wrong, it does imply a certain elitism here. It suggests, wrongly, that great revolutionaries have easily escaped or transcended the personal difficulties that bourgeois society imposes on all its members. Froelich's presentation suggests further, and equally falsely, that the personal dimension is not really worth the attention of serious political persons.

The tone of Froelich's biography is sustained eulogy. As Nettl remarks, it is "an exercise in formal hagiography,"[30] and everywhere Luxemburg is described in glowing superlatives. Clearly, she was an extraordinary person in many respects. Everyone who knew or met her agrees on that, from Lenin to Luxemburg's housekeeper, and Froelich himself must often have felt the force of her intellect and personality. But Froelich's method tends to undercut his aim, for the exemplary figure instructs not by distance but by closeness to us: not by being without faults, but by overcoming them. Froelich's Rosa Luxemburg is an unattainable ideal. So that it is not in his biography that one finds a clear evaluation of Luxemburg's personal and political limitations (even though he does concede certain errors in her criticism of the Bolsheviks). For such an evaluation Froelich must be supplemented with other sources. Her letters show both the domineering and the sentimental aspects of her nature. Georg Lukacs's 1922 essay "Critical Observations on Rosa Luxemburg's 'Critique of the Russian Revolution' " shows that Luxemburg's view of certain aspects of the early phase of Bolshevik power was far too schematic.[31] The writings of Lenin and Trotsky are an indispensable guide and an important corrective to her errors. And Nettl sheds light everywhere.

If, as Lukacs declares in the opening sentence of "The Marxism of Rosa Luxemburg," "It is not the primacy of economic motives in historical explanation that constitutes the decisive difference between Marxism and bourgeois thought, but the point of view of totality," then certainly Rosa Luxemburg's work remains permanently relevant in demonstrating the dialectical method. Lukacs concludes: "The unity of theory and practice was preserved in her actions with exactly the same consistency and with exactly the same logic as that which earned her the enmity of her murderers: the opportunists of Social Democracy."[32] Thus the essay itself progresses from focus on theory to focus on practice. Yet in his preface to the 1967 edition of *History and Class Consciousness,* Lukacs performs a self-criticism in which he notes "a—Hegelian—distortion, in which I put the totality in the center of the system, overriding the priority of economics."[33] The paradox that Lukacs notes here is as relevant today as Luxemburg herself, for his distortion will be repeated by many. Its source, as Lukacs says, is the ongoing conflict in his life between "Marxism and political activism on the one hand, and the constant intensification of my purely idealistic ethical preoccupations on the other."[34] That or similar conflict still describes the condition of many intellectuals today. It is never a waste of time to read Luxemburg. But to read her without the desire to become what she was—a revolutionary Communist in theory and in practice—is to read her in bad faith, to approach her as a curiosity, to distance the power of her work and her example. The day before Luxemburg died an article of hers appeared in *Die Rote Fahne.* Its last words were:

> Order reigns in Berlin! You stupid lackeys! Your "order" is built on sand. Tomorrow the revolution will rear its head once again, and, to your horror, will proclaim, with trumpets blazing: I was, I am, I will be![35]

To understand Luxemburg is to understand that those sentences are no mere eschatology but a statement about history that wants to lay a claim on anyone who reads it.

8

Women, culture, and revolution in Russia: Boris Lavrenev's "The Forty-first"

> This conversation took place on a quiet revolutionary evening, on a bench in Martha's garden. A machine gun tick-tocked tenderly somewhere in the distance, calling its mate.
>
> Eugene Zamyatin, "X" (1926)

How subversive is revolution, corroding even the descriptive conventions of romantic fiction! Zamyatin's Carrollesque sentences cut two ways, parodying the sentimental pieties of bourgeois romantic fiction, but also those of smug zealotry cloaked in revolutionary rhetoric. Such zealotry would in the next few years bear the sickening fruit of "socialist realist" art with its ideal stereotypes and petty-bourgeois morality, its dead style and dialogue parroting the regime's latest twist. The story from which the passage above is taken narrates the comical love-affair of one of those new village bureaucrats so soon to join NEP-men, party careerists, and disgruntled intellectuals in the social base of Stalinism.

The subversion of romantic idealism in Russian art was well under way by 1917 in the critical and creative work of the seething Russian avant-garde: futurists and formalists, Proletkult, imagists, constructivists, rayonnists, suprematists. The Russian Revolution of 1917 struck many innovative artists and scholars as the social equivalent to their own aesthetic or intellectual concerns. Yet of those who at first embraced or accepted the revolution, few survived its vicissitudes with faculties intact, if they survived at all. Zamyatin early became hysterically alienated from the necessities of national defense and social reconstruction under the Bolsheviks, and eventually left the country, his best work behind him. Mayakovsky could not endure the control and deterioration of creative life in the early Stalin era; he committed suicide in 1930. Isaac Babel was arrested in 1938 and died soon after in a prison camp; likewise the great theater director and producer V. Meyerhold. But the great majority of left-wing artists and intellectuals, whether party members or "fellow-travellers," neither killed themselves nor were physically liquidated by the regime. Instead they "went to sleep" (in Zamyatin's phrase): They accommodated to the bureaucratic regime and produced to its orders, so that, as Trotsky remarked, "The art of the Stalinist period will remain as the frankest expression of the profound decline of the proletarian revolution."[1]

Among those who quietly accommodated was the journalist, playwright, and short-story writer Boris Lavrenev (1891–1959). A minor but popular and prolific writer, Lavrenev was twice awarded the Stalin Prize, in 1946 and 1950. His work has been translated into several European languages; it continues to be published in the Soviet Union and elsewhere, including (not surprisingly) Cuba, which in 1966 brought out a Spanish edition of "The Forty-first," the story I am going to use here as a point of departure for my comments on women, culture, and revolution. "The Forty-first" (1924) is probably the most famous of Lavrenev's civil war stories, having been filmed twice: in the silent 1920s version of Yakov Protonazov, and in a 1956 color version by G. Chukrai (whose "Ballad of a Soldier" is well known in North America). The story narrates the love-affair of the fisher-girl and would-be poet Maryutka, a sharpshooter in the Red Army, with her prisoner of war, a handsome and cultured White Guard lieutenant. Hence it knits up the threads of sex, class, and culture. So, too, in its way, does Lavrenev's career, for his ac-commodation was one small symptom of the bureaucratic degen-eration of the revolution, a process also visible in the changing position of women during the 1930s and 1940s and in the increas-ing state control of the arts during the same period. Thus the story encapsulates a moment in revolutionary history—not the moment of its setting (1920), but that of its making, some four years later. That moment is, in a sense, the last when the story could have been written as it was: Not simply because in 1925 Dr. Aron Zalkind announced that "sexual attraction to a class enemy is as much a perversion as mating an ape with an alligator,"[2] but because its style, its conception of culture and its heroine would soon become impossible.

Like other of Lavrenev's stories from this period, "The Forty-first" shows that in the early 1920s the author knew how to entertain and engage the reader, that he had read the English novel to good effect and was to some extent influenced by vari-ous Russian avant-garde literary groups, and above all that he understood the often contradictory impulses of individuals and of revolution.

Much of this was renounced in subsequent years. In an auto-biographical note published in 1930, Lavrenev "self-criticized" the breadth of his reading: "European literary culture is too strong in me. 'Literaturizing.' Too much of an inveterate intellec-tual. Too much of an un-Russian writer. Bred and brought up on French and English writers."[3] Like many others, Lavrenev be-longed to RAPP (the Russian Association of Proletarian Writ-ers). In 1932 Stalin abruptly dissolved RAPP and brutally discred-ited its leaders, merging all existing writers' groups into the unitary and state-controlled Union of Soviet Writers. Though others protested publicly, Lavrenev's comment on this decisive event was complacent: "I wore the label ["fellow-traveller"] until RAPP's peaceful demise in 1932 when, having escorted the corpse to the cemetery of history, I remained just a Soviet writer. This suited me fine."[4] In contrast to "The Forty-first" and other early work, Lavrenev's stories from the early 1940s are short, terse, anti-German propaganda pieces with little literary interest, emotional impact, or sense of social complexity (though to be fair they still show considerable narrative skill). Finally, among Lavrenev's cold-war propaganda services to the regime was the play *Lermontov* (1952), in which the life and views of the nineteenth-century poet were knowingly distorted and even falsified in order to recreate the Russian literary past in the desired image of simple, committed national-patriotic militancy.[5]

It was, of course, an intolerable situation. The image that comes to mind is of a wily Brechtian survivor denying his knowledge in order to stay alive and out of prison, but that is the essence of political accommodation, to suppress the "no" one knows to be true, and there were many who did not accommodate but remained true to the revolution they had fought for. Galileo could recant and rest easy, for *"eppur se muove"* (nonetheless it [the earth] moves). But in politics it doesn't: The committed act is required so that it *will* move. In any case, the accommodations that made the real historical difference were less those of minor artists than of the well-known political figures who, despite their weaknesses, might have helped lead the struggle against bureaucratism but chose not to: the Radeks, Kollontais, Preobrashenkys, Zinovievs, and Smirnovs, who chose capitulation rather than opposition.

The laboring masses of the whole world immediately showed a readiness to regard the Russian Revolution as a whole, and in this their revolutionary instinct coincided, not for the first time, with high theoretical sense, which teaches that a revolution, with its heroism and cruelty, the struggle for individuality and the suppression of individuality, can only be understood in the material logic of its internal relations, and not by any valuation of its individual phases or separate episodes according to the price list of Right, Ethics, and Aesthetics.

Leon Trotsky, *Between Red and White* (1922)

That passage might stand to our story as theoretical gloss to fictional representation, the one asserting, the other showing the empirical/intuitive understanding of revolution by ordinary working people, the contradictions of revolution as translated into desire and necessity, and the view of revolution as an organically integrated whole.

Maryutka's affair with an enemy officer ends, with the story, when Maryutka shoots her lover as he is about to be rescued by other White Guard officers: She had been ordered not to give him up alive to the Whites. Thus the lieutenant becomes the sharpshooter's forty-first victim. On one level, then, the story is about sex and politics—or, as it would have been put at the time, love and duty. But "love and duty" is inadequate to the story, for in the post-Lenin Soviet context that phrase generally means "love versus duty" or "sex versus politics," with the latter easily and inevitably winning out. While it is true that for Maryutka, political commitment does eventually prevail, the story transcends any sense of easy or mechanical inevitability. It is less "sex versus politics" than sexual politics: an exploration of how political attitudes might be embodied in complicated individuals, how sexual attitudes and responses are shaped by social factors, including social structures as well as an intensely polarized conflict like the civil war. The ending comes (or came to me, at least) as a shock. The act is committed in fear and despair; the story closes with Maryutka's devastated lament for what she has done. That Maryutka falls in love with an enemy officer and gives herself to him; that the lieutenant is capable of generosity, gratitude, vulnerability; that both characters experience moments of ambivalence—all this keeps the story from stereotype or predictability.[6]

It is revolutionary propaganda, but propaganda that makes nothing easy.

Naturally one's sense of politics affects one's aesthetic response to the story. For a nonpolitical person, or for someone who doesn't intensely desire revolution, it is easy enough to perceive Maryutka and the lieutenant as mere social clichés, and the dénouement as inevitable. Yet part of the cauterizing effect of revolution is to cleanse social clichés of their literary-theoretical accretions: They spring to life again as social reality. To sustain that sense of historical possibility opens in turn the aesthetic possibility of seeing Maryutka and her lover as real *and* representative—the dimensions in which individuals actually exist during war, revolution, strikes, or other such polarized events—and the ending therefore as one possibility among several.

Besides sex and politics, culture is the other ingredient in the rich mix of "The Forty-first." Maryutka writes poetry, passionately felt but execrably bad verse, old-fashioned and trite, at which not only the cultured lieutenant laughs, but even newspaper editors in small Caucasian towns. (A sample of her doggerel is given in the story.) During the lovers' enforced winterlong sojourn on a deserted island in the Aral Sea, the lieutenant tells the story of Robinson Crusoe, so ironically similar to their own situation. The two debate *Crusoe* and also Maryutka's poetry: content, audience, conditions of production. The discussion of art becomes a mode of characterization and another dimension in which social attitudes are expressed.

The view of culture that emerges from the story is very far from that of high-Stalinist "socialist realism" or its predecessor, Proletkult. There is no contempt for "bourgeois culture" or for the lieutenant's booklearning. In fact his erudition saves their lives, for he has read about abandoned fishermen's huts on islands in the Aral Sea, just as he has read about Forel's hydrographic scale of blueness on which the Aral Sea rates three. Maryutka, on the other hand, knows that dried fat fish can be burned as fuel. Her experience and his education are complementary for survival. (Govorukha-Otrok is also, incidentally, an

WRITING WOMAN : *140*

accomplished seaman—a skill Maryutka appreciates on their stormy ride to the island, and which he learned on his luxurious yacht. It is clear where Lavrenev must have stood in controversies about the use of experienced czarist military men—by 1919, 40,000 of them—who were willing to work for the Reds.[7])

A few years later Lavrenev would again take up the intertwined themes of sex, culture, and revolution, confirming and developing the attitudes outlined in "The Forty-first." His *roman à thèse, The Future Is Ours* (1927),[8] has as protagonist Goudrine, a talented artist turned Red Army man and now factory director. Goudrine's wife, a puritanical, uncultured party hack, considers sensuality, comfort, and beauty contrary to the party spirit. The marriage breaks up and Goudrine resigns his position to return to his first love, painting, convinced that he can be more useful in helping to create a vibrant new culture than in performing routine supervisory tasks.

At an art exhibit and a lecture Goudrine expresses profound hatred and contempt for the theory and practice of Proletkult and socialist realism. The pictures—factory chimneys, workers' demonstrations, parades, red banners, etc.—are joyless and trivial, showing the painters' "misunderstanding of the real nature of the working class and of the party" as well as a "servile desire to serve a new master" (p. 23). (Who the new master is, we do not learn.) A young poet-scholar of the "extremist" school—an obvious parody of Proletkult—claims in his lecture that all known literature is dangerous and counterrevolutionary, an opiate of the masses, and should be replaced by factual reportage. This view the hero characterizes as ignorant petty-bourgeois nihilism; the young poet is said to "spit on the party's effort to raise the country's cultural level." Now that the civil war is over, *he* (the philistine poet) is the enemy. The new culture won't be created by such charlatans but by workers saturated in the old culture. A new culture can't be forced or legislated into existence, but must grow naturally from the new social milieu that is still being built (pp. 185–87). A good idea is a good idea, even if it comes from the other side.

But the "extremist" view is gaining ground all around Goudrine, and so are the dreadful paintings. There are disturbing hints that all is not well in party life. Only with a small group of intimates does Goudrine discuss party affairs "frankly, without those detours that diplomacy requires" (p. 33). Moreover, Goudrine's wife denounces him to his boss, and though her attempt fails, Goudrine is afraid. The episode evokes a suspicion that such attempts might well succeed in the near future. Nonetheless, laughing and joyful, Goudrine types out his resignation letter: "I too am going to wake the masses so that they can build a culture." Like a middle-aged Bolshevik Stephen Dedalus, Goudrine wants to "forge in the smithy of [his] soul the uncreated conscience" not of his race but of his class. *The Future Is Ours* is less a gesture of defiance than of revulsion against the tightening net.

The distance Lavrenev would have to travel to reach Stalinist respectability is marked in a pair of his World War II stories. In "The Portrait" (1941), the protagonist, a middle-aged painter enlisted in the Red Army, proclaims of the Germans:

> "They are not human beings. They are only images of human beings. . . . They've got no soul, only something that stinks like a polecat. And they should be destroyed like mad dogs, without mercy, to the last man. Only then will life flourish again on this earth of ours. Wipe them out, friends! For this land of ours, for our fathers and mothers, for the love that you cherish, for the honor of our womenfolk, for everything. . . ."

These sentiments are repeated in "Out at Sea": *As a nation* (i.e., not only the Nazis) the Germans "have ceased to resemble human beings but have in every respect proved to be diabolical savages."[9] Here the hero is an outstanding young naval officer who hopes to write a dissertation on German philosophy. His ship is strafed by a German plane and all aboard are killed. But before he dies the young skipper realizes that his interest in German philosophy is contemptible. His last act is to bring down the German plane—whose pilot's name turns out to be Johann Wilhelm Schelling! All is simple; all is easy. All Germans are evil; German culture is therefore not worthwhile.

To return to "The Forty-first": Maryutka desires to study in order to develop as a poet. The lieutenant has the education Maryutka needs; he is even an amateur philologist who before the war spent his evenings in a book-lined study. More abstractly: His class and its allies monopolize the culture that the rest of the population require, and that they have been systematically denied, but that the revolution had already begun to expropriate.[10] The lieutenant offers Maryutka his patronage, an offer at once sexual and cultural:

> "I've got a little place not far from Sukhumi. That's where we'll go. I'll settle down with my books and let the world go hang. . . . And you'll begin to study. You want to study, don't you? You've complained so many times that you had no chance to study. Well, here's your chance. I'll do everything for you. You saved my life and I'll never forget it." (p. 233)

(Parenthetically I note a special irony here, for after 1920, as the war journalist Lavrenev would surely know, Sukhumi was a base for Zhenotdel, the Central Committee's Department for Work Among Women, whose primary task was to educate, organize, and recruit women in the remotest areas of the country. "Teams were sent out into the mountain villages and women who had never left their native settlements before were brought down to Sukhumi. Some were shuttled off to Moscow to study, the rest went back to the mountains to organize day nurseries." The response?

> Men reacted to all this with savage violence. Women coming out of the club at Baku were assaulted by men with wild dogs and boiling water. A twenty-year-old Muslim girl who flaunted her liberation by appearing in a swimsuit was sliced to pieces by her father and brothers because they could not endure the social indignity. An eighteen-year-old Uzbek woman activist was mutilated and thrown into a well. Central Asia witnessed three hundred such murders during one quarter of 1929 alone.[11])

Angrily, Maryutka rejects his offer with its role of kept woman, its luxury of studying while the war rages, its valorization of individual over collective appropriation:

"So that's what you want me to do, is it? . . . Lie beside you on a feather-bed while people are sweating out their life's blood for the sake of justice? Fill my belly with chocolates when every chocolate is bought with somebody else's blood? Is that what you want?" (p. 233)

Her denunciation touches off a fight that eventually forces the lieutenant to abandon his escapist fantasies and for the first time to commit himself fully and consciously to class struggle. He embraces the counterrevolutionary cause of his class:

"I can see for myself that it's too soon for me to go back to my books. . . . I've come to my senses! . . . If we bury ourselves in our books at a time like this and let you do what you like with this old earth of ours, there'll be hell to pay." (p. 236)

So Maryutka converts her lover—not to revolution (that *would* be a sentimental ending) but to militant reaction.

Again, it is nowhere suggested in these exchanges that bourgeois culture is decadent per se or that what Maryutka needs, rather than *Crusoe*, is images of factory chimneys or simple hortatory verse. There is no hint that people like Maryutka should, will, or can create a new "proletarian culture" on the basis of their class and commitment. Those were the tenets of Proletkult and, later, of socialist realism, but during the 1920s they were targets of Lenin's and Trotsky's polemics.[12] Contrary to Proletkult, Maryutka aspires to appropriate the benefits of world culture in order to express her commitment more effectively in art. Her poetry is bad *despite* its commitment, and to some extent *because* of her class, which has been excluded from culture and education. To deny the badness of her poetry would be to deny the oppressiveness of oppression. Maryutka is oppressed as a woman and as a rural worker, and one sign of that double oppression is the quality of her verse. For her, decadence is not the possession of culture, but the abandonment of the struggle that will ensure the general and permanent accessibility of culture.

While Maryutka's verse might well qualify for Proletkult's notion of "worker poetry," Lavrenev's stylistic practise in "The Forty-first" certainly runs counter to Proletkult recommendation.

It shows both the influence of "bourgeois culture" (especially the eighteenth-century English novel, then much in vogue among literary intellectuals) and affinities with certain avant-garde literary groups whose mistrust of politics put them at odds with both Proletkult and the Bolsheviks. Neologisms abound in the story, as in futurist work. The sentence is nervous, economical; imagery frequent and bold. The story has a formal-symbolic structure blocked out in color-areas like a canvas: white, red, blue, and yellow are associated with certain characters and objects in the story and, through them, with a cluster of social and ethical values. There is a dream sequence when the lieutenant falls into delirious fever.

As for bourgeois literature, I have already referred to the desert-island motif borrowed from *Crusoe,* and to dialogue about that novel. (There are also the grimy, gutsy Dickensian urchins in Lavrenev's "Fast Freight," 1927.[13]) Also imitated from the eighteenth-century novel is the device of the chapter heading that Lavrenev uses, in the manner of Sterne, as an ironically distancing or (in Brecht's term) alienating technique,[14] to emphasize what Viktor Shklovsky and other formalists called the "literariness," the made quality, of the work of art. A few samples:

1. Which was written only because it had to be written.
5. Stolen from beginning to end from Daniel Defoe, except that Robinson has not long to wait for his Friday.
9. In which it is proved that, although the heart defies all laws, one's being, after all, determines one's consciousness.
10. In which Lieutenant Govorukha-Otrok hears the roar of the doomed planet, and the author dodges the responsibility of ending the story.

The headings underscore stylistically a political point made in the narrative itself. They jog the reader out of comfortable received notions of the amenities governing the relations among author, reader, and text; nudge the reader to interrogate the text just as Maryutka interrogates *Crusoe*. The creation of literature, we are forced to conclude, is artificial, selective, above all conscious; so is the reception of literature (at least it can be); and so is the making of history. The headings assert our capacity consciously to appropriate the past in order to "make it new" (the formalists would say to "make it strange"), as indeed the Bolsheviks were in the process of doing.

The emancipation of women has been, from 1917 to the present, one of the proudest boasts of Soviet Russia in its catalogue of achievements. . . . Soviet spokesmen have tended to mask the fact that a reversal in policy has occurred. . . . The terms set forth in Marxian writings as constituting the emancipation of women and the early Soviet steps taken toward their fulfillment are a matter of historical record, as, in part, are later measures toward their abrogation. . . . For investigation of widespread attitudes and behavior patterns engendered among Soviet women by the new social organization, Russian literature affords the main accessible source.

Louise E. Luke, "Marxian Woman: Soviet Variants"[15]

The figure of the fighting woman comrade or partisan is not unusual in the civil-war literature of the 1920s. In the work of later decades, though, woman's role becomes "increasingly auxiliary": "She accepts her biologically predetermined secondary status in the army, much as the Soviet woman of the 1930's accepted it in civil life, and is rewarded by peace of mind and a sense of duty well done."[16] I want to turn now to the social context in which early readers of "The Forty-first" would have been able to place its heroine. What was the role of women during these early years of revolution and civil war? How did the revolution and its subsequent degeneration affect women? What about the feminist movement?

February 23, 1917, was International Women's Day, commemorating the great strikes of about a decade earlier in New York's predominantly female garment industry, particularly the victorious "uprising of the twenty thousand" in 1909 and the 1910 cloak strike (the "great revolt"), which brought 45,000 workers into the streets. At the proposal of Clara Zetkin in 1911, the Second International adopted the day, and it was thereafter celebrated worldwide as an international proletarian holiday.[17]

Fearing premature armed confrontation, none of the political organizations in Russia called for strikes to mark the day. Nonetheless, women textile workers in Petrograd went on strike, joined by about 90,000 workers and soldiers' wives. The momentum generated on Women's Day sped into insurrection, was repeated in Moscow and provincial cities. It was the second Russian revolution (the first having occurred in 1905). It transferred state power to a liberal bourgeois parliament (Duma), forced the abdication of the czar, and brought into being soviets (elected councils) as organs of workers' power. By autumn the Bolsheviks had gained a majority in the soviets, so that the soviets were able to overthrow the weak coalition government of Kerensky and officially take the state power they already exercised in fact.[18] The civil war—against czarist White Guards, landowning Cossacks, anti-Bolshevik social democrats, and bourgeois constitutionalists, together with their German, Czech, Japanese, British, French, and North American allies—was more or less won by the end of 1920, though sporadic fighting continued for another year or more in Siberia and the Far East.

Had there been a politically autonomous women's movement in Russia to defend the special interests of women—so "socialist-feminists" often argue—then the revolution would have done more for women, and the bureaucracy would not have been able to reverse such gains as were made during the 1920s. The truth is that there was a lively feminist movement during the revolutionary period, whose inability to affect the course of events was due to its programmatic content. Already during the nineteenth century the underground non-Marxian revolutionary movement had a significant portion of female members, activists and leaders, though none of the groups had a sectoralist vision of social change: They did not imagine that the lot of any single oppressed group could be substantially improved apart from the general liberation of the Russian masses. The issue of female emancipation had occupied the intelligentsia since the 1860s, but not until 1905 did a well-organized feminist women's movement appear, stimulated by the ferment of the 1905 revolution. It is instructive to study the role of the Russian feminist organizations at a time when masses of women were ready to struggle for their rights, and important to know why those women did not see feminism as an appropriate weapon.[19]

The Russian movement was more tactically variegated than its American or British counterparts, not confined to the suffrage issue, and—in the feminist-electoral sense—sufficiently developed to include a political party. The male-exclusionist Women's Progressive party was founded on the premise that none of the existing ("male-dominated") parties could be trusted to protect the real interests of women. While its program had several demands intended to attract working women (paid maternity leave, child-care facilities in factories, equal wages for equal work, land rights for peasant women), nonetheless, its general perspective was for sex equality in context of a constitutional-democratic monarchy. The Russian Union for Women's Equality called for equal rights in employment and education, abolition of the death penalty, and universal suffrage for a constituent assembly. The union, associated with the Kadet (K.D., for Constitutional Democratic) party, was the largest of the feminist groups, peaking in 1905 with about 8000 members. The Russian Society for the Protection of Women was a patrician-intellectual charity and reform organizaiton that focussed on prostitution. The Women's Mutual Philanthropic Society—something like a Russian version of NOW—devoted itself to lobbying with friends and relatives in government and the professions for suffrage and equal rights. The Russian League for Women's Equality was also a lobbying group, primarily for suffrage; a host of smaller, more specialized student professional groups also addressed conditions in their own areas.

Like its counterparts abroad, Russian feminism was, in Stites's words, "roughly 'middle-class' with an 'upper-class' frosting."[20] This was true not only of social composition but of program, despite the occasional demand designed to entice working women to join. But by and large the feminist strategy was inadequate to the real lives of working women, urban or rural, and nowhere more obviously than on the suffrage issue. Here the feminists did not remain true to their own limited platform. When a period of reaction set in after the short-lived liberalization of 1905, the groups either abandoned their work altogether or adapted to the new climate, no longer calling for universal suffrage but now for sex-equal suffrage by class—hence the women of disfranchised classes would be equally disfranchised with their men! Later, like feminists in all belligerent nations, the Russians greeted the 1914 war as a golden opportunity to display their patriotism and earn the reward of suffrage. But the Duma continued to disappoint them. Only after the February revolution and three months before its own overthrow did Kerensky's Provisional Revolutionary Government at last, in July 1917, give Russian women the vote— not under pressure from the feminists, but from increasingly angry working men and women loyal to the soviets and readier every week to take what they wanted by disciplined force of arms. Feminist issues—inheritance laws for large fortunes, passport laws for travel, admission to professional schools, even the fetishized vote—these issues, all of them valid, all of them supportable, all of them important to women of the gentry, the intelligentsia, the professions, had little meaning for impoverished working women whose struggle was for the eight-hour day, for an end to the war in which their men were dying, for literacy, for wages, for food, for housing.

At such a time there could be no "socialist-feminism." The sharp polarization of issues rendered such a chimera impossible: "Revolution is revolution only because it reduces all contradictions to the alternative of life or death."[21] If the oxymoron "socialist-feminism" is possible now, it's in the absence of imminent revolution and expresses the acquiescence of those who are prepared to settle for perpetually unresolved social contradiction.

As for the Communists, their work among women was to address the broad issues with a program that could resolve the contradictions of the old order. They did so by organizing and recruiting working women, by intervening at feminist meetings with Communist politics, and through their journal *Rabotnitsa* (Woman Worker). On the eve of the February revolution, interestingly, the feminist organizations were operating with what Stites calls "euphoric vigor": their journals appeared regularly and their membership was on the rise (though not among working women). Three weeks after the October seizure of power, *Rabotnitsa* organized a conference of working women in the Petrograd region. A leader of the League for Women's Equality spoke, concluding her remarks with these words:

> Everywhere women are subjected; everywhere they struggle for their rights. Women from England and America arrive here and are in complete solidarity with us and wish us well in our struggle. Men cannot defend our interests; they do not understand us.

The women in attendance booed her down but were persuaded by Alexandra Kollontai, a Bolshevik leader, to let the feminist finish: "The speech marked, practically speaking, the end of Russian feminism."[22] Of the movement's leaders, some stayed in the Soviet Union and some emigrated, but there is no record of organized feminist activity after 1920 even by those who stayed: Evidently the movement had lost its raison d'être.

Almost immediately the new regime established complete economic equality for working women both in employment and wages, abolished all laws against homosexuality, outlawed the bride price, decreed the absolute right to divorce (free, immediate, and on demand of either party), and promulgated a marriage decree that protected the right of each spouse to separate identity, including name, business, friends, and place of residence. Within a few months they made education and training available to women by overhauling the school system: coeducation at all levels, free and open admissions at all universities, art and technical schools, remedial courses, no gender tracking. For mothers, fully paid maternity leave, free pre- and postnatal care, nursing breaks at work, and a network of maternity clinics, mother-and-

child homes, and preschool nurseries. The category of illegitimacy was abolished by making the biological father coresponsible
with the mother, regardless of marital status, and by giving all
children equal legal rights whether born in or out of registered
marriages.[23]

In 1920 abortion was made free and on demand. The party
amalgamated its commissions for work among women into Zhenotdel, a special department or section of the Central Committee
whose purpose was to extend organization, education, and health
care to women in all regions of the Soviet Union. The Council for
Combating Prostitution (1921) was responsible for medical treatment, education, and job placement for prostitutes; the government's policy was voluntary rehabilitation of prostitutes but se-
vere penalites for pimps and madams. In 1926 a joint property
ruling for divorce was decreed, and the validity of common-law
marriage confirmed.

In all it was an astonishing feat of social engineering, un-
equalled anywhere before or since, and certainly not imagined in
the wildest dreams of feminists. It was not accomplished without
some ambivalence; for instance, many party members, men and
women, deplored even hospital abortions as physically dangerous
and as an antisocial act on the mother's part, but they approved
its legalization as a necessary health measure. Some provisions
were not immediately enforceable everywhere, as in the most
backward Muslim areas. And it was far from perfect; for instance, contraception, so crucial to the equality and independence of women, remained a weak point in the program (though
the reasons for this weakness are not entirely clear to me).[24] No
Bolshevik imagined that law suffices for a revolution in mores,
but all understood that law is the necessary prelude.

Naturally women were conscripted into the Red Army, and
they volunteered, individually or in factory or village brigades, on
equal terms with men. Already in the world war, women in the
Imperial Army served in paramedical, communications, and
transport work, with a few in flying and combat. Armed Bolshevik women of the Red Guards fought in September 1917 against

the attempted coup by General Kornilov and again in the October insurrection. The Red Army was called into being early in 1918, after the Brest-Litovsk peace treaty had taken Russia out of the world war. Lavrenev's Maryutka would not have been an unfamiliar figure, for although most women made their contribution in industry, by 1920 (when the story evidently takes place) at least 75,000 women were enlisted at every rank and in every capacity: combat, intelligence and espionage, political propaganda, fraternization with the enemy, medical and police work, as well as construction, feeding, and sanitary projects on the home front.[25]

That Maryutka is not a Communist makes her a more representative figure, for most "Red Armyists" were not. In 1920 about 130,000 of the Army's 5.5 million were party members; like many others, Maryutka is committed to practical social justice, which she rightly sees embodied in the Bolsheviks. That Maryutka is not an urban proletarian also renders her more typical, for most of the Red Army ranks were rurals. Neither, however, is Maryutka a peasant, but an impoverished fisher-girl from a tiny village near Astrakhan in the Volga delta, on the north shore of the Caspian Sea. (Astrakhan was one of sixteen major fronts of the civil war, and the particular target of British shelling and bombs in Britain's 1918 thrust from the south by air and sea.) Certainly unusual is Maryutka's literacy and her poetic aspiration in a country where, at the moment of the revolution, fourteen of its seventeen million illiterates were women. One could say, with Stites, that "Illiteracy was essentially a woman's problem"—or, more accurately, with Trotsky, that "The 'woman problem' here, then, means first of all the struggle with female illiteracy."[26] In short, we can see that Lavrenev has made his heroine both typical enough and unusual enough to be an effective model. She has sufficient commitment and culture to focus emulation and aspiration, yet she is not so accomplished as to intimidate the reader, nor so duty bound as to deny sensuality. To fight "as a woman" would be meaningless for someone like Maryutka; to fight "for women," an evident idiocy. Her role in the story is consistent with social reality of the revolutionary period. If the heroine of later decades differs, it is because of a new social milieu: that of the bureaucracy in power.

"Our feminine hearts are overflowing with emotions," she said, "and of these love is paramount. Yet a wife should also be a happy mother and create a serene home atmosphere, without, however, abandoning work for the common welfare. She should know how to combine all these things while also matching her husband's performance on the job."
"Right!" said Stalin.
"How she has grown [spiritually]!" thought Zhdarkin.
F. Panfyorov, *Brusski*, part 4 (1937)

"Yes, it's old, but that's just why it is so terribly tenacious. It is possible to change a great deal in life, in the relations of man to man as well as in those of an individual to society. But in the domain of relations between man and woman, physiology is all-important. And you cannot change physiology. . . . What happens in life seldom coincides with our best philosophizing."
A. Koptyaeva, *Comrade Anna* (1946)[27]

These passages rather neatly summarize the reversal of earlier Bolshevik policy on women and the family. Their cynical and philistine sentiments (entirely unironical) would have been treated contemptuously by Lavrenev's heroine; indeed they seem like a throwback to some Gogolesque pen-pusher, rank #9 of the fourteen bureaucratic degrees.

Where the Bolsheviks aimed to liberate women from the social burdens of maternity (if not necessarily from the biological fact) and ultimately to replace the social and economic functions of the nuclear family with state services and support, the bureaucratic strategy on the contrary was to tie women—along with men and children—ever more tightly to the family, while simultaneously encouraging women to participate in industrial labor.

Zhenotdel was abolished in 1929, under the pretext that its job was done. In 1936 abortion was made once again illegal, except in circumstances endangering the mother's life, and divorce was made very difficult to get, through fees, delays and red tape. Coeducation was ended in 1943, the same year that Stalin obligingly dissolved the Third International as a conciliatory gesture to his allies Churchill and Roosevelt. (Coeducation was restored ten years later, after Stalin's death in 1953, but gender-track curricula and role-biased texts stayed.) A ban on paternity suits in 1944, together with denial of the legal validity of common-law marriage and of legal rights to children born out of wedlock, effectively restored the category of illegitimacy with all its injustices to mother and child. The heroine of socialist reproduction might receive a handsome state benefit after her fifth child, but only if the child were the product of a properly licensed marriage. The net effect of this program was to intensify the economic, social, and psychological dependency of women upon men. The ancient mystique of motherhood flourished; it was cultivated in tandem with the new national patriotism that became a major domestic propaganda tool in World War II, replacing the class consciousness so scrupulously maintained in civil-war propaganda and political education during the 1920s. "Holy mother Russia," "the sacred motherland," "the earth that bore and nurtures us"—this is the familiar message underscored by visual imagery in Soviet literature and in film from *Alexander Nevsky* (1938) to *Oblomov* (1980).

Why did it happen? and could it have been prevented? I want to take the long way round in answering these questions. In any society the position of women is one facet of an integrated social structure; so for the Bolsheviks, as for the bureaucratic regime. Bolshevik family legislation was part of a long-range strategy to construct a material base for eventual communism: an international, classless, stateless society. In 1919 Lenin wrote about the tasks of Communist construction, including the necessity to "foster the simple, modest, ordinary but viable shoots of genuine communism." Among these, he writes, are the public restaurants, nurseries, and kindergartens: institutions that were created under capitalism but that, in a collectivized economy and a workers' government, are able to help "really emancipate women, really lessen and abolish their inequality with men as regards their role in social production and public life":

> Notwithstanding all the laws emancipating woman, she continues to be a domestic slave, because petty housework crushes, strangles, stultifies and degrades her, chains her to the kitchen and the nursery, and she wastes her labour on barbarously unproductive, petty, nerve-wracking, stultifying and crushing drudgery. The real emancipation of women, real communism, will begin only where and when an all-out struggle begins (led by the proletariat wielding the state power) against this petty housekeeping, or rather when its wholesale transformation into a large-scale socialist economy begins.[28]

The case of architecture pointedly illustrates the intersection of political program, family legislation and the arts. During the 1920s architecture was considered both a manifestation of the new family legislation and a means to implement it: a "concrete expression" (so clichés occasionally come to life again for a moment) of the revolution's intentions toward women. The Moscow Soviet publicized in these words its 1926 competition for the design of a communal dwelling:

> It is the duty of technological innovation, the duty of the architect, to place new demands on housing and to design insofar as possible a house that will transform the so-called family hearth from a boring, confining cell that at present burdens down women in particular into a place of pleasant and carefree relaxation.
>
> A new life demands new forms.
>
> The worker does not desire his mother, wife or sister to be a nursery maid, washerwoman or cook with unlimited hours; he does not desire children to rob him and particularly their mother of the possibility of employing their free time for social labor, mental and physical pleasures. . . .

A contemporary architect wrote:

> The proletariat must at once set about the destruction of the family as an organ of oppression and exploitation. In the communal dwelling the family will, in my view, be a purely comradely, physiologically necessary and historically inevitable association between the working man and the working woman.[29]

Policies of the 1930s and 1940s were likewise integrated into overall social tasks, such as industrialization and war, but these tasks now included the maintenance of the bureaucracy itself. Programmatically this required a fundamental revision of Bolshevism because it meant, in practical terms, to not move toward full communism but instead to deliberately preserve a "transitional" state: a workers' state in its collectivized economic arrangements, but administered by a parasitically privileged caste of managers and technicians, with the political voice of workers stifled by terror, propaganda, and legislation. It was a comprehensive program—not a series of mistakes—and required a variety of tactics for implementation. In foreign policy: the "popular front," or collaboration with the international bourgeoisie. In inner-party life: the destruction of the old program and democratic-centralist party structure. This was achieved first by crushing the Left Opposition during the late 1920s, then by exterminating the entire Central Committee of the old Bolshevik party in the purge trials of the 1930s, with thousands of leadership cadre at all levels and literally millions of rank and file Communists "who had taken any direct part in the Revolution and Civil War, or had participated in party life and knew the party's structure";[30] finally by murdering the leadership of the Left Opposition in exile, including Trotsky (assassinated in 1940). In culture: rigid control of the arts and intellectual life through censorship and the prescriptive aesthetic of "socialist realism." In family life: to rehabilitate the traditional family as a microcosm of authoritarian relations and a bulwark of conservative values—what Trotsky called "40,000,000 points of support for authority and power."[31] As reflected in architecture, my exemplary case above, the bureaucratic policy meant that communal housing and the socialization of domestic labor were characterized as "utopian"; the daring new schemes were shelved for a return to traditional models more appropriate to the privatized nuclear family.

Where would she have to be in, say, 1927, a politically conscious woman who wished to defend what the revolution had accomplished for women—more, who wished to extend these accomplishments to full economic and personal liberation? First, she would need to be in the Communist party, which had initiated these gains but was now supervising their erosion. Moreover, with the Left Opposition in the party, where she would have fought to defend everything that made those gains possible. Had she been there, as numbers of women were, both in Russia and abroad, she would for the time being have lost: History doesn't guarantee victory to those who are right. But she would have made the best possible fight, and her struggle would have guaranteed—it has guaranteed—the survival of a revolutionary tradition that history continues to test and vindicate. Revolution, wrote Rosa Luxemburg, is the sole form of war "in which the final victory can be prepared only by a series of defeats." She was writing shortly after the defeat of the German revolution of 1918–19 (the so-called Spartacus revolt) and just before her own arrest and murder on January 19, 1919:

> The first flaring up of the class struggle, the 1831 revolt of the silk-weavers in Lyons, ended in a heavy defeat. The Chartist Movement in England also ended in defeat. The rising of the proletariat in Paris in June 1848 ended in an overwhelming defeat. The Paris Commune ended in a terrible defeat. . . . We stand upon those very defeats, none of which we could have done without, each of which is a part of our strength and clarity of purpose. . . . And thus the future victory will blossom from out of this "defeat."[32]

We recall that "The Forty-first," like many other civil-war stories, is a narrative of military defeat. It opens with the disorderly retreat of Maryutka's unit, the Guryev detachment, from a ruthless Cossack attack. Fewer than one-sixth of the unit have escaped; the survivors are starved, desperate, demoralized, illdisciplined. The story ends as Maryutka confronts the White Guard rescue party; in real life someone in her position would most likely be executed either on the spot or after rape or torture. Thousands of women, partisans, and comrades were. To end by saying that their deaths weren't in vain may sound like a cliché, but like every cliché it is founded in material truth.

9

Ambivalence in utopia: the American feminist utopias of Charlotte P. Gilman and Marge Piercy

Utopia may be a country without place but it is not a country without history. Its history is no placid one, for from Thomas More onward it is difficult to find a utopia that is not split by deep internal contradiction of various sorts.

Formally, as an aesthetic object, the utopia is a composite beast. It reminds us of the novel or novella yet usually lacks developed plot and character; it resembles a political tract yet generally lacks the close argumentation we require there, or the explicit agitational point. In his prefatory note to *A Modern Utopia* (1905), H. G. Wells explained his quandary in "vacillating over the scheme of this book"—argumentative essay? discussion novel? hard narrative?—and described the final result as "a sort of shot-silk texture between philosophical discussion on the one hand and imaginative narrative on the other." Again in his first chapter Wells cautions the reader: "The entertainment before you is neither the set drama of the work of fiction you are accustomed to read, nor the set lecturing of the essay you are accustomed to evade, but a hybrid of these two."

Thematically the utopia often has not a single center of gravity but a double: the negative and positive poles of exposure and advocacy, the contrary (though complementary) impulses of destruction and construction, or social criticism and social planning. In this sense utopia has a love–hate relation with history, as does satire.[1]

In tone, style, and point of view the utopia is frequently riven by ambivalence. We notice paradoxical loyalties to the very system that is to be replaced, a curious pulling of the punches, a vacillation between different sets of values as if the author's will, imagination, or desire were divided and hence restrained from fully rendering the new life, or rejecting the old.

Besides these more or less characteristic ambivalencies, and cutting across them, utopias can be divided into two categories that I would designate the programmatic and the ideological. The former stresses a comprehensive social critique and serious social planning, attempts to demonstrate what should change and what might realistically replace present arrangements; it tends to propose social reforms that give scope to human variability. In this category I would place William Morris, Edward Bellamy, the Fourierists, Wells, and Marge Piercy. The ideological group of utopias tends, on the other hand, to minimize social criticism or confine it to a few key areas of social concern, to simplify both social criticism and social planning in accordance with a specific, schematic ideology, and to offer a static social structure that emphasizes uniformity rather than variety. In this second category we might include Plato, More, Thomas Campanella, Francis Bacon, and Charlotte P. Gilman.

Before coming to my main texts I want to indicate some kinds of ambivalence or contradiction that operate in several well-known utopias. Gilman and Piercy have given us specific versions of utopia with respect to time, place, and commitment, for both *Herland* and *Woman on the Edge of Time* are feminist, American, and of the twentieth century. Yet the two works are sharply distinguished by specific social context (they were published in 1915 and 1976, respectively) and by differences between early and late twentieth-century feminism. Again, beyond the differences occur resemblances in fictional strategy, certain contradictions that seem to typify the utopian project itself.

More's *Utopia* (1516) occupies the intersection of orthodox Catholicism with the new rationalistic humanism of Renaissance Europe. That locus reflects the uneasy coexistence of feudal and bourgeois ideologies during the period of transition from feudalism to capitalism. The temporarily balanced environment produces a verbal and intellectual rhythm of continual vacillation, equivocation, paradoxicality. It is the rhythm of both/and which provides for More a stylistic equivalent to the philosophical stance called "Christian humanism." (The stance would become a good deal easier, less polarized, in the decades and generations following the Reformation, when the Christian dimension could be filled with more liberal versions of Protestant Christianity rather than with the essentially unitary and rigid Catholic doctrine.) In hindsight the fundamental contradiction of More's utopia is a historical one that no one could expect the author to have formulated as such: It is that you can't have a highly productive and fully collectivized agricultural economy such as More portrays, without a similarly productive and collectivized industrial economy. However, the tensions or ambivalencies I have in mind are textual and specific to More's own period. For instance, despite several hundred years of theoretical conflict, faith and reason are perfectly reconciled in More's text without a murmur: The Utopians think that although their beliefs (afterlife, immortality of the soul, etc.) belong to religion, "it is in accordance with reason that they be held and acknowledged." The Utopians hold both an idealist-"genetic" and a materialist-sociological theory of why some people enjoy the hunt: "They think this enjoyment in beholding deaths, even in beasts, comes from an inherently cruel disposition or from the habitual practise of cruelty in so brutal a pleasure." Nature and nurture, no need to choose. Why were the Utopians so ready to accept Christianity? "Either because God secretly incited them or because this religion is most like the belief already very strong among them." There is sexual equality, but there is sexual inequality: "Women are not excluded from the priesthood, but are chosen less often, and only if they are elderly widows." There is, in short, a will to have it both ways—which for More as a Catholic must have seemed both the essence of utopia and its outer limit.

A similar tension is evident in Thomas Campanella's *City of the Sun* (1623), written while the author, an Italian Dominican and patriot, was in prison on suspicion of treasonous conspiracy against Spanish rule. The dialogue is wooden; there is no characterization to speak of; much of the (mercifully short) fictional account consists of measurements and architectural detail. Of interest, though, is the text's odd bifurcation: on one hand a rationalistic/technological/futuristic viewpoint, on the other an ancient/classical/medieval/idealistic mythos. Thus Campanella praises the discovery of the New World first for reasons of piety—the explorations will extend Christianity worldwide—and only then succumbs to the excitement of "the coming age, and . . . our age, that has in it more history in a hundred years than all the world had in four thousand years before." He hails the development of printing, guns, and the magnet, but alongside this enthusiasm for modern technology there coexists the ancient notion of cosmic organicism. The sun is cosmic father, the earth is mother, the sea is earth's sweat or blood. Here is Campanella's most striking formulation of the ancient cosmic analogy: "The world is a great animal, and we live within it as worms live within us."[2]

Like More's *Utopia,* the immensely popular *Looking Backward* (1887) achieves a precarious equilibrium of religious orthodoxy and economic innovation, moral fervor and rational/technological efficiency. And, like *Utopia*, Edward Bellamy's book marks the juncture of old and new, balancing between them. The book repeats on many levels the classic ambivalence of the modern petty-bourgeois intellectual trapped between the Scylla of rapidly expanding capital in its early imperialist phase and the Charybdis of international proletarian revolution. It hates big capital, and it hates communism even more.[3] It was to the petty bourgeoisie that Bellamy's book appealed primarily, as did the Nationalist clubs it inspired: to teachers, ministers, doctors, journalists, farmers, and small businessmen squeezed by banks and corporations.

Bellamy's hero, Julian West, is a young intellectual and millionaire coupon-clipper who falls asleep in 1887 and wakes into the new world of 2000. The new society has "solved the labor problem" without violence, by extending capital so that everyone is a capitalist: truly the social democrat's dream! Those who "waved the red flag," it turns out, were merely the paid *agents provocateurs* of the great monopolies (chap. 24). Women work but not at the same jobs as men; they are organized into a separate labor army and have a separate judiciary. "We have given [women] a world of their own," explains Julian's instructor Dr. Leete, "and I assure you they are very happy in it" (chap. 25). Though a student of history, the heroine, Edith Leete, plays no role in instructing Julian in the history of operation of the new society. And so on, in each area, with a curious blend of past and future, conservative and iconoclastic.

Since Bellamy was a minister's son, it isn't surprising that a strong undercurrent of religious imagery reinforces the conservative impulse in *Looking Backward*. Like his fourth-century namesake, Julian is an apostate, though—with an ironic twist—not from but *to* true Christianity. Edith is an "angelic" creature, a saintly figure who watches over Julian, saving him from despair and even suicide. Christianity thrives in the new society: Chapter 26 is wholly devoted to the Sunday sermon Julian hears on the radio. The new society is frequently referred to in a millennial vocabulary as "heaven compared with what was," a "new heaven and new earth," etc. Finally, in a powerful dream sequence in the last chapter, Julian takes on the role of Old Testament prophet to the monied classes of Boston, denouncing their evil ways and predicting doom; the chapter is loaded with Biblical cadences and references.

Even the dream-vision utopia of the Marxian socialist and medievalist William Morris—*News From Nowhere* (1891), written as a deliberate "counterblast" to Bellamy—straddles future and past uncomfortably, for the stateless, classless Communist future is given the image of an idealized preindustrial English past of cottage industry, quaint villages and long silken gowns.

There are, of course, strategies for overcoming the ambivalencies I have noted. Plato's *Republic* (c. 380 B.C.) is perfectly consistent in its own terms. It is neither realistic nor desirable, but it is logically valid, ruthlessly true to its own philosophical premises. The *Republic* is an aristocrat's conservative response to the democratizing tendencies of his day. If Plato achieves a seamless structure in the *Republic,* it is by ignoring class struggle, turning his back on it with a rigor few later writers have been capable of. It is a rigor absolutely consistent with, and justified by, Plato's definition of the proper objects of contemplation; history, characterized by constant change, is not among them. Located in the space where real meets ideal, utopia can be purged of contradiction by suppressing its negative axis, the axis of present reality. This is not the only way, but it is the way Plato has chosen. (Admittedly, reality always retains a shadowy presence as the motive for writing utopia at all, even if it is granted no real textual presence; but its suppression produces a different sort of text.) Unlike More, Bellamy, Morris, Gilman, or Piercy, Plato offers no portrait of current social reality in his utopia. He suppresses the negative axis of utopia by refusing to denounce his own society.

Wells adopts another strategy, the opposite of Plato's. Intensely conscious of the aesthetic and other problems of utopian writing, Wells manages to overcome them by making them explicit, indeed by forcing the reader to become his accomplice in the exercise of imagination. "Figure the gesture . . . ," he often exhorts the reader. In general where Wells cannot reasonably specify, he does not, acknowledging the "inherent falsity" of too-specific blueprints or too-rigid theories that will work themselves out "so soon as reality is touched." Wells's new world is international, industrial, multiracial: three trends frequently ignored by modern utopian writers, though amply taken up by the dystopians—indeed in Wells's own numerous dystopias. Wells's utopia, then, is founded solidly on, projected from, the present: "The alternative is a Utopia of dolls in the likeness of angels—imaginary laws to fit incredible people, an unattractive undertaking" (chap. 1). The criticism of utopia is built into this self-reflexive text, through arguments between the narrator and his sentimental, bigoted botanist companion, through direct authorial intervention, and through the disquisitions of a blond, besandalled flower-child who wishes for a "return to nature." Social and psychological reality are rendered as fully, as novelistically, as possible; yet utopia must remain an act of the imagination, something like a soap-bubble "that becomes more fragile with every added circumstance" (chap. 11). Hence no gimmicks are required: no Rip Van Winkle sleeps, dream-visions, exotic undiscovered realms, or telekinetic journeys into the future—only imagination. It is precisely as a series of imaginative leaps that successive generations will produce their utopias, each "a little more certain and complete and real," until utopia "will be this world." So the bubble bursts. We are brought back full circle to filthy, crowded, oppressive London with a new sense of the possible created, paradoxically, by the full admission of contradictions.

Yet after all, even Wells stumbles briefly at the intersection of real and ideal—not in the future, however, but in the past. His relentless rationalism forces him to posit an entire utopian world history (chap. 9), a utopian past that might generate such a future, not lacking wars and heroes. It is an almost Hegelian vision of world history approaching perfection more and more nearly until its realization in the fictional Utopia. In this sense Wells, too, might be said to suffer at some level a failure of imagination:

For we need utopia to be possible on the foundation of *our* history.

Were it not for William Morris one might be tempted to describe utopia as the social planning of reformers without a program. Indeed, a weak spot in most utopias is precisely the question a political program must address: How will we get from here to there? This is not to deprecate utopian discourse but to place it, for I share Engels' admiration for "the stupendously grand thoughts and germs of thought that everywhere break out through their phantastic covering."[4] And I agree with his balanced assessment of the limitations of a utopian approach: its reliance on universal reason rather than class interest as source of motivation, on individual conversion rather than collective action as modality, on persuasion rather than political organization as medium. Still, utopia may be the perfect literary version of a reformist strategy (including feminism), if its formal, structural, tonal, and intellectual ambivalences express the paradox of any reformism: the inadequacy of means to end.

Another Achilles' heel of nearly every utopia is the woman question. It is a weakness, a symptom signalling the more general malaise of the mode. Even Morris and Wells, attractive and progressive in so many ways, falter here and reflect to a greater or lesser extent the sex-role stereotypes of their day. So, interestingly, does Charlotte P. Gilman, to whose feminist utopia I now turn.

In *Herland,* Gilman portrays a highly civilized, productive, and humane society of women: a new Amazonia "discovered" by three young male explorers. It is a charming book, with the three heroes delineated as three distinct (if stereotypically consistent) personality types: Jeff the dreamer-poet and doctor, Van the sensible social-scientist (who narrates), and Terry the arrogant male-chauvinist. Dialogue is clever, and the story is filled with entertaining and instructive incident. Gleeful role-reversals are a means to expose sexism in language and institutions, as when the three men try to escape their captors:

"Now for a rush, boys!" Terry said. "And if we can't break 'em, I'll
shoot in the air."
Then we found ourselves much in the position of the suffragette
trying to get to the Parliament buildings through a triple cordon of
London police. . . .
We were borne inside, struggling manfully, but held secure most
womanfully, in spite of our best endeavors. (chap. 2)

There is, though, an important difference between Amazonia
and Herland. The myth or legend (historicity is uncertain) of the
Amazons enters the Western tradition as that of an Asian nation
of warrior women conquered by the Greek culture-heroes Theseus and Hercules. The marriage of the Amazon queen Hippo-
lyta to King Theseus of Athens symbolized the restoration of
right order—that is, of dominance and submission—in international relations, domestic politics, and the family. It was an image
of independent female and foreign power subordinated to the
patriarchal Greek city-state.[5] So Chaucer used the story in *The
Knight's Tale* and Shakespeare in *A Midsummer Night's Dream*
as an instance of the literature of sexual politics. Whereas Amazonia is an image of women's realm defeated, Herland is
women's realm triumphant.

Yet paradoxically the triumph of woman, the full liberation of
woman, is something Gilman was not fully prepared to imagine—
as, indeed, few people have been, even among utopian writers. It
is a telling literary fact that Gilman's best and most powerful work
is a story of defeat: "The Yellow Wallpaper," about a woman who
goes slowly insane, trapped in marriage with a conventionally in-
sensitive man. There are two dimensions to be considered here
that, as always, interlock: the personal and the cultural.

It seems to me that the contemporary movement that has redis-
covered Gilman tends to overrate the importance of her contribution by failing to place her firmly in a cultural context. It is no
advantage to women, or to the advancement of their full liberation, to maintain as heroines or role-models figures from the past
whose limitations are as striking as Gilman's. That she "became
the leading intellectual in the women's movement in the United

States during the first two decades of the twentieth century," that she was "lionized in English and German feminist circles"[6] is beside the point: Her fame may well bespeak the intellectual poverty of feminism in that period. Of three great and original theories of her lifetime—those of Darwin, Marx, and Freud—Gilman hated the second two and misunderstood the first. When we contextualize Gilman, two things become apparent: first, that some ideas of our own day are not so new; second, that Gilman was by no means in the vanguard of social thought in her own time.

First, the genre. To write a utopia when Gilman did was to follow a literary vogue (indeed somewhat belatedly), for utopia was virtually *the* American genre of the later nineteenth century. Between 1888 and 1896 alone, more than a hundred were published in the United States,[7] a good many of them by women, some of them showing sexual equality or woman the dominant sex. Gilman herself wrote two more besides *Herland: Moving the Mountain* (1911), and a sequel to *Herland, With Her in Ourland* (1916). Utopia was no mere literary trend, for more than a hundred experimental communities were founded in the United States during the nineteenth century, by Americans and by Europeans from various countries, in accordance with one or another vision, theory, or scheme. Gilman was heavily influenced by the social ideas of that most famous American utopian author, Edward Bellamy.

Women and Economics (1898), Gilman's major contribution to theory, is a peculiar blend of lucid social comment, high moral tone, and shallow pseudoscientific myth-making. The book was extremely popular in the United States and abroad, though (or perhaps because) it represents, in my view, the epitome of American parochialism and empiricism. These features come, in part, from the main intellectual influence on the book, the American sociologist Lester Ward, whose "gynaecocentric theory" Gilman considered the most important contribution to humanity since Darwin. Ward called for equal rights for women and a positive attitude toward sexuality. As a sociobiologist Ward hypothesized that at an early stage of human development woman was the dominant "race-type," the originally superior sex, and that the historical dominance of man as "sex-type" is an organically evolved higher evolutionary phase. So that while exalting woman as "ancestress," Ward's theory actually provided a pseudoscientific rationale for male supremacy.[8] Gilman herself possessed little sense of social relativity with respect to morals (though this was a not uncommon topic of intellectual discourse in her day); indeed she considered "pure, lasting monogamous marriage" a naturally—that is, biologically—evolved feature of the human race. As well, and despite her rationalist commitment to sex equality, Gilman accepted traditional stereotypes, as did most feminists, in attributing "naturally destructive" tendencies to men and naturally conservative, nurturing qualities to women.

Politically Gilman was middle-of-the-road at best. Though nominally a member of the Socialist party for a time, she found herself in such disagreement with basic socialist ideas that she could not attend the 1896 International Socialist and Labor Congress in England as a socialist, but went as a labor delegate instead.[9] Her political education she owed to Bellamy and to the "sociocracy" of Lester Ward. Karl Marx is summarily dismissed in *Ourland* as a "German-Jewish economist" who had done nothing more than to explain "in interminable and . . . incomprehensible prolixity . . . why it was better to work together for the common good." Gilman's fundamentally antidemocratic middleclass stance is further confirmed in her heroine's comment, also from *Ourland,* that "only some races—or some individuals in a given race—have reached the democratic stage."[10] The collective of Gilman's utopia has more in common with the medieval monastery than with socialism, utopian *or* scientific.

On the woman question Gilman was equally middle-of-the-road. Abortion is presented in *Herland* as one of the worst perversions of the modern world, not because of the health problem it posed for millions of women, but because Gilman considered it an affront to motherhood. As late as 1923 she was able to write that contraception was "a free ticket for selfish and fruitless indulgence, and an aid in the lamentable behavior of our times." In 1927 Gilman did endorse contraception—not as an asset to family life or individual health but rather because of a naive neo-Malthusian belief in overpopulation as a cause of war, and in "deterioration of stock from careless and excessive breeding."[11] We need to recall that already by 1910 there were numerous public spokesmen advocating the legalization of birth control, along with many families who practiced it (often by condoms or coitus interruptus) and doctors who advised it. The trade-union movement strongly endorsed the legalization of contraception. In 1915, the year *Herland* was written, Margaret Sanger, already a well-known advocate, was indicted for disseminating contraceptive advice through the mails.

Gilman denounced temporary or multiple sexual relations, in a period that witnessed Mormon polygamy, a well-organized free-love movement with numerous public spokespersons, widespread interest in the theories of Freud, and the founding of hundreds of experimental, intentional, or utopian communities, many programmatically committed to sexual fulfillment, group marriage or serial monogamy.

Gilman's insistence on women working is laudable, yet it seems like kicking in an open door, for millions of women had not only entered the American work force (eight million in 1910) but participated in and led massive strikes. Her vehemency on this issue seems to reflect the condition of the still-homebound middle-class woman and to ignore the social reality of working women. The collectivization of housework, also a laudable aim, had been since midcentury an important aspect of the social-reform movement, especially its Fourierist-utopian branch. It had produced not only designs for cities and villages with common kitchens, dining halls, laundries, and recreational areas but, in many large cities across the country, working cooperatives for those and other services.[12] Gilman's notion of the "greatest of women's organizations" was neither the national suffrage organization, nor yet the Women's Trade Union League, but the Women's Christian Temperance Union, which supported suffrage only as a way to prohibition, and whose campaign against drink embodied the typical middle-class fear of alcohol and sex as master-solvents of civilization. With every Victorian admirer of "the angel in the house," Gilman believed that "it is the business of women to make the home life of the world true, healthful and beautiful" *(Women and Economics),* despite the evident contradiction of this view with the goals of women working outside the home and the socialization of housework.

In her personal life Gilman revealed a strong will to survive and to conquer circumstance as best she could, although it was far from an unconventional life in the main. She suffered and recovered from a nervous breakdown, as many other middle-class women did. She divorced, remarried, and let her ex-husband care for their child. She courageously committed suicide in order to preempt terminal cancer. She wrote, travelled, and spoke publicly, as did hundreds of other American women in this era of public elocution, lecture circuits, educational societies and social reform. When one bears in mind the socially imposed unconventionality of millions of working women (common-law marriage, temporary relations, abortion, labor organizing); the deliberate unconventionality of thousands of social reformers and revolutionaries (divorce, marriages of convenience, long-term common-law marriages, love-affairs, arrests, dramatic escapes, international travel, public agitation, struggle, and leadership); even the bohemian unconventionality of many apolitical middle-class women, especially in and around the arts (Frieda Lawrence and Gertrude Stein, to name only two famous examples, were Gilman's contemporaries; they seem to inhabit another world)—when one bears in mind all this, Gilman seems very much removed from the seething modernity of the period. She strikes me as representative of a day that was drawing to a close, rather than harbinger of a day that was dawning.

In short, the facts of Gilman's life, social position, and opinions seem to place her in the typical utopian stance, with a foot in each camp: a stance borne out in the text itself.

When our three intrepid young explorers set out for Herland, the big question on their minds (for both scientific and personal reasons)—and on the reader's mind—is, naturally, how do these latter-day Amazons reproduce? We also wonder, as do our heroes, why no male children are seen. The answer is that the Herlanders reproduce by parthenogenesis induced by an effort of will, and all the offspring are female. By the same token, birth control is a fairly simple matter: Think of something else and you will not conceive:

> When a woman chose to be a mother, she allowed the child-longing to grow within her till it worked its natural miracle. When she did not so choose she put the whole thing out of her mind, and fed her heart with the other babies. (chap. 6)

(Interestingly, Herland society itself is, on a larger scale, historically parthenogenetic because of a series of acts of God and intense will. The population—"of Aryan stock," we are assured—emigrated from the Old World. The men all died in wars, a volcanic eruption, and a slave revolt that the women—members of the master class if not the master sex—suppressed. So there they are, by accident (as Gilman puts it by "a series of historic misfortunes") with a whole country on their hands and no men and complete carte blanche "to clean up the place and make their living as best they could" (chap. 5).

Biology, then, is the main "gimmick" of Gilman's utopia. Several other biological wonders occur in Herland, though none so striking or so central to the plot as the human reproductive miracle. Killing and sex have been bred out of animal life to produce a rather antiseptic Disneyesque version of cloying Victorian niceness. There are no wild beasts in agricultural Herland, nor cattle: The inhabitants are vegetarian. The bird-killing instinct has been bred out of cats, along with the meow; the cats mate only once a year, and the few male cats that are born are kept shut up most of the time. There are no dogs in Herland. Sexuality has been bred out of the human inhabitants, or rather has atrophied: "They could not, with all their effort, get the point of view of the male creature whose desires quite ignore parentage and seek only for what we euphoniously term 'the joys of love' " (chap. 12). We need only add that bizarre as is all this geneticist manipulation, there were worse: In *Looking Forward* (1899) Arthur Bird has the Chinese turn white under the benevolent influence of American colonialism![13]

Uniformity of dress, uniformity of diet, uniformity of personal appearance, and uniformity of opinion characterize the Herlanders. We find, for instance, that "they all wear short hair." This makes a feminist point in rejecting the conventional ideal of long hair as a criterion for personal beauty. Yet it also ignores variety of human taste and suppresses the freedom to indulge it. The example, though small, is paradigmatic: Here, ideological rejection of the externals of traditional femininity leads to an equally repulsive and narrow repressiveness.

To return to our nation of virgins: Gilman eats her cake and has it too, by preserving virginity and maternity at once—Everywoman as the Blessed Virgin Mary. Not surprisingly, Herlanders are not at all astonished by the story of the Virgin birth of Jesus. (It was only a few years before Charlotte's birth that the Immaculate Conception, the doctrine that Mary was born without taint of original sin, was declared dogma by Pope Pius IX in 1854, a development that Charlotte may have been aware of, growing up as she did in an intensely religious and theological, although not Catholic, atmosphere.) On one level it is ironic that Gilman should preserve fictionally a central mystery of Christian faith that had been for so long an important ideological instrument in the special oppression of women. On another level the irony is that she preserves as well a central ideological notion of secular society, for chastity and maternity were the two poles of ideal womanhood in Gilman's day. She provides the miracle required to reconcile these mutually exclusive biological ideals.

This, then, is the central evasion in Gilman's utopia: a whimsical/mystical evasion of a problem crucial to the lives of women, one acknowledged and addressed as such by many writers and reformers of the period. She grasps the nettle only to drop it:

addresses the taboo topic of birth control, avoided by so many utopian writers, and evades it after all.

In part this evasion represents the pronatalism common to reform movements of the period. "Control of one's body" did not necessarily mean contraception or abortion: In the context of nineteenth-century America it often meant the right to abstain from intercourse with one's husband. And, though Margaret Sanger certainly saw contraception as a means to "control one's body" and to enhance sexuality, not everyone valued its uses beyond family planning.

A certain pronatalist tendency was also the norm among socialists, though for different reasons from those of feminists. Though the German social democracy accepted birth control in principle, the demand was not incorporated into its program. The SPD wished to dissociate itself from neo-Malthusians who saw population control as the key to social change and improved standards of living; it also wished for the ranks of the proletariat to swell, in quite accurate expectation of revolutionary upsurge during the next decades.[14] The Bolsheviks (who took power two years after *Herland* was written) legalized abortion three years after the revolution, and then reluctantly, as a lesser-evil alternative to the massive health problem created by private abortion. Contraception was available in the USSR but not profusely, so that abortion remained—and does today—the dominant means of birth control in the USSR. It was the Bolsheviks whose program took fullest account of motherhood. The most radical of sex-theorists, Alexandra Kollontai, took feminists to task for neglecting maternity-related reforms that would address the most urgent aspect of special oppression for working women. Kollontai summarized the regime's policy as follows: "To remove the cares of motherhood but leave untouched the joyous smile which is born of woman's contact with her child—such is the Soviet government's principle in solving the motherhood problem."[15] There could of course be no "official position" for or against maternity, no actual advocacy of either alternative, but there was a distinct tilt in favor. The important difference from feminist pronatalism, I would argue, is

that the Soviet tendency of the early 1920s was devoid of sentimentality, moralism, or pseudoanthropological "justification." It
was founded partly in the necessity to increase a war-depleted
population and partly in the commitment to maximum freedom
of personal choice—a commitment that had to be honored while
simultaneously enabling women to enter industrial production.

American feminist pronatalism had entirely different roots. It
preserved—and intended to preserve—the old Victorian ideals
of maternity and chastity. It was moralistic and sentimental and
often, as with Gilman, based on myth masquerading as science.
With North American and German feminists this moralism acquired a racialist thrust when combined with geneticist notions of
"racial purity" as a motive for the protection of motherhood.[16]
(We recall here Gilman's emphasis on Marx's Jewish ancestry
and her assurance that the Herland women are "of Aryan
stock . . . 'white,' but somewhat darker than our northern races
because of their constant exposure to sun and air" [chap. 5].)

For better or worse, then, *Herland* is the quintessential literary
distillation of American feminism of the later nineteenth and
early twentieth centuries, giving imaginative shape to its limited
reforms, its conservatism, its paradoxes and evasions. The book
embodies that peculiar blend of Enlightenment rationalism and
Protestant moralism that, as Richard J. Evans argues, fuses in the
nineteenth-century creed of liberalism, of which feminism is one
expression.[17] It is a vision, I suggest, especially well suited to the
utopian form, which seems to display, more than any other common feature, precisely such ambivalence.

Marge Piercy's *Woman on the Edge of Time* is not really a
utopia. It is a compelling realistic novel with utopian interludes
and so much the better for the novel. The setting is New York
City and its environs at the present time; the protagonist is Con-
suelo Ramos, who for most of the novel is confined in a mental
hospital. Connie, it turns out, is capable of telepathic travel into
the future. In this way she is able to enter the new society of 2137
in Mattapoisett, Massachusetts.

If Charlotte Gilman participated in a national vogue in writing her utopias, Piercy swims against the stream to write hers. In 1947 Vernon L. Parrington, Jr., concluded his book on American utopias with an upbeat, if rather tentative, exhortation to American optimism:

> Skepticism has reappeared inevitably. We have wanted peace so intensely that now we are afraid that we cannot keep it. Our skepticism comes partly from fear—and partly from a sense of insecurity. The weapons which brought us victory provide us with no guarantees about the future. We must have faith in a world which has yet to show that it can work together. Such faith is in our American tradition.[18]

Parrington's plea was already too late; "to most observers utopianism seemed a corpse by the 1920's and 1930's."[19] Eugene Zamyatin's *We* (1921), one of the seminal dystopias of the twentieth century, protested the rationalist collectivism of early Soviet society. It influenced Aldous Huxley's *Brave New World* (1932), George Orwell's *1984* (1948), and the work of Anthony Burgess, though clearly the historic spectacle of fascism and of Stalinism triumphant gave decisive impetus to dystopia, as did neocolonialism, the rapid development of Western science and technology, and above all cold-war propaganda. The general effect was a cynical plague-on-both-your-houses paranoia among middle-class Western intellectuals, which Northrop Frye understatedly referred to as "something of a paralysis of utopian thought and imagination" and which he rightly explained as "the result of a repudiation of communism."[20] Though the collection in which Frye's essay appeared (along with several other anthologies on the subject) testifies to a revival of scholarly interest in utopia during the 1960s and 1970s, that interest could scarcely stimulate the production of speculative myth (to use Frye's phrase) or speculative social planning, which the blatant polarizations of recent history have rendered at least temporarily obsolete. The editor of another academic collection asserts that "the utopian ideal has decayed to the point of collapse in the twentieth century," because utopia is necessarily static, ignores individuality, and assumes everyone to have the same sources of happiness. All the authors in the collection, he correctly notes, show a "counter-utopian bias"; that is, they "display little or no confidence in, or expectation of, man's attaining the secure and happy land of his heart's desire."[21]

This is the dominant intellectual climate into which Marge Piercy has had the courage to insert *Woman on the Edge of Time,* the indirect record of a "very passionate involvement with SDS" and an effort "to create a society not at all fantastic but one we can have if we fight for it, one almost attainable now. . . . "[22] It is everything Parrington could ask: The American dream revived, wearing sandals, jeans, and embroidered shirt, and probably a lapel button saying "Question Authority."

Piercy's new society is surely one of the more attractive and sophisticated in imaginative literature, a heady blend of late 1960s and early 1970s countercultures: R. D. Laing, group therapy, natural health foods, marijuana, ecology, anarchism, socialism, New Left and Yippie politics, and the radical wing of the women's liberation movement. The new society is deurbanized, regionally decentralized across the North American continent, and administered by randomly selected rotating democratic councils. It is nonhierarchal and classless, multiracial and multicultural, industrial, agricultural, highly aesthetic, and sexually liberated. Nothing is bought or sold. The nuclear family has been replaced by other arrangements for parenting, coupling, and living. Sexism does not exist, not even linguistically. Most citizens of the future are bisexual, many are androgynous in appearance. Sexual possessiveness is almost nonexistent, and sexuality is fully indulged. Following Shulamith Firestone's scenario for "the ultimate revolution" in *The Dialectic of Sex* (1970), Piercy gives us a society that has freed women from the burden of involuntary reproduction and parenting. Embryos are grown *in vitro,* and parenting is done by both sexes; this includes nursing, for which a man can get hormones to stimulate breast growth and the production of milk if he wishes to do so.

The contrast to *Herland* is obvious. Equally obvious is the inevitability of such contrast given the differences between early and later feminism. Yet I am not sure that the implications of those differences are as fully appreciated by modern feminists as they ought to be. Richard Evans states the case well:

> The tendency for supporters of Women's Liberation to look to feminists of the past for legitimation for their efforts has obscured the fact that in many respects the [former] reject the aims and beliefs of the feminists and operate on a very different set of assumptions. . . . The employment of a new political vocabulary . . . is revealing: "liberation" instead of "equal rights", stressing the inadequacy of the mere legal equality which was the principle aim of the feminists; "consciousness-raising," deriving from the ideology of Marxism with its emphasis on the need for the oppressed to liberate themselves as a group rather than—as the feminists thought—as individuals; "sexism", deriving from the concept of "racism", signifying rejection of ways of thought which the feminists themselves eventually came to share.[23]

Piercy's utopia is neither static nor trouble-free. Madness still exists in the future (though there is no apparent social causation for it). It is considered a salutary visionary experience, romanticized in the fashion of Laing as "getting in touch with the buried self and the inner mind." Capital punishment also exists (and therefore crime, though rare); it is used reluctantly and only against those who have twice deliberately hurt another person. There is controversy: debates about particular works of art and their social implications, debates about genetic intervention (which is not practiced). And, most important, the new society is at war, intermittently attacked by an unspecified enemy. The existence of this enemy shows that the new way of life is not yet established worldwide, and that it is therefore still evolving internally in a kind of protracted "permanent revolution," as Luciente, Connie's psychopomp, acknowledges (p. 328).

Utopia in transition, relative utopism: an interesting variation in the tradition, and one that brings us close to the book's problematic. The portrayal of the present is realistic and convincing; the vision of the future suffers far fewer contradictions than most utopias. What emerges as problematic, though, is the relation of present and future, crystallized, as we will see, in the war theme.

It is an ultimately uneasy coexistence of novel and utopia, for the futuristic interludes do not only intervene in the novel as the solution to its problems, but they also pose an alternate interpretation of its heroine and plot. In that sense they undercut the premises of the realistic novel, constituting an evasion that is finally as unsatisfying as Gilman's parthenogenesis.

From the novelistic point of view Connie is a lonely, passive, overweight Mexican woman who is victimized by Puerto Rican men, by pimps, by racism, by New York's inhumane, insufficient, and irrational social welfare system. In a series of psychotic episodes Connie hallucinates a better time and place. She is hospitalized and subjected to experimental surgery that will implant electrodes in her brain to activate "socially desirable" (acquiescent) responses and suppress "undesirable" (rebellious) ones. Before the experiment is completed, Connie murders several doctors and hospital staff by slipping poison into their coffee. The book ends with this episode.

From the utopian perspective Connie is a beautiful, sane, and talented telepath who makes contact with the future. Her experiences there, and the friendships she establishes there, enable her to transcend the horrors of city life and of the hospital. Her decision to kill the doctors is a principled and rational one, her first and only rebellion against the system that has robbed her of so much: her youth, health, and dignity, her daughter and her lover, her education, freedom, and creative power. Connie realizes that she is at war, that those who oppress her in the hospital represent the forces that could eventually defeat the good society of the future. Connie reveals her plan to Luciente, her contact in the other world, who replies:

> "We live by eating living beings. . . . Power *is* violence. When did it get destroyed peacefully? We all fight when we're back to the wall—or to tear down a wall. You know we kill people who choose twice to hurt others. We don't think it's right to kill them. Only convenient. Nobody wants to stand guard over another." (p. 370)

Thus Connie's act has, at least implicitly, approval from the spokeswoman of the future—if, that is, we see Luciente as "really" from the future. Of course, we can also see Luciente as part of Connie's hallucination, a projection of herself, an imaginative recreation of what she would like to be or might have been, an inner voice authorizing various of her own impulses. But then immense care has been taken to guarantee that we do believe in Luciente's reality: The chair she occupied is still warm; the slide-staining dye on her fingers leaves its faint chemical odor in Connie's apartment.

The fact of war in utopia enters this dialectic between present and future. Why does the author choose or need to show her new society at war? Evidently she does not believe—certainly Luciente does not believe—that war is a necessary part of the human condition: It can be overcome. Nonetheless, it affects the story in several important ways. First, the existence of an enemy removes the smug, quietistic atmosphere that permeates many utopias, permitting a wider range of dramatic event than is usually possible. Second, it makes the ethical/political point that struggle is necessary, that a better society will be won, not conferred. In this sense the future war of utopian and dystopian societies is a metaphor for all present social struggle. Third, the war is structurally necessary to motivate Connie's act of final estrangement, or self-assertion (whichever viewpoint one chooses), for it is Connie's participation in the future war that makes her realize that she is herself at war, that she must kill or be killed, and that any weapon is right in this struggle. War is in fact the bridge from future to present, the undifferentiated feature they share. The following passage definitively poses a problem of perspective: utopia *or* hallucination?

> She glanced around and saw all the enemy floaters zeroing in on them as if summoned to this attack. As she stared to left and right she saw that they were piloted and manned by Judge Kerrigan, who had taken her daughter, by the social worker Miss Kronenberg, by Mrs. Polcari, by Acker and Miss Moynihan, by all the caseworkers and doctors and landlords and cops, the psychiatrists and judges and child guidance counselors, the informants and attendants and orderlies, the legal aid lawyers copping pleas, the matrons and EEG technicians, and all the other flacks of power who had pushed her back and turned her off and locked her up and medicated her and

> tranquilized her and punished her and condemned her. They were
> all closing in, guns blazing. Then the air burst into golden-red
> flames and she heard Dr. Redding crow, "Right on the button. That
> does it. Okay, into the ambulance with her." (p. 336)

The objection here is not simply a political or strategic one, for the
pathetic inadequacy of Connie's private war is obvious, even if we
lend its result the theoretical credibility of what anarchists used to
call "propaganda by the deed," and see it implementing the volun-
taristic/individualistic advice of Bee, Connie's lover in utopia:

> "We're all at war. You're a prisoner of war. May you free your-
> self. . . . There's always a thing you can deny an oppressor, if only
> your allegiance. Your belief. Your co-oping. Often even with vastly
> unequal power, you can find or force an opening to fight back. In
> your time many without power found ways to fight. Till that became
> a power." (p. 328)

More fundamentally, though, the passage is an interpretive crux
because it openly and directly challenges utopia with reality—
indeed reduces utopia to reality, albeit abnormal (hallucinatory)
reality.

My intention is not to complain about multiplicity of interpretation per se. Certainly a story like Henry James's "Turn of the
Screw" sustains its ambiguity throughout: ghost story, or diseased
imagination of the governess narrator? There are numerous fictions about which we can legitimately ask, "What really happened?" Tzvetan Todorov defines the literature of the fantastic
as that about which we *must* ask that question:

> The ambiguity is sustained to the very end of the adventure: reality
> or dream? truth or illusion? . . . The person who experiences the
> event must opt for one of two possible solutions: either he is the
> victim of an illusion of the senses, of a product of the imagination—
> and laws of the world then remain what they are; or else the event
> has indeed taken place, it is an integral part of reality—but then this
> reality is controlled by laws unknown to us.[24]

In *Woman on the Edge of Time,* ambiguity is not sustained;
rather (and this is not at all the same thing), it is constantly
ruptured, sometimes in favor of utopia (as with the odor of slide

dye on Luciente's fingers), sometimes in favor of hallucination (as in the war passage). In other words, the two possibilities don't fully coexist: They cancel each other out. If we see utopia as the hallucination of a homicidal mental patient, it loses its validity as a genuine act of imagination and struggle and social planning, possible historically and to all of us. If we accept the utopia as real, then surely this trivializes Connie's heartbreaking suffering and the evils of capitalism into conditions that can be transcended by an act of will or imagination. Worse, it privileges, even glamorizes the most intensely oppressed victims of capitalism as visionaries with special access to the future. "The most oppressed are the most revolutionary" would be the fatuous political analogue; indeed, Luciente at one point does comment that most of the telepaths the new society has contacted are women, and inhabit either mental hospitals or prisons (p. 196).

We come back, then, to Wells, and to his cautionary advice against bringing the utopian soap-bubble into too close proximity with reality:

> To find the people assuming the concrete and individual is not, as I fondly imagine, the last triumph of realisation, but the swimming moment of opacity before the film gives way. To come to individual emotional cases, is to return to the earth. (*A Modern Utopia,* chap. 11)

Piercy precipitates a delicate suspension—utopian particles suspended in the medium of a realistic novel—by inviting us—forcing us, really—to choose one or the other interpretation. It is, after all, the suspension of disbelief we are talking about, for I suspect that most readers will choose the hallucination script. The novel exhorts us to revolutionary struggle yet blunts the edge of that exhortation by locating its real action where it can do no good.

Is there a future for utopia? If, as I have proposed here, ambivalence is the essential feeling of utopian writing, there probably is. Even a society we might now consider utopian will likely have its dissenters—like Wells's flower-child—to remind us of other possibilities, for better or worse.

10

A city, a room: the scene of writing in Christine de Pisan and Virginia Woolf

Unlike everyone else, it seems, I am not rereading *A Room of One's Own* but reading it for the first time. My tears come frequently in response to the angry power of the text and its controlled violence, as I mourn and protest the loss of this woman who should not have killed herself, whose passion finally turned against itself.

Her death seems a personal and immediate loss, her whose novels, when I read them years ago, puzzled and repelled me, paradoxical as they were. There was such beautiful lucidity of mind and of style, yet the novels were so full of fear and renunciation and suppressed desire: Why could not the lucidity break through the fear? Moreover, here was a woman writer, but her great heroine, Mrs. Ramsay, was a mediator of family relations, the exhausted pacifier of her husband's egotism. Was it for this that Virginia Woolf had risen above the stereotype: only to glorify the stereotype? And so, looking for models of strength, I bypassed Virginia Woolf. Her lectures on women and fiction I deferred because I expected them to be anemic and conventional, and because I did not see them as ur-text in a tradition to which I might eventually aspire. And so I am late to discover Virginia Woolf and pay tribute to her, by writing, as she asks us to do "whether it matters for ages or only for hours."

But what is the cost of such an art as hers—or even a far inferior one—in time, interiorization, renunciation? Are we not talking here about giving up the very things that might have kept Virginia from suicide: political action, children, a healthy sex life, and the daily grind of maintenance from which she was always shielded? Are those distractions the love of reality that keeps us alive? Is the choice between low productivity and self-consuming concentration? One hopes not. But that money and rooms didn't stave off breakdowns and suicide for Virginia Woolf says something about the conditions in which even the exceptional woman acquires the former. The supervalorization of marriage and coupledom, the trivialization of love among women (which was where Virginia's sensuality found its real expression), the class snobbery she shared—all contributed inexorably to the stress of an already stressful life. She felt the necessity of marriage and of subordination to a man she did not desire, a man who could only see her as Other, alien and *aliénée.* Except for writing, her choices remain the ordinary ones, and are likely to until the value structure she only partially saw through has been dismantled.

It seems obvious after, or while, reading *A Room of One's Own,* that it should be a woman writer—Virginia herself—I would be able to look to as the kind of parental figure that Harold Bloom writes about.[1] A woman writer's muse might be male, perhaps (for heterosexuals) should be male because of the creative-sexual charge a muse inspires. But the more primary identification and influence surely require a same-sex figure, since so much of what one identifies with is the process of writing, its ease or difficulty, its circumstances and assumptions. For a woman it is a different scene of writing than for a man: "a woman writing thinks back through her mothers" (*Room,* p. 101). It is not as difficult as in 1928 to have a room of one's own, especially given the relative ease of divorce, abortion, contraception; nor as difficult to have £500 a year. But it is still not easy, certainly not universally easy, and even for the privileged ones internal interdictions remain, testifying to still-present social obstacles. Most critics won't accuse the woman writer of being a dancing dog, but parents, husbands, lovers, and children might well do so: "Not married yet?" "Don't write about me!" "Come home early tonight." "Let's go to bed. You can work tomorrow." "This place is a mess." "Haven't you done anything else today?" Private desires voicing institutional desiderata.

Think of being in the hall at Gorton or Newnham College where Virginia gave the lectures that make up *A Room of One's Own.* Think of the audience of English university women hearing her, with their earnest faces and their hands clasped on tweed-clad laps. One still sees their photographs in the occasional volume of memorial essays honoring a patient-faced woman scholar who might have heard the lectures. Virginia legitimized their anger; in fact she provoked it, sparing nothing to make them feel their humiliation, right down to the beef-and-prunes dinner followed by dry biscuits and water. If I am moved to tears now, what must it have been like at Oxbridge in 1928! But perhaps it was no bombshell, perhaps they knew it already, so well that there was no shock, only recognition of familiar secrets. Or, on the other hand, were they deadened to the subversiveness of Virginia's lectures; was it too late; would they *want* to know, after decades of fitting it together so carefully? Jane Harrison, classicist of Newnham, would have understood exactly what Virginia was talking about, but Harrison had died six months earlier. One has to do Virginia's audience the charity of assuming that these women scholars and writers, most of them childless and celibate, dining on dried-out roast and excluded in principle from the best libraries, did harbor resentment as they labored at their cramped desks, stubbornly turning out classics in social and economic history, medieval studies, Greek archaeology, aesthetics. One hopes that they felt resentment. And that they still do.

The other text that I am reading for the first time is Christine de Pisan's *City of Ladies,* written about 1405.[2] Like *A Room of One's Own* it is not what I expected. The work isn't after all an early feminist utopia, no anticipation of Rabelais's Abbey of Thélème or Campanella's *City of the Sun.* Christine is not interested in the nature of the state; she imagines no ideal society. Like Woolf's lectures, Christine's lengthy treatise explores the condition of the woman intellectual. Christine not only confronts and criticizes the misogynist tradition, she rewrites it, deconstructing and reconstructing the figure of woman as it appears in myth, legend, history, and religion. The city of ladies is no social plan but a literary artifact: the text itself as city. It is an audacious and imposing piece of bricolage, architectonically planned and painstakingly built from materials gathered during years of study. It is not the first collection of women's biographies: That honor belongs to the *De Claris Mulieribus* (Of Famous Women) (c. 1360) of Giovanni Boccaccio, Christine's main and nearest source. There is also Chaucer's much shorter collection, *The Legends of Good Women* (c. 1385), clearly of ironic intention. But the originality of Christine's text (despite its frequent tedium) is as a work of self-defense and self-assertion on behalf of the author's sex, a work that fulfills its own exhortation in the act of writing about writing, a text flung in the teeth of tradition in order to make it new.

In chapter 2 of *A Room of One's Own,* Virginia tells us of her morning—doubtless the distillation of many mornings—in the British Museum. Books about women, she finds, are written by men "who have no apparent qualification save that they are not women." While waiting for several volumes to come down she reflects on various things that male writers have written about women, and while pondering she draws a sketch:

> It was the face and the figure of Professor von X. engaged in writing his monumental work entitled *The Mental, Moral And Physical Inferiority of the Female Sex.* He was not in my picture a man attractive

to women. He was heavily built; he had a great jowl; to balance that he had very small eyes; he was very red in the face. His expression suggested that he was labouring under some emotion that made him jab his pen on the paper as if he were killing some noxious insect as he wrote, but even when he had killed it that did not satisfy him; he must go on killing it. (p. 31)

The sketch prompts an effort of introspection:

Had anger, the black snake, been lurking among [my emotions]? Yes, said the sketch, anger had. It referred me unmistakeably to the one book, the one phrase, which had roused the demon; it was the professor's statement about the mental, moral and physical inferiority of women. My heart had leapt. My cheeks had burnt. I flushed with anger. . . . One does not like to be told that one is naturally the inferior of a little man—I looked at the student next me—who breathes hard, wears a ready-made tie, and has not shaved this fortnight. (p. 32)

And introspection leads to analysis of its cause:

Soon my own anger was explained and done with; but curiosity remained. How explain the anger of the professors? Why were they angry? For when it came to analysing the impression left by these books there was always an element of heat. This heat took many forms; it showed itself in satire, in sentiment, in curiosity, in reprobation. But there was another element which was often present and could not immediately be identified. Anger, I called it. But it was anger that had gone underground and mixed itself with all kinds of other emotions. To judge from its odd effects, it was anger disguised and complex, not anger simple and open. (p. 32)

The opening scenario of *City of Ladies* is startlingly similar. The setting is another library, Christine's study; and her professor von X. is one Matheolus, a thirteenth-century misogynist whose *Lamentationes* had recently been translated into French. Though Christine finds the work malicious and dishonest, the book nonetheless provokes her to introspection and analysis "as a woman naturall." Why do so many men slander women? How is it that so many wise philosophers, clerics, poets, and rhetoricians have agreed in erroneous opinions about women? She knows that they are wrong but it is a long and authoritative tradition. How could God have made such an abominable creature as woman? Christine begins to doubt her own judgment and to grow depressed: "There sprang in me a grete dyspleasaunce and sorowe of courage in dyspraysynge myselfe and all womenkynde" (I.I).

The work is a *consolatio* modelled on one of Christine's favorite sources, the *De Consolatio Philosophiae* of Boethius. The confessional mode gives way to a dream-vision enclosing personification allegory—so often in medieval literature the method of choice for reestablishing the narrator's personal equanimity or resolving some dilemma. Like the Boethian text, Christine's is a theodicy, for her lack of equanimity, like that of Boethius, is at bottom doctrinal uncertainty, in this case in the question of the goodness of God's works. Christine's dream-vision encounter with three crowned ladies, Reason, Righteousness, and Justice, establishes the correct philosophical stance for thinking about women. In doing so it also restores Christine's self-confidence as woman and as writer and provides the material for the *City of Ladies*. Indeed that encounter *is* the text gradually built up as we read, each of its hundred and thirty or so stories another stone, pillar, or tile in the edifice.

The crowned ladies begin with the most urgent task: to comfort Christine, to bring her out of depression and back to herself. This they accomplish by asserting the superiority of experience to authority on this question, for Christine has forgotten that "that thou knowes is of very certayne science" (what you know is truly certain knowledge) and instead has begun to believe "that which thou felest not ne seest not ne knoweth otherwyse than by pluralyte of straunge opynyones" (what you neither feel nor see nor know except through many eccentric opinions). It is a fool who believes false sayings rather than "the certaynte of his beynge." Gold is tested in the furnace; the most important issues are the "moost debatous & most arguous." Philosophers can be wrong; poets exaggerate and tell fables; tradition is full of contradictions, so use what's valuable and leave the rest (I.2).

Lady Reason—at once Christine's own capacity for reason, and human reason generally—carries a mirror that shows everything in its true proportions and qualities. Her mission is to cheer up Christine, to destroy the misogynist error, and to establish a "cloystre of defense." For this task, she tells Christine, "the pre-rogatyve is gyven to the amonge al other women." Repeating the *aere perennius* topos, she assures Christine that this fortress will be "more durable than ony marble . . . and of perpetuall dur-ynge;" Troy, Thebes, and Amazonia fell, but this refuge must be stronger (I.4). Thus Christine, self-conscious writer of a self-re-flexive text, psychs herself up to the massive project at hand.

This accomplished, the author can proceed to justify theologi-cally her iconoclastic project. To slander women is unnatural, Reason argues, for men and women were made to love one another. Some women may be evil, but this doesn't justify blame of the sex as a whole. Woman, like man, was made by God in his image (I.9). With this use of Genesis 1:27 Christine has already begun her revision, for the usual approach was based on Genesis 2:21–23, where God creates Eve from Adam's rib, the version usually considered to prove the subordination of women. But Christine also revises this second version, arguing that if God had intended woman to be inferior he would have taken her from Adam's foot instead of his side. We begin to appreciate what Reason means when in chapter 8 she directs Christine to found the City in the Field of Scripture and to dig there with the pick of her sharp, inquisitive intellect.

As for misogynistic writers, some are old and impotent, unable to do what they'd like to do and hence urging chastity on all. Others envy the superior understanding and social rank of certain women; still others are woman-haters or, like Ovid, dissolute lechers who try to corrupt youth through their writings. So much for the forefathers of Professor von X. The field now clear of the stones that impeded her work, Christine is able to begin, depres-sion dissipated and the certainty of her being confirmed. Here perhaps is the therapeutic advantage to allegory: that it permits the externalization, the distancing of inner conflict so that the latter can be scrutinized and resolved. Virginia seems to have found a similar stability in her writing ("the one dependable thing in a world of strife, ruin, chaos"[3]), though even it couldn't finally preserve the certainty of being that would have enabled her to survive.

As might be expected, Christine exercises considerable poetic license in rewriting woman good. To be sure, tradition abounds with figures of good women, and the bulk of Christine's work repeats or expands their stories. But what about the famous bad women, who can scarcely be ignored? Here Christine's effort is not only scholarly or selective but creative: She must rethink the story from her character's point of view or provide a new story. Figures who live through the centuries as exempla of crime or vice are given new reputations, their sins or faults suppressed or reinterpreted. Medea, known as witch and as murderer of her two children by the fickle Jason (as well as murderer of her rival for Jason's love) appears twice: once as a great sorceress-technocrat and again as generous, constant lover who used her art to help Jason win the Golden Fleece. There is no mention of the children. Circe, another great manipulator of nature, is also vindicated: she justifiably transformed Odysseus's men into beasts because she thought they were hostile. Lovelorn Dido becomes an exemplum of prudence rather than of uncontrolled passion (here Christine follows Boccaccio) and Socrates' traditionally nagging wife Xantippe is a devoted, tolerant mate, to be praised for her lifelong loyalty to a difficult old man. Cleopatra is omitted, as are Cressida and Guinevere.

Reason's exposition of the nature of tradition has prepared the ground for these revisions, though she does not explicitly pose their implications. How, after all, do we know? All we know is what writers—usually men, and often clerics—have told us. What is tradition, then, if not the motives and biases of writers? Since historical reality must remain conjectural, Christine's conjecture has equal epistemological status with any other. The unreliability of *fama*—tradition, documentary authority, human communication—was the problem that Chaucer had confronted some decades earlier in *The House of Fame*. Though he was by far the better artist, he resolved the dilemma with less aplomb than did Christine.

The text has an integrated dual structure, its encyclopedic and metaphoric systems of classification neatly dovetailed. We learn first of women who have benefitted Christianity (St. Augustine's

mother, whose tears converted her son, the Virgin Mary, various
women Jesus spoke with); then of those who have exercised temporal or military rule, figures from myth, legend, and history.
With these the foundation is laid and we proceed to the City's
walls, moving from physical to intellectual prowess: women who
have excelled in the sciences, humanistic studies, arts, or crafts.
Here we find the poet Sappho, the great sorceresses Medea and
Circe, a contemporary illuminator named Anastasia, and a series
of euhemeristic culture-heroines, Minerva, Ceres, Ariadne, and
Isis, inventors of the various arts of civilization. (These last figures and the rationalistic methodology are imitated from Boccaccio.) Next comes the category of morality, presided over by Righteousness: dutiful women, chaste women, generous women.
Should the women of contemporary France be invited to inhabit
the City? Christine thinks so, for in addition to many virtuous
aristocratic women (painstakingly listed, doubtless in part a bid
for patronage), of "ladyes & gentylwomen burgeyses wyves & of
al estates there ben ynowe bothe good & fayre maulgre the evyll
sayers." So the City is built and populated. The last section belongs to Justice: It is the construction of battlements and towers,
the stories of holy women and saints. Now the City, perfect and
complete, is open to every "woman of worshyp" as a shelter from
the enemies of womanhood. The book ends with Christine's exhortation to women that they be virtuous, humble, and patient,
and with her memorable warning against seducers and depreca-
tors of the sex: woman-haters all, she says, who would entrap you
as one does a wild animal. Flee their acquaintance under whose
laughter is concealed deadly venom. Thus Christine dispatches
the vaunted "humor" of the antifeminist tradition.

It is testimony to Christine's artfulness that she assimilated an
encyclopedic collection of good-woman stories to the architectural metaphor. Yet there is a certain contradiction in this dual
structure: on one hand, the arch-medieval genre of the sprawl-
ing, arbitrarily divided compilation; on the other, the tight, self-
consciously literary-rhetorical organization that seems to herald
a renaissance aesthetic of shapely and harmonious unity. The
dual structure is perhaps emblematic of the ambivalent historical

moment when Christine wrote—that of the transition from feudalism to capitalism in Europe—and of Christine's own paradoxical consciousness. For if Christine does what the Wife of Bath imagines—

> By God! if wommen hadde writen stories,
> As clerks han withinne hir oratories—
> (693–94)

nonetheless she is no rebel, and her rationalistic revisionism goes only a short way. Why, Christine inquires, do women not occupy "the syege of pleadynge" (as lawyers, judges, and magistrates)? Reason replies that it is foolish to ask why God did not ordain women to do the offices of men and vice versa, for God "hathe gyven to every kynde such nature and inclynacion as to do his office competently." Besides, she adds, it would be inconvenient, for there there are already enough lawyers and judges! Christine believes in the innate intellectual capacity of women—their apparent deficiency is due only to limited opportunity and experience (II.27); yet nowhere does Christine propose expanded opportunity. Despite many portraits of military leaders and queens, only three women are shown actually triumphing physically over a man.[4] Nor, despite her belief in the physical strength of many women, does Christine depict the labors of peasant women or, except for the painter Anastasia, allude to the toil of the artisan or businesswoman of her own day. Hers is the courtly milieu; rarely will she step outside it. In the peroration of her book, Christine urges married women to swallow their pride. Do not disdain subjection to your husband, Christine exhorts her readers, for as God said to the prophet, those who are free fall into sin. This is the counsel of accommodation, for like her older contemporary Geoffrey Chaucer, Christine depended on the goodwill of aristocratic patrons. I don't want to imply that Christine was, underneath, a raging radical; her conservatism was doubtless sincere and, given her epoch and social position, normal. The quality of her "feminism"—if such it can be called—is consistent with renaissance Christian humanism, resembling, for example, Edmund Spenser's view of women as capable of independent moral, intellectual, even physical action, yet in the great eternal scheme of things destined for subordination to men (see Book 5 of *The Faerie Queene*).

The juxtaposition of Virginia Woolf and Christine de Pisan is one that Virginia might have found—as I have found it—engaging and disturbing, as she found other juxtapositions such as this one:

> The honorary treasurer's glance seemed to rest upon a little scrap of paper upon which were written two dull little facts which, since they have some bearing upon the question we are discussing . . . may be copied here. The first fact was that the income of the W.S.P.U. upon which Mr. Joad has based his estimate of their wealth was (in the year 1912 at the height of their activity) £42,000. The second was that: "To earn £250 a year is quite an achievement even for a highly qualified woman with years of experience." The date of that statement is 1934. . . .
>
> To take the first fact first—that is interesting because it shows that one of the greatest political changes of our times was accomplished upon the incredibly minute income of £42,000 a year. . . .
>
> But the second fact is the more startling and the more depressing of the two—the fact that now, almost 20 years, that is, after they have been admitted to the money-making professions " to earn £250 a year is quite an achievement even for a qualified woman with years of experience." (*Three Guineas,* chap. 2)

How much more startling and depressing that women writers separated not by twenty years but by half a millenium should confront the same task; how dismaying to feel the continuing truth not only in Woolf's lectures but even in Christine's long-obsolete personification allegory! Many texts of the earlier period have become, in their social dimension, historical curiosities. Anyone may be amused or instructed by Boccaccio, Chaucer, or Dante, but how many of us live with a vision of heaven and hell? Anyone may be bored by Christine's relentless recital of female excellence, but half the population of earth continues to know what it is to encounter sexism and to internalize it as self-doubt or self-destructive behavior.

Other points of contact between the two writers occur, less distressing than the similarity in their scene of writing. Both occupied a somewhat paradoxical social position, elevated and privileged but not immune from financial insecurity. Christine, daughter of an Italian scholar at the French court, was married at fifteen to a civil servant, secretary to King Charles V. Widowed at twenty-five, she was thereafter dependent upon aristocratic patrons—as vicious a crew as have ever congregated at the head of a state—in order to support herself and her children by the production of ballades, *débats,* dream-visions, and flattering biographies. Virginia, better pedigreed than Christine, was related to, and all her life moved in, circles of titled wealth. Despite her parents' comfort and status, her father constantly worried about finances in scenes that filled his daughter with rage and frustration. Virginia herself experienced periods of panic over money during the early years of her marriage when her modest patrimony was heavily depleted in medical expenses.

Both women were distinctly their fathers' daughters, and both fathers were distinguished intellectuals of international reputation. Tommasso di Benvenuto da Pizzano, physician and professor of astrology at the University of Bologna, counsellor of the Venetian Republic, was asked by King Louis I of Hungary and by Charles V of France to live at their courts; he accepted the latter invitation. Leslie Stephen was one of the foremost essayists, critics, biographers, and editors of his time, friend of Henry James, Alfred Lord Tennyson, and other eminent men. Despite his distinction, neither parent was a vanguard intellectual. Both were practitioners of dated ideas in a turbulent modern world: Tommasso of obsolete astrology amid the new Parisian nominalistic science and philosophy, Leslie Stephen "the most typical of Victorians" in an England careening toward world war ("our surroundings were at least fifty years behind the times" wrote Virginia in a 1939 memoir.) Both fathers oversaw the education of their gifted daughters; neither girl went to school, and both daughters, largely self-taught later in life, maintained an ambivalent attitude toward their early homebound education, at once appreciating its breadth relative to that of other women, and deploring its deficiencies. Interestingly, both women had brothers, whose systematic education in comparison with their own produced bitter resentment and strong opinions on the education of women, reiterated throughout the corpus of their work.

In *City of Ladies* Christine tells us that although her father did not share the common prejudice against educating daughters, her mother's objections retarded her development. Lady Righteousness tells the story:

> "Thy father that was a naturall phylosophre had not that oppynyon that women sholde not lerne letters but in so moche that he sawe the enclyned to lernynge as thou knowest well he had grete pleasure of it. And by the blame of thy moder whiche by the comune opynyon of women thou were taryed in thy youthe to entre more in the depnesse of scyences. But as the proverbe saythe, that nature gyveth maye not be taken awaye." (II.36)

May we hypothesize that this interference was responsible for the bitterer tone in an earlier version of this story, and for Christine's effacement of her biological mother there? For in *La Mutacion de Fortune* (1400), Christine mythifies her father while replacing her real mother with an allegorical figure. Her father, writes Christine in the earlier text, was a wealthy scholar who possessed two magic jewels taken from the muses' fountain on Mount Parnassus: One of them enabled him to predict the future; the other to cure maladies. Her mother was a big, strong woman, braver than the Amazon Penthesilea, superior to her father in understanding, power, and merit; indeed, she was a queen (339–46). This wondrous figure turns out to be "dame Nature," mother of us all. Although her father wishes for a son as first-born, Mother Nature wants a daughter, "a female like herself" (391). Nevertheless she makes Christine resemble her father in every way but sex: in features, manner and build, and especially in her intellectual inclinations. Here Christine bitterly denounces the "cursed custom" (437–38), so contrary to justice and to her own desire, that kept her from the full education that would have allowed her to inherit her father's jewels. Nonetheless, she did inherit some things from her father, and these she has kept to the present day.

Virginia's attitude toward her mother was very different from

Christine's. Far from effacing Julia Stephen, she worshipped her, thought and wrote of her obsessively for more than thirty years (Julia had died when Virginia was thirteen), and recreated her in the powerful figure of Mrs. Ramsay in *To the Lighthouse*. Nonetheless it was not upon Julia Stephen that Virginia modelled herself primarily but upon Leslie, with whom she always felt a special (if ambivalent) bond, whom she was considered to resemble physically, and whom from earliest childhood she imitated in her commitment to the profession of writing.

The idea of androgyny was important in the life and work of both writers, perhaps in response to strong paternal influence as well as the privileged position of men. Christine frequently wishes she had been born a man, though there is a certain irony in her remark, in *City of Ladies*, that as a woman she is less to blame for the imperfection of her work—that she'd be a better writer were she a man. Compare Virginia's cutting retort to a literary article that endorsed the inferiority of women:

> That Mr. Bennett can name fifty of the male sex who are indisputably her [Sappho's] superiors is . . . a welcome surprise, and if he will publish their names I will promise, as an act of that submission which is so dear to my sex, not only to buy their works but, so far as my faculties allow, to learn them by heart.[5]

In the *Mutacion,* Christine describes her actual transformation into a man at the hands of Fortune. The death of her husband—figured as a shipwreck—required this metamorphosis so that Christine could steer the ship herself; that is, she had to become financially self-supporting. The transformation was economic and literary at once, for Christine's self-sufficiency came through her writing. "My voice became a man's," she specifies, for through the vagaries of Fortune Christine took up her pen in her late twenties and began to earn her living as a writer, the first woman in Europe that we know to have done so. If man is the writing subject, the master of discourse, then, indeed, Christine became a man, constituted as such by circumstance and society. In another work Christine tells us that if her husband had not died she would not have been able to study (and, we may add, to write), for household occupation would have prevented her.[6]

Hence, she concludes, the reverses of Fortune can be turned to good—in this case the termination of one of those "silences" so movingly documented by Tillie Olsen.[7]

Virginia also links androgyny to writing in proposing, in *A Room of One's Own,* a theory of the androgynous creative mind. Stripped of its gender labels the theory itself seems to find some support in recent neuropsychological work on right–left brain hemisphericity. That it was put forward with gender labels, though, is as clearly due to social role-definitions—men are logical; women, intuitive—as was Christine's "mutation."

Finally, in my list of similarities, there is the architectural image in the title of both texts discussed here. Does its presence confirm the opinion of psychologists who argue, in an extension of "biology-is-destiny," that women naturally tend to imagine closed, womblike spaces? I think that there are more interesting and more accurate ways to account for the image. More accurate because one is rarely, if ever, physically conscious of one's womb as such: unlike the external genitalia or the stomach, it has few nerve endings. More interesting because the function of enclosed space in both texts is as protection, security, and shelter, so that what it points to is the socially and psychologically *embattled* scenario in which the writer locates herself.

Equally important, though, is the difference in the image, the contraction from city to room. For Christine the city is the peak of civilization, precisely the locus of protection: of the royal court, of patrons and their libraries, of economic opportunity, of relative freedom. Thus Christine approvingly cites Boccaccio's criticism of self-deprecating women who consider themselves good only to embrace men and raise children, "as if they were born in the mountains" (I.28). It is not quite a notion of rural idiocy, but it is certainly a notion of how *"Stadluft macht frei"* (city air makes free), especially for the late-medieval woman. For postromantic, postindustrial Europe, though, the city no longer walls out what is dangerous and stultifying but rather encompasses it. It is at the heart of the city—courts of law, Parliament, banks and social clubs—that Virginia finds social contradiction and the exclusion of women most vividly manifested in the robes, wigs, uniforms, ermine capes, business suits, and decorations of its inhabitants:

> Now we must fix our eyes upon the procession—the procession of the sons of educated men.
> There they go, our brothers who have been educated at public schools and universities, mounting those steps, passing in and out of those doors, ascending those pulpits, preaching, teaching, administering justice, practising medicine, transacting business, making money. It is a solemn sight always—a procession, like a caravanserai crossing a desert. Great-grandfathers, grandfathers, fathers, uncles—they all went that way, wearing their gowns, wearing their wigs, some with ribbons across their breasts, some without. . . . On what terms shall we join that procession? (*Three Guineas,* chap. 2)

There is, then, a withdrawal into the home as a general thing. Particularly for Virginia Woolf—born "of well-to-do-parents, born into a very communicative literate, letter writing, visiting, articulate, late nineteenth century world"[8]—the home is what the city was to Christine: the source of culture, social life and income. It is the space one clears for oneself, in short, the place where one can be a writer.

Thinking back—whether through mothers or fathers (and it is Proust, not Jane Austen, whom Virginia says she tries to imitate)—thinking back is one part of the story; thinking forward is another.

Christine had no mothers to think back through; no near contemporaries to use as models. Since she had only woman as object, written by men predominantly misogynistic, she must create mothers for herself: woman as mistress of discourse (the poets and scholars and rhetoricians), technique (the great sorceresses and inventors), and temporal rule (queens and military leaders). Because she must fabricate her mothers, Christine's work takes shape at a far more archaic level than that of a man confronting the sources. Her "anxiety of influence" cannot be about herself as writer only, because it is first about herself as woman. Until that effort of existential self-justification is unnecessary (rendered irrelevant by changed forms of social life), the possibility is fore-closed, as Virginia Woolf saw (or at least it is limited) to "live more than other people in the presence of . . . reality . . . to find it and collect it and communicate it to the rest of us" (*Room,* chap. 6). Until then there will always be a "Shakespeare's sister" among us: Virginia's invention (*Room,* chap. 3), whose lack of opportunity to develop her talent leads to suicide.

Equally foreclosed, for Christine, was any meaningful specula-tion about the future in general or the position of women in particular. Those who did engage in such speculation during those pre-Enlightenment centuries were heretics, and it is in the heretical sects that one sniffs the first breezes of utopian rational-ism: against war, against private property and temporal rule, anarchistic, communalistic, for free sexuality within or without marriage, for the right of women to preach and hold office. But for an orthodox Catholic, the subordination of women—like the weather or the existence of social classes—was a natural conse-quence of the Fall, to be remedied only in the afterlife; there is no paradise now.

If Christine is no utopian, Virginia is. Her social program in *Three Guineas* is abstentionism and separatism ("the Outsiders' Society"), pacifism, wages for housewives, and an open univer-sity; in "Evening over Sussex" it is automated housework. Her program for the novel was much bolder, utopian in the very best sense of that word, not impossible but merely nonexistent:

> The novel of a classless world should be a better novel than the old novel. The novelist will have more interesting people to describe—people who have had a chance to develop their humour, their gifts, their tastes, real people, not people cramped and squashed into featureless masses. ("The Leaning Tower")

There is a revision to be wished and worked at, to be imagined and embodied in texts as different as a political program and a novel. It inscribes a reality in which a Shakespeare's sister—or a Virginia Woolf—will not take her own life, but in whose presence she will want to live, "in order to achieve the prodigious effort of freeing whole and entire the work that is in [her]."

Notes

Chapter 1: Confessions of an ex-handkerchief head

1. There is a large bibliography on sexism in socialization, language, scholarly disciplines and the arts. Some samples are: *Woman in Sexist Society*, ed. Vivian Gornick and B. K. Moran (New York: Basic Books, 1971); *The Prism of Sex*, ed. Julia Sherman (Madison, WI: University of Wisconsin Press, 1979); *Liberating Women's History*, ed. Berenice A. Carroll (Urbana, IL: University of Illinois Press, 1976); Robin Lakoff, *Language and Woman's Place* (New York: Harper and Row, 1975); Katharine M. Rogers, *The Troublesome Helpmate* (Seattle, WA: University of Washington Press, 1966); Mary Ellman, *Thinking About Women* (New York: Harcourt, Brace and World, 1968); Annette Kolodny, *The Lay of the Land* (Chaptel Hill, NC: University of North Carolina Press, 1975); *Feminist Literary Criticism*, ed. J. Donovan (Lexington, KY: University Press of Kentucky, 1975); and of course Kate Millett, *Sexual Politics* (New York: Doubleday, 1970).

2. Lillian S. Robinson, *Sex, Class and Culture* (Bloomington, IN: Indiana University Press, 1978), p. 4. Her definition is evidently borrowed from Simone de Beauvoir, *The Second Sex* (New York: Knopf, 1952).

3. Of much material on the suffrage movement, I have found most useful Carrie C. Catt and Nettie R. Shuler, *Woman Suffrage and Politics* (Seattle, WA: University of Washington Press, 1926); Eleanor Flexner, *Century of Struggle* (Cambridge, MA: Belknap Press of Harvard University Press, 1959); and Aileen Kraditor, *The Ideas of the Woman Suffrage Movement 1890–1920* (New York: Columbia University Press, 1965). A few qualifications to my remarks. Michigan did not segregate its suffrage clubs, and Kraditor relates the response at the 1899 convention of the National American Woman Suffrage Association to a motion presented by a black delegate from Michigan. Appeals to racism did not always work; as Catt recounts, several southern states did not ratify the federal suffrage amendment. Sporadic efforts were made to attract women workers, especially during the period of the great textile strikes of 1909–14; but these did not succeed, based as they were on expediency (desire for a larger base) rather than on serious programmatic orientation to the needs of working women. See, beside Flexner and Kraditor, two articles by Nancy Schrom Dye in *Feminist Studies*, vol. 2, no. 2–3, and vol. 3, no. 1–2 (both 1975): "Creating a Feminist Alliance: Sisterhood and Class Conflict in the New York Women's Trade Union League, 1903–1914," and "Feminism or Unionism? The NYWTUL and the Labor Movement." Also in *Feminist Studies*, vol. 3, no. 1–2, Robin Miller Jacoby, "The Women's Trade Union League and American Feminism."

4. Carol Bacchi, "Divided Allegiances: The Response of Farm and Labour Women to Suffrage," in *A Not Unreasonable Claim: Women and Reform in Canada 1880s–1920s*, ed. Linda Kealey (Toronto: Women's Press, 1979), pp. 89–107.

5. Richard J. Evans, *The Feminist Movement in Germany 1894–1933* (London: Sage Publications, 1976), p. 258. See also Jean H. Quataert, "Unequal Partners in an Uneasy Alliance: Women and the Working Class in Imperial Germany," in *Socialist Women: European Socialist Feminism in the Nineteenth and Early Twentieth Centuries,* ed. Marilyn J. Boxer and J. Quataert (New York: Elsevier North-Holland, 1978). Quataert seems mainly concerned to boost the German Social Democratic party (SPD) at the expense of bourgeois feminism without analyzing the serious weaknesses that pushed such SPD leaders as Rosa Luxemburg and Clara Zetkin into opposition. It is significant that much of the SPD's work among women was pioneered and led by oppositionists, who constituted the Spartacist faction and eventually seceded to form the KPD (Communist party) and affiliate with the Third International. My point is that while feminism certainly can't fight effectively for women, neither can reformist social democracy. This is also shown in essays on France and Italy in the same volume: M. J. Boxer, "Socialism Faces Feminism: The Failure of Synthesis in France 1879–1914," and Claire La Vigna, "The Marxist Ambivalence Toward Women: Between Socialism and Feminism in the Italian Socialist Party."

6. David J. Mitchell, *The Fighting Pankhursts* (London: Jonathan Cape, 1967). Lenin's book *Left-Wing Communism, an Infantile Disorder* (1920), was directed partly at Sylvia (chap. 9), and she was warmly welcomed at the second Comintern Congress in Moscow that year. Cf. also Lenin's long letter to Sylvia of August 28, 1919 (*Collected Works,* vol. 29). Sylvia was expelled from the CPGB in 1921 for breach of discipline in publicly discussing internal debates, though it seems likely she would have resigned soon because of other disagreements. In "The Truth About the British Suffragettes," in *Feminist Revolution,* ed. Redstockings of the Women's Liberation Movement (New York: Random House, 1975), Faye Levine does not mention the personal and political split but refers to Sylvia as coleader with her mother and sister of the suffrage movement! Some "truth"! Sylvia's son Richard Pankhurst has published a memoir, *Sylvia Pankhurst, Artist and Crusader* (London: Paddington Press, 1979), that includes reproductions of Sylvia's drawings and paintings.

7. Richard Stites, *The Women's Liberation Movement in Russia: Feminism, Nihilism and Bolshevism 1860–1930* (Princeton, NJ: Princeton University Press, 1978); William Mandel, *Soviet Women* (New York: Anchor Books, 1975).

8. Sarachild's essay, "The Power of History," the statement of principles, and excerpts from the manifesto appear in *Feminist Revolution,* pp. 12, 205, and 82, respectively. The Attica rebels were demanding twenty-eight reforms, including improvement in general prison conditions and special demands to end race discrimination. They were crushed by order of New York Governor Nelson Rockefeller. The Alpert quotation is "I will mourn the death of 42 male supremacists no longer," and its sordid history is recounted in Alpert's memoir, *Growing Up Underground* (New York: Willima Morrow & Co., 1981).

9. Gregory J. Massell refers to the veil as not only "the most tangible publicly perceived embodiment of physical and symbolic apartheid, but . . . the very linchpin of seclusion itself." See *The Surrogate Proletariat: Moslem Women and Revolutionary Strategies in Soviet Central Asia, 1919–1929* (Princeton, NJ: Princeton University Press, 1974), p. 232. Massell gives a fascinating account of the cam-

paign against the veil, including mass unveilings at demonstrations celebrating International Women's Day in 1927, when about 10,000 women in several Uzbek cities burnt their veils. By May the number of public unveilings in Uzbekistan alone reached 90,000 (pp. 244–45).

10. Millett, *Sexual Politics*.

11. The Gilgamesh epic is available in an inexpensive Penguin version edited by N. K. Sandars. On the rivalry and gradual separation of king and temple priesthood, see F. R. Kraus, "Le Rôle des Temples depuis la Troisième Dynastie d'Ur . . . " *Journal of World History*, vol. 1, no. 3 (January 1954): 518–45, and, in the same journal, A. Falkenstein, "La Cité-Temple Sumérienne," vol. 1, no. 4 (April 1954): 784–814.

An especially interesting text in connection with sexual politics is *The Exaltation of Inanna*, ed. W. W. Hallo and J. Van Dijk (New Haven: Yale University Press, 1968). It restores to history the Sumerian poet/priestess/princess Enkeduanna and suggests some immediate political referents in Sumerian theological poetry.

12. From "Tell it like it is," *Small Press Review*, vol. 3, no. 3, cited in Suzanne Juhasz, "The Feminist Poet: Alta and Adrienne Rich," in *Feminist Criticism: Essays on Theory, Poetry and Prose*, ed. Cheryl L. Brown and Karen Olson (Metuchen, NJ: Scarecrow Press, 1978), p. 168.

Chapter 2: Flore et Jehane

1. For a collection of clerical/courtly views of women, see Joan Ferrante, *Woman as Image in Medieval Literature* (New York: Columbia University Press, 1975).

2. See chap. 5.

3. The phrase is from a brief introduction to *Flore et Jehane* by its editors Moland and d'Héricault, *Nouvelles françoises en prose du XIIIe siècle* (Paris, 1856). The *conte* was published earlier by F. Michel in 1838 and in 1842. All quotations in my text are from d'Héricault's edition; the translations are mine. The story has been translated (though not always accurately) by Eugene Mason in *Aucassin and Nicolette and Other Medieval Romances and Legends* (London: J.M. Dent and Sons Ltd., 1910). The English critic George Saintsbury described the *conte* as "a kind of version of Griselda," evidently focussing on the test-motif but ignoring Jehane's determined self-assertion; see *A Short History of French Literature* (1882), p. 120.

4. "Patriciate" is the term of Henri Pirenne: *Histoire de Belgique* (Brussels: H. Lamertin, 1909) or *Medieval Cities* (Princeton, NJ: Princeton University Press, 1925). See also: C. V. Langlois, *Histoire de France* (Paris: Hachette, 1911); Robert Fawtier, *The Capetian Kings of France* (London: Macmillan, 1960); Maurice Dobb, *Studies in the Development of Capitalism* (New York: International Publishers, 1947); Carl Stephenson, *Borough and Town: A Study of Urban Origins* (Cambridge, MA: The Medieval Academy of America, 1933); Georges Picot, *Histoire des Etats Généraux,* (2nd ed. 1888); Achille Luchaire, *Social France at the Time of Philip Augustus,* trans. E. Krehbiel (New York: H. Holt, 1912).

5. It might be objected that since men, too, can generate offspring, the author could have made the same point about bourgeoisie and royalty by giving us a

knight who becomes a bourgeois and marries a princess or a childless queen. Here emerges the story's underlying and paradoxical commitment to conventional social mores. Jehane leaves home to follow her husband and enters business to support him, thus establishing her credentials as model wife. Her reward is the fulfillment at a higher social level of woman's biological function and "moral duty," motherhood. But a knight could not honorably leave home to enter business. He would be accused of abandoning his social obligations, of greed for money, and of lack of bravery or fighting ability. Further, if there is any marginal distaste for the process of making money, the plot permits a woman to do the actual "dirty work" while, conversely, the principle of male domination is upheld in having the ruler a man.

6. Worker-artisans and petty-bourgeois would be hostile to the patriciate because the latter enriched itself at their expense and used municipal government in its own interest, frequently sacrificing the interests of less substantial producers. Class struggle frequently erupted into open war—in Flanders most notably with the widespread rebellions of 1280–81 of Flemish artisans against the urban patriciate. But our author does not concern himself with these classes—a fact that may suggest a date of composition prior to the rebellions or that may simply testify to his desire to present the patriciate in its progressive rather than its exploitive aspect.

7. As Dobb notes (*Studies*, p. 120), once the bourgeoisie won its privileges, it was quite ready to compromise with the aristocracy in business partnerships, intermarriage, political alliances and the acceptance of court and ministerial posts. Its desire for aristocratic gentility and life-style was also expressed in the purchase of estates (or portions thereof) of impoverished knights and nobles, a practice vehemently denounced in the thirteenth-century French fable, "The Lai of the Little Bird," in *Aucassin and Nicolette*, trans. E. Mason. So it is not surprising that the businesswoman Jehane keeps one foot in the lower landowning class of her origin, and that part of her income is land-rent: some from her father's estate (not inherited but won in tournaments), some forfeited by Raoul to make good his sin against Jehane, and some won by Robert also in tournaments. It is significant that our author emphasizes the tournament not as an occasion for chivalric display or military training, but as a source of income: in ransom for prisoners, in saleable horses and equipment, in wagered land that could be sold or kept for rents.

8. The motif, common in European folktale, is also found in Boccaccio's *Decameron* (IX, 2) and Shakespeare's *Cymbeline*. For other examples in medieval literature, see G. Paris, "Le Cycle de la Gageure," *Romania*, XXXII (1903), 481–551.

9. Dobb, *Studies,* p. 121. Elsewhere (pp. 92, 116 ff.) Dobb notes other examples of legislation intended for the same purpose of regulating the urban market and guild control over it. For background to this section of the chapter, see A. Abram, "Women Traders in Medieval London," *The Economic Journal,* vol. 26 (1916); Alice S. Green, *Town Life in the Fifteenth Century,* 2 vols. (Boston, 1894); Alice Clark, *Working Life of Women in the Seventeenth Century* (London: Frank Cass & Co., Ltd., 1919); Sylvia Thrupp, *The Merchant Class of Medieval London* (Ann Arbor, MI: University of Michigan Press, 1962); R. Thompson, *Women in Stuart England and America* (London: Routledge & Kegan Paul,

1974); Ivy Pinchbeck, *Women Workers and the Industrial Revolution* (London: G. Routledge & Sons, 1930); Georges Renard, *Guilds in the Middle Ages* (1918; repr. New York: A. M. Kelley, 1968). The condition, rights, and duties of peasant women in the Middle Ages is another topic entirely, with a (growing) bibliography of its own.

10. In England the silk industry was not organized into a guild, though in France it was.

11. See R. H. Tawney, *Religion and the Rise of Capitalism* (London: J. Murray, 1926); Michael Walzer, *The Revolution of the Saints* (Cambridge, MA: Harvard University Press, 1965); Edmund S. Morgan, *The Puritan Family* (Boston: Trustees of the Public Library, 1944).

12. Diane Owen Hughes, "Urban Growth and Family Structure in Medieval Genoa," *Past and Present,* vol. 66 (February 1975), pp. 3–28.

13. *Ibid.,* p. 14.

14. *Town Life,* vol. 2, p. 46.

15. Clark, *Working Life of Women,* p. 103.

16. Attempts were made to introduce the factory system in England as early as the late sixteenth century. However, until the development of mechanical power, the factory system was not sufficiently productive to make it qualitatively more profitable than cottage industry, and it was forbidden by the (predominantly aristocratic) government on the grounds that collective labor offered too much occasion for insubordination and combination by workers. Cf. Clark, *Working Life of Women,* pp. 99–100.

17. For evidence supporting my assertion about feminist historiography, see Kathleen Casey's essay, "The Cheshire Cat: Reconstructing the Experience of Medieval Women," in *Liberating Women's History,* ed. Berenice A. Carroll (Urbana, IL: University of Illinois Press, 1976).

Chapter 3: *Womanliness in* The Man of Law's Tale

1. See Bernard Duffey, "Intention and Art of the *Man of Law's Tale," ELH,* vol. 14 (1974). On other sources and antecedents see Margaret Schlauch, *"The Man of Law's Tale,"* in *Sources and Analogues of Chaucer's Canterbury Tales,* ed. W. F. Bryan and Germaine Dempster (New York: Humanities Press, 1941), pp. 155–206; Margaret Schlauch, *Chaucer's Constance and Accused Queens* (New York: New York University Press, 1927); A. H. Krappe, "The Offa–Constance Legend," *Anglia,* vol. 61 (1937): 361–69.

2. John Speirs, *Chaucer the Maker* (London: Faber and Faber, 1951), p. 135.

3. B. Huppé, *A Reading of the Canterbury Tales* (Albany: State University of New York Press, 1964), p. 95. For his complete discussion, see pp. 91–107.

4. The use of the love between man and woman as a figure for the relation between God and humanity has a long and distinguished literary tradition. Its origins are to be found in Old Testament prophetic books (particularly Hosea), in the Song of Songs, in the New Testament parable of the wise and foolish virgins, and of course in patristic interpretation of these texts. The tradition is continued in the work of many scholastic commentators and preachers, in Part III of An-

dreas Capellanus's *De Arte Honesti Amandi,* in the "Luve Ron" of Thomas de Hales, and in the "Quia Amore Langueo" group of lyrics.

5. Morton Bloomfield emphasizes this aspect of Constance in *"The Man of Law's Tale:* a Tragedy of Victimization and a Christian Comedy," *PMLA,* vol. 87 (May 1972): 384–90. Bloomfield fails, in my opinion, to reconcile the terms of his title in any unified aesthetic response.

6. All quotations from Chaucer are from *The Works of Geoffrey Chaucer,* 2nd ed., ed. F. N. Robinson (Boston: Houghton Mifflin, 1957).

7. E. T. Donaldson's phrase; cf. his essay on *Troilus and Criseyde* in *Chaucer's Poetry* (New York: Scott, Foresman & Co., 1958), pp. 965–80.

8. *De Consolatione Philosophiae,* V, prosa 6, 294–303. The translation is Chaucer's, from Robinson, *Works of Chaucer,* p. 384.

9. From *The Chronicles of Jean Froissart. In Lord Berners' Translation,* ed. Gillian and William Anderson (London: Centaur Press, 1963), p. 161.

Chapter 4: Slaying Python

1. *The Physician's Tale* is end-linked to *The Pardoner's Tale,* the two works composing a fragment (VI) that is not connected to other tales. *The Manciple's Tale* constitutes a fragment by itself (IX), with no explicit links at beginning or end, although several critics have attempted to show that it is an appropriate prelude to *The Parson's Tale.* The ms. tradition usually places *The Manciple's Tale* just before *The Parson's Tale,* but the text indicates that other material would probably have been inserted between the two; cf. *The Works of Geoffrey Chaucer,* 2nd ed., ed. F. N. Robinson (Boston: Houghton Mifflin, 1957), p. 765. (All Chaucer quotations in this chapter are taken from Robinson.) The suitability of tale to teller is also debatable for both works, although as my study of animal imagery in *The Manciple's Tale* indicates, I think there may be more tale/teller consistency for the Manciple than for the Physician. Both tales are thought to have been composed early in the Canterbury period, although dates and chronology are not firmly established.

2. Ed. Elaine Marks and Isabelle de Courtivron, *New French Feminisms* (New York: Schocken Books, 1981), p. xii.

3. Sigmund Freud, "On the Universal Tendency to Debasement in the Sphere of Love: Contributions to the Psychology of Love II" (1912), Pelican Freud Library, vol. 7. This essay has also been translated under the title "The Most Prevalent Form of Degradation in Erotic Life." The attitude has certainly left its mark in modern literature: Witness the well-known plot of the working woman seduced and abandoned by the gentleman, as in Hardy's *Tess of the D'Urbervilles,* or the gentleman's obsessive love for the brutalized working girl, as in Maugham's *Of Human Bondage.* Such affective split would be in part a reaction against the real inhibitions of "well-brought-up" young ladies, as Freud notes in "The Taboo of Virginity" (1917), as well as in the essay cited and elsewhere. Moreover, the stereotypes held by middle-class men about working-class women are not necessarily without some sociological foundation, such as the general acceptance by nineteenth-century European proletarians of common-law marriage. In the category of psychic impotence Freud includes not only physical incapacity but lack of

pleasure or difficulty in performance. He adds: "We cannot escape the conclusion that the behavior in love of men in the civilized world today bears the stamp altogether of psychical impotence" ("Tendency," p. 254).

I don't intend my use of Freud in this chapter to be construed as across-the-board endorsement of all his theories. Freud's work has its contradictions that reflect those of his epoch. Some of his work clarifies our condition; other parts, especially his theories of femininity, only further mystify it.

4. A similar motion of mind can be discerned behind *The Merchant's Tale,* with its heavy sarcasms about virtuous women and the value of wives. One can hypothesize that only a disillusioned idealist ("women are wonderful") could become so cynical ("women are terrible") without finding a realistic middle way.

5. Talbot Donaldson, "Chaucer the Pilgrim," *PMLA,* vol. 69 (1954): 928–36, reprinted in *Speaking of Chaucer* (New York: W. W. Norton & Co., 1970).

6. J. B. Severs, "Is the *Manciple's Tale* a Success?" *JEGP,* vol. 51 (1952): 1–16. The primary source is Ovid's *Metamorphoses,* II, with various details borrowed from other texts, such as the early fourteenth-century *Ovide Moralisé,* Machaut's *Le Livre du Voir Dit,* and *The Seven Sages of Rome;* cf. also Richard L. Hoffman, *Ovid and the Canterbury Tales* (Philadelphia: University of Pennsylvania Press, 1966).

7. P. R. Watts, "The Strange Case of Geoffrey Chaucer and Cecilia Chaumpaigne," *The Law Quarterly Review,* vol. 63 (1947): 491–515; T. F. T. Plucknett, "Chaucer's Escapade," *LQR,* vol. 64 (1948): 33–36. Plucknett does not rebut the earlier article but modifies it in some particulars. The release document, dated May 1380, appears in *Life Records,* ed. M. Crow and C. Olson (Oxford: Clarendon Press, 1966), p. 343. Skeat held the rape as a distinct possibility, coyly connecting it with the fact that the "Litel Lowys" whom Chaucer addresses as "my sone" in dedicating to him the *Treatise on the Astrolabe,* was ten years old in 1391; cf. *Complete Works,* ed. Walter W. Skeat (Oxford, 1894), vol. 1.

8. Robinson, *Works of Chaucer,* p. xxiii.

9. Russell Krauss, in *Three Chaucer Studies,* ed. Carleton Brown (London: Oxford University Press, 1932), part 1, chaps. 1, 2, and 9. The heraldic argument about Thomas Chaucer had already been made in the 1880s but had been rejected on grounds of Victorian morality. George Williams, *A New View of Chaucer* (Durham, NC, 1965), suggests that Chaucer knowingly did John of Gaunt the favor of marrying Philippa, whose first child, Elizabeth, was supported all her life in a convent by John. Williams successfully recreates the (rather unsavory) atmosphere of ruling circles in Chaucer's London, but many of his literary interpretations are in my view vitiated by a dogged *roman-à-clef* method. In *The Life and Times of Chaucer* (New York, 1977), John Gardner seems to accept the liaison between John and Philippa but not any effects (offspring); he also finds it hard to accept the continuation of the affair six years after the marriage with Chaucer, when the conception of Thomas would have occurred.

10. In "Imaginary and Symbolic in Lacan: Marxism, Psychoanalytic Criticism, and the Problem of the Subject," *Yale French Studies,* vols. 55–56 (1977); 338–95, Fredric Jameson notes "the taboo on biographical criticism" and the necessity "to have a closer look at the ideological function of that taboo." The kind of biographical criticism Jameson envisions would understand the author's life less as

"a cause . . . that . . . would explain the text" than as "a text on the level with the other literary texts of the writer in question and susceptible of forming a larger corpus of study with them," a criticism to take account of "the specificity of those registers of a text in which authorial wish-fulfillment . . . is deliberately foregrounded" (p. 340, n. 4). Donald Howard insists on the authorial presence in Chaucer's work: "Chaucer the Man," *PMLA,* vol. 80 (1965): 337–43.

11. For Augustine's life-long attention to the Pauline corpus, see Peter Brown, *Augustine of Hippo* (Berkeley, CA: University of California Press, 1967). The dualism I refer to here is obviously not the one distinctive of Manichaeanism (two creative principles) but more generally that of the mind–body split that for Western philosophy probably originated in Orphism; cf. Alban D. Winspear, *The Genesis of Plato's Thought* (New York: Russell & Russell, 1940). On Augustine's verbal epistemology and his expression of it in rhetorical terminology, see Marcia Colish's study (primarily of the *Confessions*) in *The Mirror of Language* (New Haven, CT: Yale University Press, 1968).

12. *City of God,* trans. Marcus Dods (New York: Random House, 1950), XII:27.

13. *Ibid.,* XI:18.

14. *Ibid.,* XI:28.

15. Brown, *Augustine of Hippo,* p. 63. Augustine's statement has the virtue (or rather, advantage) of letting the incest-wish show through less obscurely than is usually the case.

16. The quotation is from an interview with a young rapist, in Nancy Gager and Cathleen Schorr, *Sexual Assault: Confronting Rape in America* (New York: Grosset & Dunlap, 1976), p. 215.

17. The *Ovide Moralisé,* an anonymous allegorization of the *Metamorphoses* that Chaucer is known to have used in numerous works, says, *"Par Phitoun . . . /Est li diables entendus"* ("By Python . . . is the devil understood [meant]") (I:2665). Phebus is Christ, who fights the devil for man's salvation, and the Pythian games are glossed as the continual moral struggle necessary to resist diabolical assaults; cf. *Ovide Moralisé,* ed. C. de Boer (Amsterdam, 1915). A fourteenth-century Latin prose redaction of this same material says, *"Serpens significat carnem que veneno deliciarum suarum premit et occupat totum mundum"* ("The serpent signifies the flesh which with its venom of pleasures oppresses and invades the world"); cf. *Petrus Berchorius Reductorium morale (Ovidius Moralizatus) . . . a magistro Thoma Walleys . . . explanata* (Utrecht: Rijksuniversiteit, 1962), p. 40.

18. The *Ovide Moralisé,* taking up the old exegetical tradition of Christ as lover (also a conventional theme in Middle English lyric), gives this interpretation of the murder: Phebus is divine sapience who loves our humanity so long as it holds the right way without envy, pride, or avarice. But when the soul joins itself to the devil, angering its loyal lover, then God punishes it. When the soul repents, God is reconciled with it (II:2549 ff).

19. L. Bayard, "Pytho-Delphes et la légende du serpent," *Revue des Études Grècques,* vol. 56 (1943): 25–28.

20. Jane E. Harrison, *Epilegomena to the Study of Greek Religion and Themis: A Study of the Social Origins of Greek Religion* (Cambridge, 1912 and 1921, respectively; repr. together New York: University Books, 1962), p. 396. My scenario in these paragraphs is necessarily condensed and schematic; it is indebted to various sources, among them J. E. Harrison; Gilbert Murray, *Five Stages of*

Greek Religion (Oxford: Clarendon Press, 1925); Nicholas Hammond, *A History of Greece to 322 B.C.* (London: Oxford University Press, 1959, 1967); Eva M. Sanford, *The Mediterranean World in Ancient Times* (New York: The Ronald Press, 1951); W. K. C. Guthrie, *The Religion and Mythology of the Greeks*, vol. 2, chap. 40 of *The Cambridge Ancient History* (Cambridge: The Cambridge University Press, 1961); R. A. Crossland, *Immigrants from the North*, vol. 1, chap. 27 of *CAH*. Joseph Fontenrose's *Python* (Berkeley, CA: University of California Press, 1959), strictly synchronic, was not useful for my purpose here.

21. It is relevant, if tangential, to the present essay, to relate this history to the theory of the anthropologist Lewis Morgan, adapted by F. Engels in *The Origin of the Family, Private Property and the State*, to the effect that the purpose of monogamy was to ensure undisputed transmission of the father's private property. Cf. Engels, "The Monogamous Family" in *Origin* (New York: International Publishers, 1942), p. 55.

22. Harrison, *Epilegomena . . . ,* p. 468. Guthrie emphasizes the syncretic nature of Greek religion, stressing that we must not expect to find two sharply defined, mutually exclusive, competing yet historically coexistent sects, chthonic versus Olympian. "Yet," he continues, "the two contrasting elements remain, seeming to form as it were the warp and woof of the fabric upon which, in later centuries, was embroidered the intricate and many-colored pattern of Greek religion" (*Religion and Mythology of the Greeks*, p. 5).

23. "Phallogocentric" is the coinage of Jacques Derrida in "The Purveyor of Truth," *Yale French Studies*, vol. 52 (1975), where it is used ("phallogocentric transcendentalism") to describe the privileged locus of the privileged signifier, the phallus, in the work of Jacques Lacan. Given the Gnostic assault on the Judaeo-Christian concept of a jealous god, and its valorization of self-knowledge, it isn't surprising that some Gnostic texts maintain the archaic meaning of the serpent; cf. "The Hypostasis of the Archons" (in which the prelapsarian snake appears as "the Female Spiritual Principle . . . the Instructor") and "The Testimony of Truth," in *Nag Hammadi Library* (San Francisco, CA: Harper & Row, 1977). The Gnostic Ophites, who were a serpent cult, wrote: "Our bowels, thanks to which we nourish ourselves and live, do they not reproduce the form of the serpent?" Cited in Jean Doresse, *The Secret Books of the Egyptian Gnostics* (London: Hollis & Carter, 1960).

24. See "Cinderella" and "The Three Little Birds" in *Grimm's Fairy Tales* (complete ed., New York: Grosset & Dunlap, 1944); Stith Thompson's lists of speaking birds and helpful birds in the *Motif Index*, B 211.3 ff and B 450 ff.; the Arab tale of the bird named Hamah, narrated in the Koran (Sale ed., London, 1888, p. 16); or Munro Leaf's *Watchbird* series of children's books from the late 1930s ("This is a watchbird watching a nailbiter. This is a watchbird watching you. Are you a nailbiter?")

25. A rapid survey of Chaucer "phallic criticism" (I borrow Mary Ellmann's phrase) shows that D. W. Robertson (*A Preface to Chaucer*), B. Huppé (*A Reading of the Canterbury Tales*) and Robert C. Burlin (*Chaucerian Fiction*) ignore *The Manciple's Tale*. Donaldson's edition of the poetry has a scanty paragraph in its 120 pages of commentary; it does barely more than summarize the plot. John H. Fisher's *Complete Works* mentions Ovid and quarrels among pilgrims, little else. Severs ("Is the *Manciple's Tale* a Success?") saw "a warning

against jangling" as the tale's "central thesis," its moral that even the best of husbands with the worst of wives will act as Phebus does! Donald Howard *(The Idea of the Canterbury Tales)* skips over the murder and also seems to accept the crow as the real center of the story. The most offensively sexist criticism of the tale is, to my mind, that of William Cadbury, "Manipulation of Sources and the Meaning of the *Manciple's Tale," Philological Quarterly*, vol. 43 (1964): 538–548. Following Severs, Cadbury offers this melodrama: The crow becomes "a loving and moral being who does his best for truth;" the action is not felt tragically because it is "of no account;" and the real victim is none other than Phebus: "We know that Phebus, in killing his wife and in his subsequent self-laceration, is the *victim* of two very *natural* and very *human* impulses. . . . " (My italics.) Such a critic would more suitably narrate than interpret the tale.

A happy exception to the consensus is Britton J. Harwood, "Language and the Real: Chaucer's Manciple," *Chaucer Review*, vol. 6 (1972): 268–79. Harwood sees the tale as "a covert indictment in which the Manciple sneers at those who can be distracted from empirical reality by language, which creates a bogus reality of its own. . . . Those who listen to the word rather than see the thing are gullible." The interpretation applies to Chaucer's modern as well as his medieval audience.

26. Arlyn Diamond, "Chaucer's Women and Women's Chaucer," in *The Authority of Experience*, ed. A. Diamond and Lee R. Edwards (Amherst, MA: University of Massachusetts Press, 1977). In the same volume and along similar lines, the essay by Maureen Fries, " 'Slydynge of Corage': Chaucer's Criseyde as Feminist and Victim," lets Criseyde off the hook, exempting her—and, implicitly, why not all women in Chaucer's time and ours?—from criticism by presenting her lack of moral strength as the "almost inevitable result" of a culture that emphasizes the weakness of women. Elsewhere, in "The Portrayal of Women by Chaucer and His Age," in *What Manner of Woman*, ed. Marlene Springer (New York: New York University Press, 1977), Ann Haskell writes that the rapist-knight of *The Wife of Bath's Tale* "yields totally to the superiority of a woman and of women," neglecting to add that this yielding gets the knight exactly what he wants, and on the most sexist, snobbish terms; it also in effect rewards him for the rape committed at the beginning of the story.

27. Paul de Man, "Criticism and Crisis," in *Aesthetics Today*, ed. M. Philipson and Paul Gudel (Cleveland: World Pub. Co., 1961), p. 344.

28. Jonathan Culler, "Apostrophe," *Diacritics*, vol. 7, no. 4 (Winter, 1977): 59–69.

29. *A General Introduction to Psychoanalysis*, 21st lecture, trans. Joan Rivière (New York: Washington Square Press, 1924, 1966), p. 336.

Chapter 5: Sexual economics, Chaucer's Wife of Bath, and The Book of Margery Kempe

1. Chaucer quotations are from F. N. Robinson, *The Works of Geoffrey Chaucer*, 2nd ed. (Boston: Houghton-Mifflin, 1957). Robinson notes that "the reputation of the cloth made in Bath was not of the best."

2. On marriage settlements in fourteenth- and fifteenth-century England, see Paul Murray Kendall, *The Yorkist Age* (New York: W. W. Norton Co., 1962), chap. 10; Edith Rickert, *Chaucer's World* (New York: Columbia University Press, 1948), chap. 2; H. S. Bennett, *The Pastons and Their England* (Cambridge; University Press, 1922), chap. 4.

3. A chronology of Margery Kempe's life and times, together with the evidence for these dates, is provided in the edition by S. B. Meech and Hope E. Allen (London, 1940; EETS o.s. 212, vol. 1).

4. Only with the Reformation was the city's name changed to King's Lynn. For much of the following information about Lynn, I am indebted to Alice S. Green, *Town Life in the Fifteenth Century* (Boston, 1894), 2 vols.

5. *Ibid.*, vol. 1, pp. 277–78.

6. Nearly a century later, feelings still ran high. Richard Dowbigging's account of a confrontation between the bishop and the mayor of Lynn concludes: "And so then the Bishop and his squires rebuked the mayor of Lynn, and said that he had shamed him and his town forever, with much other language, etc. . . . And so at the same gate we came in we went out, and no blood drawn, God be thanked." Item 200 in *The Paston Letters*, ed. John Warrington (London, 1924; Everyman ed. no. 752), 2 vols.

7. For the convenience of readers not familiar with Middle English I have taken quotations from the modernized edition of W. Butler-Bowden (London: Jonathan Cape, 1954).

8. In the introduction to the Bowden edition, p. xx.

9. F. Engels, *The Origin of the Family, Private Property, and the State* (New York: International Publishers, 1942), pp. 65–66.

10. See H. E. Allen's "Prefatory Note" and textual notes to the Meech-Allen edition.

11. Karl Marx and Friedrich Engels, *Manifesto of the Communist Party*, in *Collected Works* (London: Lawrence & Wishart, 1976), vol. 6, pp. 486–87.

12. On the creative power of money, see Karl Marx, "The Power of Money in Bourgeois Society," in *Economic and Philosophic Manuscripts of 1844* (Moscow: Foreign Languages Publishing House, 1961), pp. 136–41.

13. Beryl Rowland, "On the Timely Death of the Wife of Bath's Fourth Husband," *Archiv*, vol. 209 (1972).

14. "I shall suddenly slay thy husband" (p. 27). In the manuscript a marginal note inserts after "slay" the phrase "the fleshly lust in." this scribal insertion seems gratuitous, and especially unjustified in view of the contents of the next chapter. There Margery's husband poses a conundrum: If he were forced under pain of death to "commune naturally" with Margery, would she consent, or see him killed? Her answer: "I would rather see you being slain, than that we should turn again to our uncleanness" (p. 30). A few lines further on, Margery says, "I told you nearly three years ago that ye should be slain suddenly. . . . " Clearly, she is speaking of her husband's life, not his lust. Meech also believes that the emendation is "quite wrong."

15. Cited in the Meech-Allen edition, p. 261.

16. From the introduction to Marx's *Contribution to the Critique of Hegel's*

Philosophy of Right, in *Marx and Engels on Religion* (New York: Schocken Books, 1964). Emphasis in original.

Chapter 6: Sex and politics in Pope's Rape of the Lock

1. Cleanth Brooks, "The Case of Miss Arabella Fermor," in *The Well-Wrought Urn* (New York: Harcourt, Brace, 1947).
2. Pope's letters are quoted from the *Correspondence,* ed. George Sherburn (Oxford: Clarendon Press, 1956), vol. 1. There is some possibility that the congratulatory letter to Fermor was contrived especially for Pope's edition of his own letters (1737), in which it first appeared. The letter is not dated; there is no authority for it besides Pope's own edition; and other incidents show that Pope was never above such conscious manipulation of his public image. Although it is beyond the scope of this chapter to discuss the psychoanalytic aspects of Pope's attitude toward women, the paragraph quoted offers rich material for such a discussion.
3. *Epistle to Dr. Arbuthnot,* lines 201–202.
4. For a summary of these laws and their effect on Pope and his family, see A. Beljame, *Men of Letters and the English Public in the Eighteenth Century* (London: K. Paul, Trench, Trubner, 1948), pp. 373–75.
5. The text of *The Rape of the Lock* is quoted from the Twickenham edition, vol. 2, ed. Geoffrey Tillotson (London: Methuen, 1940; 3rd ed., 1962).
6. *An Essay on Criticism,* part II, lines 201–14.
7. *Windsor Forest,* lines 393–96.
8. J. H. Plumb, *England in the Eighteenth Century* (Baltimore: Penguin, 1950), p. 17.
9. *An Essay on Man,* epistle II, lines 265–66.
10. This excerpt from the anonymous *The Mall: or, the Reigning Beauties* (1709) appears in the Twickenham edition of *The Rape of the Lock,* Appendix A.
11. *Moral Essays,* epistle II, lines 213–14.
12. *Ibid.,* lines 263–68.
13. *An Essay on Man,* epistle I, lines 285–86.
14. For discussion of the radical attitude toward these events, see Carl B. Cone, *The English Jacobins: Reformers in Late Eighteenth-Century England* (New York: Scribner, 1968).
15. This is not, of course, to imply that sexism is unique to capitalist economy; rather that sexism in any society is an institutionalized attitude that helps to preserve an oppressive system.

Chapter 7: Red Rosa

1. V. I. Lenin, "Notes of a Publicist," in *Collected Works,* vol. 33 (Moscow: Progress Publishers, 1973), p. 210.
2. The major texts are as follows: *Lettres à Karl et Luise Kautsky,* trans. Nadine Stchoupak and A. M. Bracke-Desrousseaux (Paris: Presses Universitaires de Paris, 1970); Paul Froelich, *Rosa Luxemburg: Her Life and Work,* newly trans. Johanna Hoornweg (New York: Monthly Review Press, 1972); Robert Looker,

ed., *Rosa Luxemburg: Selected Political Writings* (London: Jonathan Cape, 1972); Horace B. Davis, ed., *The National Question: Selected Writings by Rosa Luxemburg* (New York: Monthly Review Press: 1976); Rosa Luxemburg, *The Industrial Development of Poland,* trans. Tessa deCarlo (New York: Campaigner Publications, 1977); Stephen E. Bronner, ed. and trans., *The Letters of Rosa Luxemburg* (Boulder, CO.: Westview Press, 1978); Elzbieta Ettinger, ed. and trans., *Comrade and Lover: Rosa Luxemburg's Letters to Leo Jogiches* (Cambridge, MA: MIT Press, 1979).

Other, earlier texts mentioned are J. P. Nettl, *Rosa Luxemburg,* 2 vols. (London: Oxford University Press, 1966); Bertram D. Wolfe, ed., *The Russian Revolution and Leninism or Marxism?* (Ann Arbor, MI: The University of Michigan Press, 1961).

For further background, see Werner Thönnessen, *The Emancipation of Women: The Rise and Decline of the Women's Movement in German Social Democracy 1863-1933* (Bristol, England: Pluto Press, 1973); Eric Waldman, *The Spartacist Uprising of 1919* (Milwaukee, WI: Marquette University Press, 1958); Peter Gay, *The Dilemma of Democratic Socialism* (New York: Columbia University Press, 1952); Carl Schorske, *German Social Democracy 1905-1917* (New York: J. Wiley, 1955); Jean H. Quataert, *Reluctant Feminists in German Social Democracy, 1885-1917* (Princeton, NJ: Princeton University Press, 1979); Karen Honeycutt, "Clara Zetkin: A Left-wing Socialist and Feminist in Wilhelmian Germany" (Ph.D. diss., Columbia University, 1975).

3. Rosa Luxemburg to Hans Diefenbach, letter dated 3/8/17, in Bronner, *Letters,* p. 185.

4. The quotation is from Konrad Schmidt, a follower of Bernstein, cited in Rosa Luxemburg, *Reform or Revolution* (New York: Pathfinder Press, 1970), p. 20.

5. V. I. Lenin, *Imperialism, the Highest Stage of Capitalism,* in *Collected Works* (Moscow: Progress Publishers, 1974), vol. 22.

6. Luxemburg, *Reform or Revolution,* p. 8.

7. *Ibid.,* p. 56.

8. Herbert Marcuse, *Counter-Revolution and Revolt* (Boston: Beacon Press, 1972), pp. 55-57, 132.

9. Looker, *Luxemburg . . . Writings,* p. 35.

10. Rosa Luxemburg, "Either/Or," in Looker, p. 212.

11. Letter to Jogiches, dated 5/1/1899, in Bronner, p. 76.

12. Honeycutt, p. 249.

13. Letter to Mathilde Jacob, dated 11/10/15; in Bronner, p. 165.

14. Letter to Luise Kautsky, undated (mid-August 1911); in Bronner, p. 145.

15. Letter to Mathilde Wurm, dated 2/16/17; in Bronner, pp. 179-80.

16. Cited in Quataert, *Reluctant Feminists,* p. 215.

17. Letter to Hans Diefenbach, dated 1/7/17, in Bronner, p. 174.

18. Letter to Sonja Liebknecht, dated 5/2/17, in Bronner, p. 203.

19. Letter to Robert and Mathilde Seidel, dated 23 June 1898; excerpted in Froelich, p. 39.

20. Letter to Mathilde Wurm, dated 12/28/16; in Bronner, p. 173.

21. Letter to Hans Diefenbach, dated 6/29/17, in Bronner, p. 217.

22. Rosa Luxemburg, "The Old Mole" (May 1917); in Looker, p. 227.
23. Rosa Luxemburg, "The Russian Tragedy" (September 1918); in Looker, p. 235.
24. "Old Mole," in Looker, p. 234.
25. Froelich, chaps. 13 and 14.
26. Wolfe, "Introduction," pp. 1–24.
27. *Ibid.,* "The Russian Revolution," p. 29.
28. Georg Lukacs, "Critical Observations on Rosa Luxemburg's 'Critique of the Russian Revolution,' " in *History and Class Consciousness* (Cambridge, MA: MIT Press, 1971), pp. 276–77.
29. Rosa Luxemburg, "The Russian Revolution" (1918), in Wolfe, pp. 34–35, 38.
30. Nettl, *Rosa Luxemburg,* vol. 1, p. 14.
31. Lukacs, "Critical Observations," pp. 272–94.
32. Lukacs, "The Marxism of Rosa Luxemburg," in *History and Class Consciousness,* p. 44.
33. *Ibid.,* Preface, p. xx.
34. *Ibid.,* p. x.
35. Rosa Luxemburg, "Order Reigns in Berlin" (January 14, 1919); in Looker, p. 306.

Chapter 8: Women, culture, and revolution in Russia

1. "Art and Politics in Our Epoch," in *Leon Trotsky on Literature and Art,* ed. Paul N. Siegel (New York: Pathfinder Press, 1970), p. 109. I have used Zamyatin's phrase somewhat differently than he intended it. In "On Literature, Revolution, Entropy and Other Matters" (1923), Zamyatin writes of entropy as a "hereditary sleeping sickness" afflicting most of mankind and whose effect on artists is to leave them content with what they have already done: It is an aesthetic, not a political, category.
2. Cited by Richard Stites, "Women and the Russian Intelligentsia: Three Perspectives," in *Women in Russia,* ed. D. Atkinson *et al.* (Stanford, CA: Stanford University Press, 1977), p. 52. Zalkind was professor at Sverdlov University and founder of the Society of Marxist Psychoneurologists. The extreme conservatism and philistinism of his views is representative neither of Marxism nor of Freud's work (though there has been no shortage of conservatives or philistines associated with either movement). See also David Jorawsky, "The Construction of the Stalinist Psyche," in *Cultural Revolution in Russia 1928–1931,* ed. Sheila Fitzpatrick (Bloomington, IN: Indiana University Press, 1978), pp. 105–28.
3. In Gleb Struve, *Soviet Russian Literature 1917–50* (Norman, OK: University of Oklahoma Press, 1951), p. 118.
4. Xenia Gasiorowska, *Women in Soviet Fiction 1917–1964* (Madison, WI: University of Wisconsin Press, 1968), p. 256. For a detailed study of the dissolution of RAPP in context of general state control of literature, see Chaké Der Melkonian-Minassian: *Politiques Littéraires en URSS* (Montreal: Les Presses de l'Université du Québec, 1978). The head of RAPP, L. Averbach, got off relatively easily at first (denunciation and exile) because his uncle, Yagoda, was head of Security. After his uncle's fall in 1937, Averbach

was shot as a traitor. With rather remarkable naiveté Katerina Clark suggests that the dissolution of RAPP had as its selfless motivation "to halt RAPP's persecution of independent writers' groups . . . ; not to oppress the literary profession but to rid it of ugly and counterproductive faction fighting"; see "Little Heroes and Big Deeds: Literature Responds to the First Five-Year Plan," in Fitzpatrick, *Cultural Revolution,* p. 204.

5. See discussion and an analysis of the play by Spencer E. Roberts, *Soviet Historical Drama* (Hague: M. Nijhoff, 1965).

6. In "Such a Simple Thing" (also 1924), Lavrenev gives another variant on the theme of desire and necessity, permitting his hero a great deal more ambivalence then even Maryutka. The hard-nosed young Orlov, Cheka commissar and intelligence agent, trying to save an unjustly arrested peasant from torture at the hands of Whites, foolishly jeopardizes himself, is outwitted by a clever White officer, and captured. Before going to his execution, Orlov at first declines, then accepts, the handshake of an honorable White Officer who has unsuccessfully interviewed him. The story appears in an anthology of the same title. "The Forty-first" is quoted throughout from *The October Storm and After* (Moscow: Progress Publishers, 1967).

7. Statistic from Edgar O'Ballance, *The Red Army* (New York: F. A. Praeger, 1964), p. 61. Their motive was patriotism: to defend the homeland against foreign invasion. The question of ex-czarist officers provoked one of the earliest Stalin–Trotsky confrontations. At Tsaritsyn, where toward the end of 1917 Stalin was senior political commissar, he ordered the removal of former czarist officers serving the Red Army. Trotsky, as commissar of war, demanded and obtained from Lenin Stalin's transfer to the Ukraine. In Lavrenev's *Wind* (1924) the Red Army man does recruit an enemy officer.

8. Quotations and pages are taken from a French version, *L'Avenir est à Nous!* (Geneva, Switzerland: Jeheber, 1944); my translations.

9. Both stories in *Stout Heart and Other Stories,* trans, and ed. D. L. Fromberg (Moscow, 1943).

10. On Bolshevik educational and cultural policies, see Sheila Fitzpatrick, *The Commissariat of Enlightenment* (Cambridge: Cambridge University Press, 1970).

11. Both quotations from Richard Stites, *The Women's Liberation Movement in Russia* (Princeton, NJ: Princeton University Press, 1978), pp. 339–40. Further on Zhenotdel, see Robert H. McNeal, "The Early Decrees of Zhenotdel" in *Women in Eastern Europe and the Soviet Union,* ed. Tova Yedlin (New York: F. A. Praeger, 1980), pp. 75–86.

12. For Bolshevik attitudes toward Proletkult, see Fitzpatrick, *Commissariat;* Lenin's 1920 speech "On the Tasks of the Youth Leagues" in *Collected Works* (Moscow: Progress Publications, 1974), vol. 31; Trotsky, *Literature and Revolution* (Ann Arbor, MI: University of Michigan Press, 1960).

13. "Fast Freight," in *An Anthology of Russian Literature in the Soviet Period,* trans. and ed. B. G. Guerney (New York: Random House, 1960). The philandering Toutkov in *The Future Is Ours!* (1927) is described as an "office Romeo," "a Lovelace," and there is the very Balzacian story of the old painter in the same novel.

14. On the relation between the two notions, see Stanley Mitchell, "From

Shklovsky to Brecht," *Screen,* vol. 15, no. 2 (Summer, 1974): 74–81, and reply by Ben Brewster in the same issue.

15. Luke's article appears in *Through the Glass of Soviet Literature,* Ernest J. Simmons, ed. (New York: Columbia University Press, 1953), pp. 27–28. In the thirty years since Luke wrote, a wide variety of other material—memoirs, sociological studies, party documents—has become available to sovietologists. Nonetheless, literature retains its illustrative value.

Not all scholars consider the Stalinist policies on women and family to be a reversal. Beatrice B. Farnsworth argues that the legislation of the 1930s "represented not a reversal of policy but rather the triumph of certain traditionalist strains within Bolshevism that had been strong throughout the 1920's"; see "Bolshevik Alternatives and the Soviet Family: The 1926 Marriage Law Debate," in *Women in Russia,* ed. Atkinson, p. 139. In the same volume, Gail Warshofsky Lapidus writes in a similar vein: "Revolutionary change in the USSR has brought not a total rupture with the past but a partial assimilation and even reintegration of prerevolutionary attitudes and patterns of behavior that are not merely 'bourgeois remnants' destined to evaporate in the course of further development but defining features of a distinctive political culture" (p. 117). She develops this approach in *Women in Soviet Society* (Berkeley, CA: University of California Press, 1978). What both ignore, I believe, is the decisive nature of the fact that "traditional strains" were unable to triumph during the period of Lenin's leadership. That they triumphed later is precisely the reversal. Lapidus seems to me needlessly pessimistic: Prerevolutionary attitudes will not evaporate, of course, but there is reason to think that they can be overthrown.

Stites claims that "a clear understanding of social history is impeded by the traditional obeisance to the year 1917 as a watershed" (*Women's Liberation,* p. xix) and manages even to find a "positive" side to the puritanism of the 1930s: to stabilize society via the family. To be sure this was one of its purposes, as Trotsky noted in *The Revolution Betrayed* (London: Faber and Faber, 1937). Nonetheless the massive evidence of Stites's superb study supports both the view of 1917 as a watershed, and the retrograde effect of Stalinist family legislation.

The "continuity thesis" is scrutinized and challenged by Stephen F. Cohen, "Bolshevism and Stalinism," in *Stalinism: Essays in Historical Interpretation,* ed. Robert C. Tucker (New York: W. W. Norton & Co., 1977), pp. 3–29.

16. Gasiorowska, *Women in Soviet Fiction,* p. 156. See also Luke, as above, and Vera S. Dunham, "The Strong-Woman Motif" in Cyril Black, *The Transformation of Russian Society* (Cambridge, MA: Harvard University Press, 1960), pp. 459–83, for the extension of the theme into post-Stalin literature.

17. February 23 was the date in Russia, which at that point kept the Julian calendar, thirteen days behind the Western or Gregorian calendar. The Soviet government adopted the Western calendar in February 1918, so that the date of IWD is now March 8 everywhere. I stress the proletarian origins of the day in order to counterpose it to the "sisterhood" celebration that tends to be typical of North American feminists, and to the "sentimental Soviet version of Mother's Day" into which IWD has been metamorphosed in Soviet children's books; cf. Mollie Schwartz Rosenhan, "Images of Male and Female in Children's Readers," in *Women in Russia,* ed. Atkinson, p. 302.

18. For an overview of conditions of female labor, see Rose L. Glickman, "The Russian Factory Woman, 1880–1914" in *Women in Russia*, ed. Atkinson, pp. 63–83. A detailed account of the 1917 events is Trotsky's three-volume *History of the Russian Revolution*, available in editions from Gollancz (London, 1965) and the University of Michigan Press (Ann Arbor, 1960).

19. On nineteenth-century women radicals, see Nina Selivanova, *Russia's Women* (New York: Dutton, 1923, repr. Westport, Conn: Hyperion Press, 1976), chaps. 9–11; the documentary collection by Barbara A. Engel and Clifford N. Rosenthal, *Five Sisters: Women Against the Tsar* (New York: Knopf, 1975); Stites, *Women's Liberation*, chaps. 1–6, and "Women," in Atkinson, ed.; Robert H. McNeal, "Women in the Russian Radical Movement," *Journal of Social History*, vol. 5 (Winter, 1971–72); 143–63.

20. Stites, *Women's Liberation*, pp. 227–28.

21. Trotsky, *My Life* (New York: Pathfinder Press, 1970), p. 474. There is a curious and perverse tendency among some feminist scholars to label as "feminist" socialist women who not only would have rejected the term indignantly but who spent their lives opposing feminism. I have in mind, for instance, Barbara E. Clements's biography of Alexandra Kollontai, *Bolshevik Feminist* (Bloomington, IN: Indiana University Press, 1979), and Beatrice Farnsworth's "Bolshevism, the Woman Question and Aleksandra Kollontai," in *Socialist Women*, ed. Marilyn J. Boxer and Jean Quataert (New York: Elsevier North-Holland, 1978). In the latter volume, the editors write: "Socialist women in imperial Germany . . . vehemently rejected the label 'feminist' . . . not only to distinguish themselves from middle-class 'women's righters' but to emphasize their adherence to the *workers'* struggle for liberation. To us, however, these German socialists appear decidedly feminist" (p. 6)! Claire LaVigna, writing of Anna Kuliscioff, a founder of the Italian Socialist party, refers to Kuliscioff's commitment to socialism over feminism as "ambivalence" (*ibid.*, p. 149).

22. Stites, *Women's Liberation*, p. 307 for both quotations. I am indebted to Stites for much of the information in this section of my book.

23. *Ibid.*, part 4; Lapidus, *Women*, chap. 2; Fitzpatrick, *Commissariat*, on educational reform; H. Kent Geiger, *The Family in Soviet Russia* (Cambridge, MA: Harvard University Press, 1968); *The Family in the USSR, Documents and Readings*, ed., Rudolf Schlesinger (London: Routledge & Kegam Paul, 1949).

24. Schlesinger has a section on "Soviet Justice and Administration in their fight for the emancipation of women in the Soviet East." Also in Schlesinger, cf. the speech of D. I. Yefimov, Health Commisar for the Ukraine at a 1927 conference of gynecologists: "Fighting abortion means replacing it by contraception. . . . At present, the production and sale of contraceptives is left to private speculators and quacks. Contraceptives are sold in the streets like any other commodity, without medical control" (p. 183).

25. On women in the Imperial Army, see Stites, *Women's Liberation*, pp. 278–81. Stites tells the story of the well-known soldier Maria Bochkareva, founder in 1917 of the Women's Battalions, some members of which defended the Winter Palace against the Bolsheviks on October 25. Bochkareva travelled in the United States with Mrs. Pankhurst on a patriotic speaking tour, and wound up with the Whites during the civil war. On the Red Army, see Leonard Schapiro, "The Birth

of the Red Army," and Col. E. Lederry, "The Red Army During the Civil War," both in *The Soviet Army,* ed. B. H. Liddell Hart (London: Weidenfeld and Nicolson, 1956); Edgar O'Ballance, *The Red Army* (New York: F. A. Praeger, 1964); M. Bonch-Bruyevich, *From Tsarist General to Red Army Commander* (Moscow: Progressive Publishers, 1966); Trotsky, *My Life,* chaps. 32–37.

I have located the story in 1920 because of the reference to Commander Yevsukov's belief in "the Soviets, the International, the Cheka. . . ." The Third International was not founded until March 1919; since the story opens in February, it must be February of 1920. Maryutka volunteered into "what was then called the Red Guards," hence before the creation of the Red Army proper in April 1918, so that she has been in the army for about two years.

26. Stites, *Women's Liberation,* p. 397; Trotsky, "Leninism and Library Work," in *Problems of Everyday Life* (New York: Monad Press, 1973), p. 153. It should be added that Zhenotdel's attack on illiteracy produced striking results: By 1926, 43 percent of Soviet women could read.

27. The passages are cited respectively in Gasiorowska, *Women in Soviet Fiction,* p. 53, and Vera S. Dunham, *In Stalin's Time: Middleclass Values in Soviet Fiction* (Cambridge: Cambridge University Press, 1976), p. 218.

28. V. I. Lenin, "A Great Beginning," in *Collected Works,* vol. 29, p. 429.

29. Both quotations from Vladimir Zelinsky, "Architecture as a Tool of Social Tranformation," *Women and Revolution,* no. 11 (Spring, 1976): 6–14. See also S. Frederick Starr, "Visionary Town Planning During the Cultural Revolution," in Fitzpatrick, *Cultural Revolution,* pp. 207–40. Starr notes that innovative work was "hobbled" by a party decree of June 1931, and that new ideas were "smothered" under the standardized town plans imposed by the Second Five-Year Plan. Although cost was usually given as the reason for the return to conventionality, the Gosplan economist Stanislav Strumilin showed that the new communal and deurbanized schemes were far more economical than the old system.

30. M. Agursky, cited by Roy Medvedev in *Stalinism,* ed. Tucker, p. 220. See also Medvedev's *Let History Judge* (New York: Knopf, 1971).

31. Leon Trotsky, *The Revolution Betrayed,* chap. 7, "Family, Youth and Culture." On the trials, see, among many other sources, Medvedev, *Let History Judge* and "New Pages from the Political Biography of Stalin" in *Stalinism,* ed. Tucker, pp. 199–235.

32. Rosa Luxemburg, "Order Reigns in Berlin," in Robert Looker, ed., *Rosa Luxemburg: Selected Political Writings* (London: Jonathan Cape, 1972), p. 304.

Chapter 9: Ambivalence in utopia

1. In *The Shape of Utopia* (Chicago: University of Chicago Press, 1970), Robert C. Elliott argues that the exposure/advocacy division is typical of Roman satire and that More's *Utopia* belongs to the "literary kind" of satire. The argument doesn't account for the frequently encountered dual impulse in other utopias, nor, in my view, does it do so fully for More. There are of course many ways to classify utopias and their dualisms. Robert Philmus uses Kenneth Burke's terms "dialectical" and "ultimate" to designate the exposure/advocacy division, and calls the results "satirical" or "visionary" according to which impulse pre-

dominates; cf. "The Language of Utopia," *Studies in the Literary Imagination,* vol. 6, no. 2 (Fall, 1973): 61–78.

2. On the uses and fate of analogical thought in several types of discourse during the Middle Ages and Renaissance, see Sheila Delany, "Undoing Substantial Connection: The Late Medieval Attack on Analogical Thought," MOSAIC, vol. 5, no. 4 (Summer, 1972): 31–52, and "Substructure and Superstructure: The Politics of Allegory in the Fourteenth Century," *Science and Society,* vol. 38, no. 3 (Fall, 1974): 257–80. The former has been reprinted in *Chaos and Form: History and Literature,* ed. Kenneth McRobbie (Winnipeg, Canada: University of Manitoba Press, 1972).

3. Though I admire the work of Franklin Rosemont, I believe that his wish to recover an American tradition of revolutionary vision has produced a distorted evaluation of Bellamy. See "Free Play and No Limit: An Introduction to Edward Bellamy's Utopia," in *Surrealism and Its Popular Accomplices,* ed. F. Rosemont (San Francisco, CA: City Lights Books, 1980), pp. 6–16.

4. Frederick Engels, *Socialism: Utopian and Scientific* (1878), part 1.

5. See Mandy Merck, "The Patriotic Amazonomachy and Ancient Athens," in *Tearing the Veil. Essays on Femininity,* ed. Susan Lipshitz (London: Routledge & Kegan Paul, 1978), pp. 95–115.

6. From Carl Degler's introduction to *Woman and Economics* (New York: Harper & Row, 1966), pp. xiii and xix. Other examples of the tendency to overrate are Alice Rossi, "The 'Militant Madonna,' " in *Feminist Papers* (New York: Bantam Books, 1973), and Ann J. Lane's introduction to *Herland* (New York: Pantheon, 1979).

7. According to Jean Pfaelzer, "American Utopian Fiction 1888–1896: The Political Origins of Form," in *Minnesota Review,* ns, no. 6 (special supplement: Marxism and Utopia) (1976): 114–17.

8. Summary of and quotations from Ward in Samuel Chugerman, *Lester F. Ward, The American Aristotle* (Duke University Press, 1939; repr. New York: Octagon Books, 1965). This volume also contains Gilman's fulsome dedication to Ward of *The Man-Made World* (1911), p. 379. One could, I suppose, trace two current descendants of sociobiology: the male-chauvinist branch (Lionel Tiger, Robert Ardrey, Konrad Lorenz) and the feminist (Evelyn Reed, Elizabeth Gould Davis).

9. Mary A. Hill, *Charlotte Perkins Gilman: The Making of a Radical Feminist, 1860–1896* (Philadelphia, PA: Temple University Press, 1980). See also Ann J. Lane's introductory chapter to *The Gilman Reader* (New York: Pantheon, 1980).

10. Both quotations from *Ourland* are cited in Lane, *Herland,* pp. xvii and xviii.

11. Quotations from "The New Generation of Women," *Current History* (August 1923), cited in Degler, *Woman and Economics,* p. xvi; and from Gilman's article, "Progress Through Birth Control," in *North American Review,* vol. 224 (1927): 622–29.

12. Dolores Hayden, "Two Utopian Feminists and Their Campaigns for Kitchenless Houses," *Signs,* vol. 4, no. 2 (Winter, 1978): 274–90. See also Hal D. Sears, *The Sex Radicals* (Lawrence, KS: Regents Press, 1977); Linda Gordon, *Woman's Body, Woman's Right: A Social History of Birth Control in America*

(New York: Grossman, 1976); James Reed, *From Private Vice to Public Virtue: The Birth Control Movement and American Society Since 1830* (New York: Basic Books, 1978); Taylor Stoehr, *Free Love in America: A Documentary History* (New York: AMS Press, 1979).

13. Pfaelzer, "American Utopian Fiction," p. 115.

14. See Jean Quataert, *Reluctant Feminists in German Social Democracy, 1885–1917* (Princeton, NJ: Princeton University Press, pp. 98, 265.

15. Rudolf Schlesinger, *The Family in the USSR: Documents and Readings* (London, 1949), p. 53. Kollontai's critique of the feminists appears in the same volume. Cf. also "Decree on the Legalization of Abortions" (November 18, 1920), p. 44 in the same volume.

16. See, for example, Richard J. Evans's account of Ruth Bfe's rural maternity colonies, the Mutterschützbund, in *The Feminist Movement in Germany 1874–1933* (London: Sage Publications, 1976), and almost any American material from the later nineteenth century in connection with blacks or immigrants.

17. Richard J. Evans, *The Feminists: Women's Emancipation Movements in Europe, America and Australasia, 1840–1920* (London: Croom Helm, 1977), chap. 1.

18. V. L. Parrington, Jr., *American Dreams: A Study of American Utopias* (Providence, RI: Brown University Press, 1947), p. 218.

19. Frank Manuel, Introduction to *Utopias and Utopian Thought*, ed. F. E. Manuel (Boston: Houghton Mifflin, 1965), p. ix.

20. Northrop Frye, "Varieties of Literary Utopias," in Manuel, *Utopias*, p. 29.

21. Jack I. Biles, *Studies in the Literary Imagination*, vol. 6, no. 2 (Fall, 1973): xi.

22. Letter from Marge Piercy in *Frontiers: A Journal of Women's Studies*, vol. 2, no. 3 (Fall, 1977): 64. All page references to *Woman on the Edge of Time* are to the Fawcett edition (New York, 1976). The letter says that *Dance the Eagle to Sleep* is the record of Piercy's involvement with SDS (Students for a Democratic Society, a popular New Left national student organization of the late 1960s; it split in 1971 and soon disintegrated), but the experience is equally evident in the later novel.

23. Evans, *The Feminists*, p. 244.

24. Tzvetan Todorov, *The Fantastic: A Structural Approach to a Literary Genre*, trans. Richard Howard (Ithaca, NY: Cornell University Press, 1975).

Chapter 10: A city, a room

1. Harold Bloom, *The Anxiety of Influence* (New York: Oxford University Press, 1973). For *A Room of One's Own* I have used the Harvest/HBJ paper edition (New York: Harcourt, Brace and World, 1929). For *Three Guineas* I have used the Penguin edition (1977), and for the essays, *Collected Essays* (London: The Hogarth Press, 1966), vol. 2.

2. For the *Livre de la Cité des Dames* I have used the critical edition by Maureen Curnow (Ph.D. diss., Vanderbilt University, 1975), 2 vols. My quotations are from the 1521 translation of Bryan Anslay (London: Henry Pepwell). A new translation by Earl Jeffrey Richards, *The Book of the City of Ladies* (New York: Persea Books, 1982), was not available to me before the chapter was